WORLD CULTURES IN PERSPECTIVE

# ANCIENT GREECE AND ROME

Harry A. Dawe

CHARLES E. MERRILL PUBLISHING CO.
A Bell & Howell Company
Columbus, Ohio

# Author

Harry A. Dawe is currently serving as Headmaster at The Harvey School in Katonah, New York. His previous professional experience includes the Assistant Headmastership at The Beaver Country Day School in Chestnut Hill, Massachusetts, where he also taught and served as Chairman of the History Department. Mr. Dawe received his B.A. degree from Oberlin College and his M.A. degree from Columbia University. He is the author of *The Ancient Near East* in Merrill's World Cultures in Perspective series. He has contributed a number of articles to professional journals and is a member of the American Historical Association and the New England History Teachers' Association.

# Acknowledgements

Thanks are due the following authors and publishers for the material quoted on the pages indicated: pp. 9, 10, 11: Homer, *The Odyssey*, trans. E. V. Rieu (Harmondsworth, Middlesex, England: Penguin Books, 1946); reprinted by permission. p. 10: Walter F. Otto, *The Homeric Gods: The Spiritual Significance of Greek Religion* (Boston: Beacon Press, Inc., 1964). pp. 16, 44-45: Leonard Cottrell, *The Anvil of Civilization* (New York: The New American Library, Inc., Mentor Books, 1957); reprinted by permission. p. 19: Truesdell S. Brown, ed., *Sources in Western Civilization*, Vol. II: *Ancient Greece;* copyright © 1965 by The Free Press, a division of the Macmillan Company; reprinted by permission. pp. 23, 24: Kathleen Freeman, *The Work and Life of Solon* (London: H. Milford, 1926). pp. 24, 31-33: George Rawlinson, trans., *History of Herodotus*, Vol. II, IV (London: John Murry, 1875). pp. 33-35: Herodotus, *The Histories*, trans. A. De Sélincourt (Harmondsworth, Middlesex, England: Penguin Books, 1955); reprinted by permission. pp. 39-40, 54, 55, 66-71: Thucydides, *The Peloponnesian War*, trans. Rex Warner (Harmondsworth, Middlesex, England: Penguin Books; copyright © 1954 by The Bodley Head); reprinted by permission. p. 44: Arnold Toynbee, *Hellenism: The History of a Civilization* (New York: Oxford University Press, 1959). p. 45: Sophocles, *The Theban Plays*, trans. E. F. Watling (Harmondsworth, Middlesex, England; Penguin Books, 1947); reprinted by permission. p. 51: Plutarch, *The Rise and Fall of Athens*, trans. Ian Scott-Kilvert (Baltimore: Penguin Books, 1960). pp. 58-59, 61-62, 62, 62-63, 63-64: Plato, *The Last Days of Socrates*, trans. Hugh Tredennick (Harmondsworth, Middlesex, England: Penguin Books, 1954); reprinted by permission. pp. 59, 60: Plato, *Protagoras and Meno*, trans. W. K. Guthrie (Harmondsworth, Middlesex, England: Penguin Books, 1956); reprinted by permission. pp. 61, 104-110: B. Jowett, trans., *The Dialogues of Plato* (New York: Macmillan, 1892). p. 61: James B. Pritchard, ed., *Ancient Near Eastern Texts Relating to the Old Testament* (Princeton, New Jersey: Princeton University Press, 1955). pp. 92, 93, 94, 95, 96: From *Essential Works of Stoicism*, edited by Moses Hadas. Copyright © 1961, Bantam Books, Inc.; reprinted by permission. pp. 103, 118: Dorothy Mills, *The Book of the Ancient Romans* (New York: G. P. Putnam's Sons, 1937). pp. 110-111: Francis Conford, trans., *The Republic of Plato* (New York: Oxford University Press, 1945). pp. 121-122: From *A History of Rome: From Its Origins to 529*, by Moses Hadas. Copyright © 1956 by Moses Hadas. Reprinted by permission of Doubleday & Company, Inc. pp. 131-132, 140: A. H. Clough, trans., *Plutarch's Lives* (Boston: Little, Brown & Co., 1859). pp. 153-157: Evelyn S. Shuckburgh, trans., *The Histories of Polybius* (London: Macmillan, 1889). pp. 162, 164, 173: Edward Gibbon, *The Decline and Fall of the Roman Empire and Other Selected Writings*, ed. Hugh R. Trevor-Roper (New York: Washington Square Press). p. 171: William G. DeBurgh, *The Legacy of the Ancient World* (Baltimore: Penguin Books, 1923). pp. 171-172: William G. Sinnigen, ed., *Sources in Western Civilization*, Vol. III: *Rome;* copyright © 1965 by The Free Press, a division of the Macmillan Company; reprinted by permission. p. 178: C. Warren Hollister, *Medieval Europe: A Short History* (New York: John Wiley and Sons, Inc., 1964). All biblical quotations: *The Holy Bible*, Revised Standard Version (New York: Thomas Nelson & Sons, 1953).

ISBN 0-675-01281-3

Copyright © 1970 by
CHARLES E. MERRILL PUBLISHING CO.
A Bell & Howell Company
Columbus, Ohio 43216

*All rights reserved. No part of this book may be reproduced in any form, by any method whatsoever, without permission in writing from the publisher.*

Printed in the United States of America

# Preface

In the early twentieth century, ancient history was a substantial and important course in secondary schools throughout the United States, an unquestioned part of a liberal education. Today, however, ancient history is, in many cases, no longer a noticeable element in the normal course of study. New courses, such as psychology and urban sociology, have often supplanted ancient history by offering the promise of greater "relevancy." Ancient history, however, still stands as an extensive and usable record of human experience. As is true for all past eras, its relevance must be exposed and articulated. When this is done, the unique characteristics and educational value of ancient history can be seen as an essential element of modern education.

Ancient history can serve today's young people in a number of ways. First, it can be used as a vehicle for instructing students in the vocabulary of history; it can teach essential historical terms, uncluttered by modern facts and biases—terms such as *dictatorship, revolution* and *religion.* Second, ancient history can serve to assist students in developing the ability to interpret events; by studying the classic structure of certain human events in ancient times, they can become better prepared to understand and interpret the more complex events of modern history.

Third, ancient history can teach students a most vital historical skill—perspective. Examining the civilizations of the Greeks and the Romans will better equip students to comprehend the larger picture of history, into which fits the Peloponnesian War as well as the Crusades and the World Wars of the twentieth century. Finally, citizens of the Western world neglect at their peril the germinal ideas and beliefs of their own culture—ideas and beliefs embodied in Graeco-Roman civilization. Thus, it is with these goals in sight that *Ancient Greece and Rome* has been written; the book serves as an introduction to the study of human culture, as relevant as any of the "new" social studies courses.

The spatial and temporal limits of the book are the Mediterranean basin and its immediate hinterland from the emergence of Hellenic civilization around 1000 B.C. to the disintegration of Roman rule in the West around 500 A.D. Attention is given to the fundamental ideas of Christianity, seeing them as an integral part of the ancient world.

*Ancient Greece and Rome* is an interpretive essay rather than a comprehensive, chronological textbook. It has been conceived in the belief that an interpretive account is a kind of cutting edge which provokes critical thinking and provides a flexible instrument of instruction. Ample original sources have been included in order to permit individual analysis and interpretation. These original sources are in the form of primary documents placed both in the body of the text and in the collection of Readings at the ends of the units; thus, the Readings, because they are an integral part of the text, are designed to be read in conjunction with the appropriate chapters. The experience of the Graeco-Roman world is used in the book in two ways: to provide raw material for the development of critical thinking, and to provide some factual knowledge of the ideas and events which shaped the early period of Western civilization. Conceptual skills are meant to grow from a direct exposure to historical substance.

The author is grateful to The Beaver Country Day School, its Headmaster, faculty and student body, who all provided the environment for the writing of this book. Portions of the book in manuscript form were used by students whose frank comments helped to give its final form a genuine relevance of both style and content. Special thanks are extended to Miss Ann Grayson and Mrs. Ruth Selig, who helped to shape the book by graciously using sections of it with their students. Their cooperation helped to make the book an account designed for students and teachers, for whom it is intended. The author welcomes the comments of other teachers who may have occasion to read it. Throughout the process of publication, the intelligent editorial help of Jean Diederich Stouffer of Charles E. Merrill Publishing Co. has been appreciated.

Harry A. Dawe<br>Katonah, New York

# Table of Contents

**UNIT I**    **The Creation of Civilization**

| Chapter 1 | The Greek Mind | 2 |
| Chapter 2 | The Athenian State | 16 |
| Reading I | The Hellenic Mind | 31 |

**UNIT II**    **The Flowering of Greek Civilization**

| Chapter 3 | The Golden Age of Athens | 38 |
| Chapter 4 | The Agony of Hellas | 51 |
| Reading II | Greek Society: Unity and Disunity | 66 |

**UNIT III**    **Greek Civilization and the Mediterranean World**

| Chapter 5 | The Growth of a Universal Culture | 74 |
| Chapter 6 | The Hellenistic World | 88 |
| Reading III | Greek Philosophy | 104 |

**UNIT IV**    **The Roman Empire**

| Chapter 7 | Italy and the Republic | 114 |
| Chapter 8 | The Mediterranean and the Empire | 127 |
| Chapter 9 | The Empire and the Roman Constitution | 137 |
| Reading IV | The Merging of Greece and Rome | 153 |

**UNIT V**    **The Climax of Mediterranean Civilization**

| Chapter 10 | The Ancient World and the Roman Order | 160 |
| Chapter 11 | The Great Transformation | 173 |
| Reading V | The Transformation of Values | 190 |

Epilogue: The Legacy of Greece and Rome    203

Index    210

## Maps

| The Mediterranean World (c. 1000 B.C.) | 8 |
| Hellas (c. 5th Century B.C.) | 48 |
| The Empire of Alexander the Great | 84 |
| Rome and the Western Mediterranean (c. 3rd Century B.C.) | 135 |
| The Roman Empire: Greatness and Decline (c. 300 A.D.) | 184 |

The Greeks did not invent civilization. The basic elements of human culture —a control over nature, a system of cooperation, a method of communication and the development of the human mind and spirit—had been attained before the Greeks had even existed as a distinct people. However, the Greeks living in small groups on the land in and around the Aegean Sea created distinct ideas and established patterns of thought which were truly unique. What they borrowed from earlier peoples, they molded into new forms. They gave their peculiar and indelible stamp to the fabric of human civilization.

In this unit, the basic intellectual, social and political achievements of the ancient Greeks are presented. Some distinctive Greek ideas and institutions are introduced, and the political evolution of one Greek state, Athens, is traced. Two chapters and two selections from the writings of a Greek historian comprise this unit. From these, a clear sense of the Greek style of life and thought should be gained.

# UNIT I
# The Creation of Civilization

# 1

# The Greek Mind

Compared with the natural fertility of Egypt and Mesopotamia, the lands around the western Mediterranean Sea seem poor indeed. The Greek peninsula is a rocky land with rivers no larger than streams. The fact that the first civilization had not been created in Greece is quite logical—the ingredients were not there. However, there are excellent harbors on the eastern coast, and so Greece faces the area in which civilization was born. Also, the island of Crete, home of a very old civilization, is only seventy-five miles from the southernmost tip of the Greek peninsula. Therefore, when the arts of civilization began to spread out from the Near East, Greece was in a geographical position to receive them.

## The Mycenaean Civilization

Just who the Greeks were and where they came from is still difficult to say for certain. We do know that an Indo-European people moved into the peninsula around the year 2000 B.C. as part of a major migration, including also the Hittites and Persians. Most of what we know of these early inhabitants of Greece has come from recent archaeological excavations in the ancient Greek cities of Pylos (PIE luhs) and Mycenae (my SEE nee). The early settlers, called *Mycenaeans* (my suh NEE uhns), learned some of the arts of civilization from the Cretans, who at that time dominated the Aegean Sea and the bordering lands.

**Cretan Influence.** The Mycenaeans used a Cretan pictographic script for writing, borrowed their art form from the Cretans and at one time paid tribute to the kings of Crete. Although we are able to read the script used by the Mycenaeans, the language of Crete has not yet been deciphered. Therefore, it is difficult to know the full extent of the relationship between Crete and the mainland of Greece. It does seem clear, however, that the stimulus for the creation of civilization in Greece came from the Cretans, a people whose art and sculpture show a spirit of freedom and grace which was unique in the ancient world, a people whose buildings display not only a sense of beauty but a keen intelligence. The early culture of Greece was based on a vigorous and lively tradition.

**Social and Economic Forces.** The remaining buildings from the Mycenaean period of Greek history indicate that the people who lived in them spent much of their time fighting. Most of the structures are heavily fortified. There is enough evidence of wealth in these palaces to indicate that the people had a fairly good control over their environment. The sea was an important part of that environment, and piracy might well have been the major source of wealth. The land, however, was not capable of sustaining a large population, and so there was a good deal of migration to other lands around the Aegean Sea. One important settlement was Troy (also known as Ilium) in western Asia Minor. This city was in a position to control the passage of ships through the Hellespont, a narrow strait leading to the Black Sea. It is quite likely that ships laden with grain from southern Russia passed through this strait, a fact which made Troy an important city.

Much later in the history of Greece, the poet Homer told of a great battle on the plains of Troy, a battle between the Trojans and the warriors from Greece who wanted to destroy the city. This poem is called the *Iliad*; it describes the kidnapping of Helen of Troy and the ten-year war (the Trojan War) which followed. Until recently, the *Iliad* was regarded as a legend and the city of Troy as a product of the poet's imagination. Now, archaeologists have not only uncovered the ruins of Troy but have discovered evidence of battles for the control of the city. The approximate date of the seige and destruction of Troy is 1184 B.C.

The Mycenaeans had a written language, used bronze tools and weapons, and managed to spread their influence over a wide area. Their land was too poor to support a civilization equal to those near the Nile or Euphrates, so the Mycenaeans were a kind of semi-civilized group standing between the centers of civilization to the southeast and the stone-age barbaric civilizations to the north and west. Around the year 1200 B.C., the discovery of iron and the

Dating from the sixteenth or fifteenth century B.C., this golden mask may have covered the face of a Mycenaean nobleman or warrior in death. This work of art attests to the wealth and artistic skill of the Mycenaean Greeks.

*Hirmer Fotoarchiv, München*

rapid influx of new people from the north brought about a turmoil from which would emerge Greek civilization.

**The Invasions.** The waves of invaders from the north, armed with iron weapons, destroyed both Mycenaean and Cretan civilization and threw the entire Aegean area into confusion. This rapid pressure of people caused large-scale migrations which had an impact upon the Near East itself. Raiders from the sea, perhaps displaced Mycenaeans, attacked Egypt and settled in Palestine; some of them were the Philistines spoken of in the Old Testament. In Greece itself, the invasions ushered in what could be called a "dark age" in which even literacy disappeared.

However, the spread of civilization which had been activated by inventions such as iron, the alphabet and coinage could not be stopped. Gradually, with the dawning of the Iron Age, Greece came out of its dark period: iron tools made it possible to increase agricultural production, while control of the sea through trade and piracy produced wealth. Around the eighth century B.C., literacy returned to Greece in the form of the alphabetic script which had originally been developed by the Phoenicians. The formation of Greek civilization occurred roughly at the same time as that of the Hebrews. Each of these peoples, Greeks and Hebrews, developed during the early Iron Age, and each of them made distinctive contributions to human civilization.

## The Hellenic Civilization – Greece

The Greeks did not call themselves Greeks. "Greek" is actually a Latin word; it is what the Romans were to call the inhabitants of this peninsula. The Greeks believed that they were all descended from the god Hellen and therefore called themselves *Hellenes* (HELL eens), and their land *Hellas*. Therefore, the word "Hellenic" is often used to describe Greek culture, and the word "Hellas" is used to indicate any land where Greek culture predominated. As the Greeks settled throughout the Mediterranean area, Hellas became more than just Greece. Hellenic culture could, and frequently did, exist outside of the Greek peninsula itself.

**Political Organization.** The Greeks gathered into many small, rather than large, states. Perhaps this political grouping was caused by the fact that the land is broken up by many valleys and hills. Joined to the mainland of Greece by a narrow isthmus is a secondary peninsula, on which the early civilization of Greece, the Mycenaean, had developed. This southern peninsula is called the *Peloponnesus* (pel uh puh NEE suhs).

One important Peloponnesian area, called *Lacedaemonia* (las uh duh MOE nee uh), was dominated by the city of *Sparta*. On the isthmus itself was the city of *Corinth*, located in an excellent position to control trade routes. North of Corinth was Attica, ruled by the city of *Athens*, a city destined to become the most important in the history of Greece. It is not quite accurate to call these political divisions "cities," for during the ninth and eighth centuries B.C., they were more like villages based primarily on agriculture. Although there was a common Hellenic culture, there was no Greek nation, but rather a collection of separate, small states, each jealous of its independence.

**Religion.** The religion of the Greeks was a nature religion filled with many gods, each corresponding to the natural forces. *Zeus* (zoose), like the Sumerian god Enlil, was the god of the storm. *Poseidon* (puh SIDE uhn) was the god of the sea; *Aphrodite* (af ruh DITE ee) was the goddess of beauty and fertility; *Apollo* was the sun god who drove his flaming chariot across the sky each day. These gods were worshipped and sacrificed to in order to gain various favors, such as fertile soil, calm seas and good sailing breezes. The Greeks were *polytheists*, that is, persons who believe in the existence of many gods. (In contrast, *monotheists* are persons who believe in the existence of only one God.) Around the Greek gods, an elaborate mythology* developed.

**Geography.** Unlike Egypt, Greece was not dominated by a major river which flooded with regularity each year. The weather was changeable, and although the climate was generally warm, Greece was colder in winter than the rest of the Near East. The climate was irregular and stimulating. The land surface was also irregular, having stark contrasts and sharp outlines. If a visitor from Egypt had gone to Greece in the eighth century B.C., he would have found there a vigorous and rather uncivilized people. However, the natural setting was pleasant, and if a way could be found to provide a surplus of wealth, the land could be the home of a creative people. Such was to be the case, for the Greeks were intelligent, and they had easy access to the accomplishments of earlier civilizations.

## The Ionian Civilization

Around the year 1000 B.C., a considerable number of Greeks migrated to the coast of Asia Minor, a land which they called Ionia (i OH nee uh). The cities which were built there were in a position to act as "middlemen," standing between the civilized lands to the east and the barbarian lands to the north and west. In addition to carrying goods, the Ionian Greeks turned to manufacturing and made such things as pottery and textiles, two commodities much in demand. As a result, the Ionian cities became wealthy trading and manufacturing centers. The most important of these cities was Miletus (my LEET uhs).

The Ionian cities were close enough to the ancient seats of civilization to learn from them, yet they were far enough away to escape political or military domination. Because of this excellent location, Greek creativity was nourished by the ideas of others, yet was permitted to develop along its own lines. The wealth produced by trade and manufacturing provided the economic basis for civilization, and during the first half of the first millennium,† no major Near Eastern empire ruled the western half of Asia Minor. The Ionian cities were free, independent and wealthy and were

---

\* A *mythology* is a collection of myths or stories dealing with the gods and legendary heroes of a people, usually involving supernatural elements.

† A *millennium* is a period of a thousand years.

composed of adventurous people who had been willing to move there in the first place. It was here, in Ionia, that the basic elements of Hellenic culture were created.

**Homer.** The first clear indication of the shape of Greek civilization came from Ionia in the form of the poet *Homer,* who lived and wrote around 850 B.C. Homer's two long epic poems, the *Iliad* and the *Odyssey,* both revolve around the Trojan War and its aftermath. The best, and perhaps the only, way to fully grasp the spirit and shape of Greek culture is to read both of these poems. A work of art must speak directly to the mind and senses of each person. It cannot easily be described and talked about. The ideas expressed by Homer and the style of his poetry form the basis of Greek civilization. With the creation of these two works, we can speak of the birth of civilization in the land of Hellas.

The *Iliad* is more than a gory battle story, and the *Odyssey* is more than a travel story. They are expressions of the Greek view of man, the universe and the gods. Just as the prophets of Israel created a new concept of man and God, the Homeric poems struck a new note in the history of human civilization. Both men and gods appear in these poems, but Homer used his artistic imagination to portray the gods as something more than personified forces of nature.

**Mythology—A Humanistic View.** Although the gods were immortal, Homer infused them with humanity and made each of them represent a distinct human quality, thereby linking them to humanity. Apollo represented wisdom; Athena (uh THEE nuh), quick wit; Aphrodite, physical beauty; Hermes (HER meez), craft and speed. Zeus was the father of the gods who represented order, but at times, he too acted in what we would call a human manner. The diversity, or variety, of the Greek gods reflected the diversity of man's character and emotions. Even the ability to lie with style was considered to be a divine gift.

The gods inhabited the heavens—in Homeric language, *Mount Olympus* (uh LIM puhs)—but they frequently moved into the world of men, usually by means of human disguises. In this way, Homer blurred the distinction between the human and divine spheres. Different gods favored different men, but not because the men obeyed divine laws or led moral lives. Rather, men were admired for distinctly human traits. In the *Odyssey,* for example, the goddess Athena favored Odysseus (oh DIH see us) not because he was a Greek or because he was an upright man who wor-

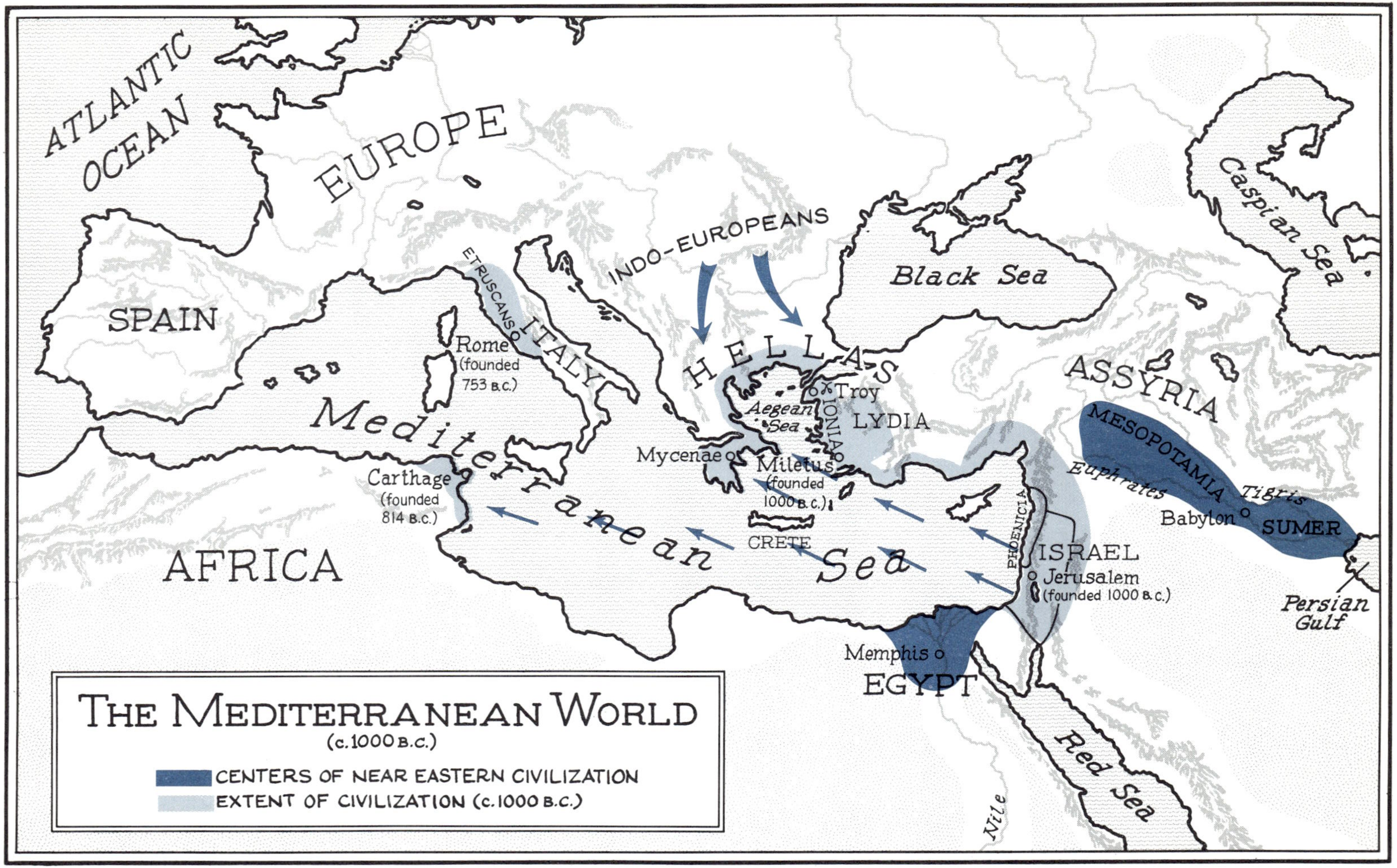
THE MEDITERRANEAN WORLD
(c.1000 B.C.)
CENTERS OF NEAR EASTERN CIVILIZATION
EXTENT OF CIVILIZATION (c.1000 B.C.)
ATLANTIC OCEAN
EUROPE
SPAIN
AFRICA
INDO-EUROPEANS
ETRUSCANS
ITALY
Rome (founded 753 B.C.)
Carthage (founded 814 B.C.)
Mediterranean Sea
HELLAS
Aegean Sea
Troy
IONIA
LYDIA
Mycenae
Miletus (founded 1000 B.C.)
CRETE
Black Sea
Caspian Sea
ASSYRIA
MESOPOTAMIA
Euphrates
Tigris
Babylon
SUMER
Persian Gulf
PHOENICIA
ISRAEL
Jerusalem (founded 1000 B.C.)
Memphis
EGYPT
Nile
Red Sea

shipped only her. She favored him because he was brave and clever—she admired his distinctly human qualities.

The world of the gods was intertwined with the world of men. In the Homeric poems, the gods were portrayed as superhumans often feeling the very human emotions of love, envy or jealousy. Yet at the same time, they represented the perfection of many noble human attributes. Man was portrayed as being almost godlike, and the focus of both the *Iliad* and the *Odyssey* was on man, even when Homer was talking about the gods. "Greek religion did not make divinity human, but regarded the essence of humanity as divine." Therefore we might say that humanism, a belief in the supreme importance of man, was at the heart of Greek civilization.

**Religious Attitudes.** This strong humanistic point of view was not found in the religions of other peoples. To the Babylonians, man was the plaything of the gods, regarded by them as a mere nothing. Even the Hebrews, who conceived of man as having been made in the image of God, saw humankind as totally separated from the divine. For example, when the prophet Isaiah had a vision of God, he exclaimed with holy terror:

> ... I saw the Lord sitting upon a throne, high and lifted up; and his train filled the temple. And the foundations of the thresholds shook at the voice of him who called, and the house was filled with smoke. And I said: "Woe is me! For I am lost; for I am a man of unclean lips, and I dwell in the midst of a people of unclean lips; for my eyes have seen the King, the LORD of Hosts!"
> ISAIAH 6:1, 4-5

To gaze upon God was, for the Hebrews, to risk death.

But in the *Odyssey*, when Athena wished to communicate with Telemachus (tih LEH muh kuhs), the son of Odysseus, she acted in the following manner.

> When Athene had finished, she bound under her feet her lovely sandals of untarnishable gold, which carried her with the speed of the wind over the water or the unending land, and she seized her heavy spear with its point of sharpened bronze, the huge long spear with which she breaks the noble warrior's ranks, when she, the Daughter of the almighty father, is roused to anger. Thus

---

**The map on page 8 shows the Mediterranean world a short time before Greek civilization began to emerge from its "dark age." Also shown is the Etruscan civilization in central Italy, a civilization which reached its height about 500 B.C., before the rise of Rome.**

*Hirmer Fotoarchiv, München*

This detail from a bronze statue of either Poseidon or Zeus shows the confident, commanding and aggressive quality which was characteristic of early Greek civilization. The statue was discovered in 1929, after lying for more than two thousand years beneath the waters of the Aegean Sea.

she flashed down from the heights of Olympus. On reaching Ithaca she took her stand on the threshold of the court in front of Odysseus' house; and to look like a visitor she assumed the appearance of a Taphian chieftain named Mentes, bronze spear in hand. When Telemachus had to deal with this divine visitor, he expressed none of the fear and awe experienced by Isaiah. The Greek spoke with calmness:" 'As for my guest he introduced himself as Mentes, the son of a wise man Anachialus, and chieftain of the sea-faring Taphians.' In this way Telemachus described the visitor who in his heart he knew for an immortal goddess."

In order to gain a knowledge of the gods, there was no need to bridge a gap of holiness and terror. Homer urged the Greek to seek divinity by living his life as fully as possible as a human being, by exerting the powers of humanity to the greatest possible extent. According to one authority, "Instead of raising his powers and virtues to heaven by pious fantasy, [the Greek] perceived the outlines of divinity in the delineations of his own nature." Consider Homer's description of the king of Sparta.

> Dawn had just touched the East with crimson hands, when the warrior Menelaus put on his clothes and rose from bed. He slung a sharp sword from his shoulder, bound a fine pair of sandals on his shapely feet and strode from his bedroom looking like a god.

The emphasis in Homer is so much on man and on mortal life that the gods of the dead are not important characters in his poems. There is no Greek god who attained the power of the Egyptian god Osiris (oh SIE ruhs), the judge of the underworld. When Odysseus visits the land of the dead, he sees the great heroes of the past wandering around as mere shadows of their former selves. He addresses Achilles (uh KILL eez) as prince of the land of the dead, and Achilles answers him, saying, "My lord Odysseus, spare me your praise of Death. Put me on earth again, and I would rather be a serf in the house of a landless man with little enough for himself to live on, than king of all these dead men that have done with life."

**The Homeric Image of Man.** The Homeric epics described a rough, almost barbaric society where the qualities of the warrior predominated. Men in Homer's poems neither read nor wrote; they fulfilled their destiny in action unhampered by the restraints of an elaborate civilization. Only the upper classes, the few who ruled by right of birth, appeared in the stories. They were fighters by trade and were scornful of those who earned a living by means of buying and selling goods.

Yet in the midst of this raw power, Homer's men were never small-minded, never sordid in their actions, and they represented a constant striving for excellence, a quality which the Greeks called *arete* (a ruh TAY). This word is one of the keys to Greek civilization. For Homer, *arete* meant courage, loyalty and physical skill. As Greek ideas developed, the image of man as a warrior changed, but the Homeric ideal of human excellence—*arete*—remained as a permanent element in Greek thinking. The *Iliad* and the *Odyssey* served as great educating forces in the lives of the Greeks. Young men committed them to memory, and so the values described by Homer were woven deep within the fabric of Greek civilization.

The Homeric poems were to the Greeks what the Old Testament was to the ancient Hebrews, and much of the Old Testament was written at the same time that the *Iliad* and the *Odyssey* were composed. The Old Testament, as we might expect, was different from these two poems. It dealt not only with the action of the Hebrew God, but provided a full explanation of the origin of the world and of man; it also contained a record of the destiny of the Hebrew nation. The Old Testament became a sacred book, the sole source of truth. The Greeks had no official single repository of truth, and the Homeric poems dealt with only some aspects of man and religion. This very incompleteness of Homeric religion left the Greeks free to pose a variety of questions and to seek many different answers to them. Zeus, for example, was not a creator-god, and the Greeks had no official religious explanation for the origin of the universe.

## Ionian Scholars

The free atmosphere of Ionia which had produced Homer produced other thinkers who were not poets. Thinkers can be called *philosophers*—men who practice *philosophy* (*philos* meaning lover and *sophia* meaning wisdom). The Ionian philosophers turned their attention to nature and to the origin and structure of the universe. They attempted to work out a philosophy of nature. During the sixth century B.C., in the city of Miletus, a man by the name of *Thales* (THAY lees) became the first natural philosopher.

**Thales.** Like most Greeks, Thales traveled a great deal. We know that he visited Egypt and absorbed much of the thought of Near Eastern civilization. In his thinking about the origin of the world, Thales developed a theory that all things had originated from water. He believed that at one time, all the different elements of the universe had been in a watery form. With this simple idea, Thales began to open the secrets of nature and to see the universe as it had never been seen before, just as Homer had looked upon man as had never been done before.

It is understandable why Thales developed his "water theory" of the universe. In Egypt, it was possible to see the "creation" of new soil each year through the flooding of the Nile. The Babylonian creation story stated that the god Marduk (MAR dook) created the universe out of a watery chaos. According to the Hebrews, water was the one thing which God did not create. In the words of the Old Testament, ". . . and the spirit of God was moving on the face of the deep." Also in the Old Testament was the belief that man was created out of clay and mist.

Thales, however, lived in a cultural atmosphere which had no clear concept of a creator-god, and so this philosopher stated that all things came from the water—*without the action of any god or gods.* The four basic elements (earth, fire, air and water) all separated out of the original water and took their present forms. Thales believed that the earth was floating on a body of water, a view not unlike the Egyptian belief in an underground Nile or the Hebrew belief in "the waters under the earth." The ideas of Thales have been recorded in very fragmentary form, and it may seem to us that his theory was not very complete. His importance lies in the fact that he saw the universe as being formed by a natural process requiring no divine intervention.

**Anaximander.** Another Ionian philosopher was *Anaximander*. He disagreed with Thales, believing that the original substance was an unknown quantity which once contained the four elements. The hot portion of this original substance operated on the wet portion, thereby causing dry land to appear through a process of evaporation. Mist was caused by this heating, and the excess vapor built up enough pressure to cause an explosion, thereby creating fire. Fire pushed upward and outward from the earth and was enclosed above the earth in a tube of air so dense that the fire could be seen only through small holes in the tube. According to this theory, when man saw the stars, what he was really seeing was glimpses of this fire. Anaximander proved to his satisfaction that fire covered the earth when he observed that all fires on earth seemed to reach upward toward their true home in the sky.

According to Anaximander, the four elements had their proper place, but they continually infringed on each other. He called this action "injustice," an action which upset the balance of nature. From this mixing of elements, individual things, including man

This bronze statue of the god Apollo was cast in about the sixth century B.C. Note the quality of reflection and alertness that surrounds it. The statue speaks eloquently of the clarity, serenity and openness of the Greek spirit.

*Hirmer Fotoarchiv, München*

himself, came about. Eventually, the balance of nature corrected the injustice, and the elements returned to their proper places. This theory explained the existence of physical change in the world, and seemed to have been based upon actual observation. When a man died, his body disintegrated, and the various elements left him. Water (blood) dried up, earth (flesh) returned to the earth, and air (breath) returned to the atmosphere. Creation, therefore, was an upsetting of the balance of nature, and this imbalance was not permanent, for nothing existed forever.

The ideas of Thales and Anaximander are significant because they are examples of men using facts to construct theories without the aid of religious doctrines. The Ionian philosophers saw nature following a natural pattern, a pattern which could be grasped by the mind of man. These theories may sound primitive to us, but it was these men who first developed the idea of *natural law*. Their thinking asserted the belief that the forces of nature are not unpredictable actions of the gods but rather are movements determined by certain laws which can be understood by the reason of man. If these laws of nature were rational (capable of being discovered by use of reason), man could understand the universe of which he was such a small part; he might even be able to control it.

In the year 494 B.C., the city of Miletus was conquered by the expanding Persian empire; with this conquest, the focus of Greek civilization shifted from Ionia to the mainland of Greece itself. However, the creations of the Ionians—humanism and natural law—were to serve as the basis for the full flowering of Greek civilization. It would be inaccurate to say that the Greeks discovered man and nature, but they did look at these two parts of creation in a unique manner.

**Herodotus.** Perhaps the most remarkable of the early Greeks was *Herodotus* (hih RAHD uh tuhs), a native of Ionia who spent his mature life in Athens. Therefore Herodotus, in his own life, represented the shift in focus from Ionia to the Greek mainland. He was a historian, but for the Greeks, history meant more than a recording of past events. History meant "inquiry," and Herodotus' writings show man inquiring into all that he saw about him. Herodotus had both the Ionian faith in a rational universe and the Homeric interest in man as an important subject of study. To understand the Greeks, it is necessary to read Herodotus as well as Homer. Two selections from Herodotus' writings are included in Reading I at the end of this unit. These selections serve to illustrate the way Greek interest in both the order of physical nature and the order of human society could be combined in the mind of one man. They also serve as a transition from our look at early Greek ideas to our study of the development of Greek government.

Herodotus composed his thoughts on government during the fifth century B.C., a century of greatness in Greek history. Why and how were the Greeks able to think about the various forms of government in such a perceptive manner? To find this out, it will be necessary to examine the political experience of the Greeks during the years leading up to the time of Herodotus. We must trace the political history of Greece.

## Define

Mycenaeans
Hellas
Hellenic
Zeus
Poseidon

Aphrodite
Apollo
Hermes
humanism
*arete*

philosopher
Thales
Anaximander
natural law

## Review and Answer

1. What are some of the geographical features of Greece; why were they important in the development of Greek civilization?
2. What reason other than the kidnapping of Helen of Troy can be given for the Trojan War?
3. What seems to account for the creativity of the Greeks who lived in Ionia?
4. Describe Homer's view of man.
5. Why was the Ionian philosopher's view of nature so remarkable?

1.) rocky land with rivers no larger than streams. Excellant harbors because of irreg. coastline. Near Crete home of old civiliz.
2.) Greeks wanted to capture Troy because it could control the passage of ships through the Hellespont.
3.) Ionia was between civilized + barbaric lands Ionia turned to manufact., pottery + textiles thus, became wealthy

# 2

# The Athenian State

In the early days of Greece, the period described by Homer, leadership was held by a warrior class. Power was in the hands of members of leading families, and the right to rule was passed on by birth. People of noble birth were free to live a full and vigorous life, while the rest of society, the lowborn common people, labored for the benefit of the few. This form of government is called *aristocracy*, which means, literally, "rule of the best." Who was best was determined by birth; the gift of leadership was transmitted by means of inheritance. In the words of a Greek poet:

Ne'er yet from the root of a squill did rose or hyacinth wave;
Nor came a son of freedom from out of the womb of a slave.

The poems of Homer are reflections of this style of political organization.

## Political Organization

During the time of Homer, Greek states were small and were separated from each other. Each political group was called a *polis* (PO luhs); it is from this word that our word "politics" is derived. We usually translate *polis* as "city-state," for we have nothing like the polis in our political culture. It was a small but independent political unit about the size of a city but having the power of a state. The center of the polis, where the rulers met, was usually on high ground in a well-fortified position. This was called the *acropolis* (uh CROP uh luhs), meaning "high city." Here political and religious functions took place. The *agora* (AG uh ruh) was the public marketplace where economic activity, the buying and selling of goods, was transacted. Beyond this area were the farms of the nobility, the sources of their wealth.

**The Role of the Aristocracy.** The Greeks had a primitive kind of government, one in which the ruling class was a law unto itself. There were no written laws; the aristocratic code of conduct was inbred into every man. A true aristocrat needed no laws to restrain him, as he always acted properly—or so people thought. In such a society based on birth, the family was an important social and political unit. If a member of one family insulted or killed a member of another family, it was proper to take revenge on the other. There was no central government with fixed laws or formal courts. It was a rough and direct kind of government in which an insult to one's honor could lead to war. In fact, it was the abduction of a woman which touched off the massive Trojan War!

However, during the seventh and sixth centuries B.C., more wealth came to Greece. Greek ships increasingly became the major carriers of goods. Greek wine and olive oil were valuable products, as were the skillfully designed pottery vessels in which they were carried. A nobleman with vineyards or olive orchards could amass a great deal of money. Also, the introduction of coinage into Greece made the accumulation of wealth easier. In time, the pur-

This reconstructed drawing of the Acropolis of Athens has attempted to recapture in a model the fullness of the ruins. Athena herself, spear in hand, guards the entry, presiding over a religious procession which is about to enter the city.

suit of wealth displaced the pursuit of military glory as the driving goal of the aristocracy.

**The Shift to Oligarchy.** The word aristocracy, although it literally means "rule of the best," resists an iron-clad definition. In common usage, it describes a ruling class usually resting upon an economic basis of agriculture but unconcerned with the actual earning of wealth. The aristocrat turns his attention and energies to other pursuits, such as the art of war or the collection of knowledge. However, a ruling class whose major goal is the gaining of wealth, whether through agriculture, manufacturing or commerce, is usually called an *oligarchy* (AHL uh gahr kee). The shift in Greek values to the pursuit of wealth can be seen as the transformation of the Greek ruling class from an aristocracy to an oligarchy.

Peasant farmers with smaller plots of land found it difficult to compete with the wealthy oligarchs, and they were often forced to borrow money from them. In order to do this, they had to offer their lands or even themselves as security for the loan. If the harvest was bad one year, and the farmers were unable to pay the debt, they would have to give up their land to the lender or finally even work for him as a slave. This particular institution was called *debt slavery*. Such a situation produced a decline in the number of peasant farmers and led to a widening gap between rich and poor.

## Social Problems and Change

The Homeric view of life served as a model for the warrior aristocracy. Although it did not take into account the merchant oligarchy which developed in Greece, it had nothing but scorn for the peasant farmer. As long as these values persisted, the downtrodden poor had no way to show that they were being treated unjustly. The unbridled rule of the few seemed to be the natural order of society, and the oppression of the poor was not thought of as being unjust.

**Hesiod.** About 700 B.C., however, a challenge to this set of values was made by a peasant farmer by the name of Hesiod (HEE see uhd). Hesiod compiled a book, not about nobles and warriors, but about farmers and sheepherders. His book, *Works and Days*, was a series of poems dealing with the life of the average farmer. In this book, Hesiod placed the mark of the gods' approval on humble labor, rather than on military exploits. In so doing, he expanded the notion of *arete* beyond the range of the military aristocracy and showed that human excellence could be gained in farming as well as in fighting. As Hesiod wrote:

> There is not only one kind of strife on earth, but two. And one the thoughtful man would praise, the other is blameworthy, for they are widely separated in spirit. The first is cruel, fostering evil war and battle. Nor does anyone love this one, but only from necessity and because the immortals have so decreed do men honor this baneful strife. Dark night bore the other earlier one, and Cronus' son on his lofty throne in heaven placed it in the roots of the earth, much more beneficial to man. For this strife urges on to toil even the idle man. For when, not working himself, he sees another become rich, then he is eager to plough, to plant and improve his property. Neighbor emulates neighbor desirous of wealth. This strife is good for mortals, and potter vied with potter, carpenter with carpenter, beggar with beggar and bard with bard.

In other words, the favorable kind of strife was not fighting, but rather ambition, which drives men in all walks of life. Hesiod directed his words to the average man and gave that way of life some of the dignity and grandeur which once had been reserved only for the nobility.

**Social Inequality.** In addition, Hesiod sensed the deep injustice committed when the arrogant rich dominated the poor through the power of money.

> There is confusion when Justice is manhandled by bribe-devouring men who pervert the law with crooked judgments. But Justice pursues covered with mist, complaining about the city and the behavior of the people, and bringing evil to men who drive her away and deal unfairly.
>
> O Kings, do you yourselves reflect on this punishment. For the immortals are present among men and they take note of those who grind one another with crooked judgments, disregarding the gods. Three times ten thousand of Zeus' immortals on the all-nourishing earth watch out for mortal man. They easily keep track of judgments and evil deeds; wrapped in mist they wander through the land . . . . Guard against these things, Kings, make your words straight, you bribe-swallowers; avoid all kinds of crooked judgments. The man who harms another also harms himself, and an evil plot damages most the one who concocts it. The eyes of Zeus are everywhere and he knows everything. And if it be his wish, he sees this too, nor does it escape his notice what kind of justice any city contains inside itself. Now may I not be a righteous man among men, nor my son either, for it is pointless to be just if the unjust man is to prevail. But I cannot believe that all-wise Zeus will ever permit that.

Here we see Zeus portrayed as being not interested in the courage of an individual warrior but rather in the moral evil of a selfish and wicked oligarchy. According to Hesiod, Zeus was a god angered by the uneven nature of society and was prepared to correct the imbalance. In the phrase, "But Justice pursues covered with mist . . . bringing evil to men who drive her away and deal unfairly," we can see the sense of natural order and balance which was grasped by the Ionian natural philosophers being applied to human affairs. Hesiod provided the poor with a powerful moral argument.

**Defense Strategies.** There were more than just moral arguments against an unbalanced state. During the seventh century B.C., the style of warfare gradually changed; a group of mounted warriors was no longer the most effective kind of fighting force. A well-trained and disciplined group of foot soldiers, *hoplites* as the Greeks called them, could defeat the nobility mounted on horses. Therefore, if most of the peasants of a land were in debt or enslaved, they would be unable to equip themselves in order to serve in an infantry; the state would be exposed to attack. Only a rearrangement of economic power—to keep the poor from getting poorer—could make an adequate army possible. Here we can see the moral idea of a balanced society and the practical necessity of military defense working together for a change in the form of government.

**Limited Resources.** In a very fertile land such as Egypt, a large population could be easily provided for, even if wide differences of individual wealth remained. In lands such as Greece, however, the pressure of population on a limited amount of fertile land was bound to cause friction and perhaps civil war. Some solution to this kind of social and economic problem was necessary, especially among people as restless and argumentative as the Greeks.

One solution to the problem lay close at hand. Greeks were willing and able to take to the sea and start over again in new lands. From the seventh century B.C. on, small groups established colonies abroad, as far north as Russia and as far west as Spain. The Greek city of Syracuse, on the island of Sicily, eventually became a wealthy and powerful city, the equal of any city in Greece itself. In fact, there were so many Greek cities in Sicily and on the lower half of Italy that the Romans called this area Greater Greece. Although all of these colony cities regarded themselves as free and independent, they all shared a common heritage of Greek culture,

Shown here is a long view of what remains of the Acropolis, the heart of Athenian culture. The Greek sense of order, discipline and balance can still be seen in the half-ruined Parthenon, which commands the heights of the city.

a culture which was not bound to one land but rather existed wherever there were Greeks. This willingness to seek new lands served to spread the ideas of the Greeks over a large area, into lands of earlier civilizations to the east, and into the lands of the barbarians to the north and west. Because of this dispersal, it seemed to many non-Greeks that the Greeks were everywhere. The Greeks took their language and culture wherever they went; Hellas was where the Greeks were.

## Changing Forms of Government

**Sparta.** There was another solution to the problem of limited resources and social inequality. In Lacedaemonia, the citizens of Sparta banded together and conquered a large number of people who lived in the surrounding lands. These enslaved people, who were called *helots*, were put to work providing food for the Spartans. The helots were slaves, but they were not owned by individual Spartan masters. In fact, no Spartan had any personal property at all. Among the Spartans, there was complete equality and a fair share in the government. The government owned everything, including the helots, and loyalty was given not to an individual leader but to the state as a whole. The enslavement of the helots and the use of their labor made it possible for Sparta to rid itself of friction between rich and poor because all Spartans were equal. Even money was forbidden.

Through this kind of social organization, the Spartans produced both political stability and a powerful army. A Spartan man lived most of his life as a soldier, taking his meals with other soldiers and spending most of his time in the service of the state. The Spartan government and army was the envy of many other Greek states who were faced with the problem of getting individuals to pull together. In Sparta, the Homeric ideal of individual *arete* was transformed into the driving force of community or collective excellence.

The success of Sparta did not come without a price. A permanent army had to be maintained in order to prevent a helot uprising. In time, the possession of a permanently subjected population led to a brutalization of Spartan culture. Sparta was an army with a state rather than a state with an army. Once this system had been imposed, very few poets, artists or creative minds came out of Sparta. Although the Spartans attained almost perfect equality and the power of self-government, the very sustaining of these seemed to stifle individual thought and creativity.

**Athens.** In Athens, migration abroad had eased some of the pressure of population, but the possibility of war between rich and poor was still present. The Athenians did not have enough internal solidarity to follow the Spartan pattern, nor did they have docile neighbors who could be easily subdued. Someone had to devise the political forms necessary to bring about stable human cooperation, or Athens would fall prey to better-organized states such as Sparta.

In the year 691 B.C., a man named *Solon* (SO luhn), himself a member of the nobility, was given full power to create a workable form of government for Athens. The nobles wanted things to remain as they were, and the poorer people wanted to see the wealth of the rich divided among themselves. For Solon to support either of these extreme positions would bring about a civil war. Solon had to discover and apply the laws of human society just as the Ionian philosophers had grasped the laws of nature. He had to develop a science of politics.

**Solon's Reforms.** In the writings of Solon, we can see one striking characteristic of Greek thinking—a sense of balance and order. Solon realized that these were desirable qualities to have in a state. The economic laws which he devised abolished all existing debts and made debt slavery illegal. He also put restrictions upon the wealthy, forbidding them to display their wealth in an arrogant manner. He did not order a division of the nobility's lands, but he made it difficult for the poor to become poorer and so made it possible for the gap between rich and poor to be bridged. Solon tried to make all classes of Athenians secure and content with their position in society, rather than to equalize wealth as had been done in Sparta. In his own words:

> The people will best follow its leaders if it be neither given undue liberty nor unduly oppressed; for excess bears arrogance, whenever great prosperity attends on men whose minds are not well balanced.
> Tame the strong will in your hearts, you who have made your way to the enjoyment of lavish prosperity; keep your high thoughts within moderate bounds; for neither shall we yield to you, nor for yourselves will this course prove expedient.

In order to obtain this balance, Solon devised a constitution for Athens. He did away with the practice of automatically giving a person power because of his birth. Rather, he gave important influence in that state to the rich. The poorer members of society had less power, but they had some control over the actions of the government. They also could gain political power by increasing their wealth. Solon's government was neither a rule of the few nor a rule of the many, but was rather a mixture—a balanced constitution.

> To the people I have given just as much power as suffices, neither taking away from their due nor offering more; while for those who had power and were honored for wealth I have taken thought likewise, that they should suffer nothing unseemly. I stand with strong shield flung around both parties, and have allowed neither to win an unjust victory.

**A Government of Laws.** Solon wanted to see the government of Athens as a government of laws rather than a government of men. To him, laws were not a list of particular rules but rather were an innate sense of justice and balance, a pattern of living together. Law should serve to direct human affairs just as the law of nature determined the forces of nature. This kind of outlook was expressed by Herodotus when he recorded a description of the Greeks given to the Persian king as he was about to invade Greece:

They are free—yes—but not entirely free; for they have a master, and that master is Law, which they fear much more than your subjects fear you.

In the words of Solon:

These are the lessons which my heart bids me teach the Athenians, how that lawlessness brings innumerable ills to the state, but obedience to the law shows forth all things in order and harmony and at the same time sets shackles on the unjust. It smoothes what is rough, checks greed, dims arrogance, withers the opening blooms of ruinous folly, makes straight the crooked judgement, tames the deeds of insolence, puts a stop to the works of civil dissension, and ends the wrath of bitter strife. Under its rule, all things among mankind are sane and wise.

A friend of Solon's mocked him for thinking that written laws could check the injustice of men. Laws, he said, were no more than spiders' webs which would hold the weak and poor but would be torn to pieces by the rich and powerful. Solon had hoped that men would abide by the laws if and when they had nothing to gain by breaking them. Solon's friend observed that in Greece, wise men spoke on public affairs but fools decided them.

The restraint and balance which Solon spoke of did not come easily to a people living in the shadow of the Homeric warrior who threw caution to the winds. Homer's concept of *arete* could not be easily absorbed by an increasingly crowded and complex society. In order to achieve order and balance in Athens, the energy of the

The "Calf-Bearer" is an example of early Greek sculpture (sixth century B.C.) in which the human figure is presented quite formally, with few individual human traits noticeable.

*Alinari*

Greek spirit had to be channeled into paths which would not destroy a complex and delicate social structure. The Homeric idea of human excellence had to be expanded and given a different shape to cope with a more settled existence. The famous Greek motto, "Nothing in excess," emerged because the Greeks realized how easy it was for them to break through limits. No people can avoid the heritage of their past, and so in Greece, the restless spirit of Homer continued to influence the history of the people in a number of ways.

All parties were satisfied with Solon's reforms only for awhile. Friction and discord will always occur in a free and open society where change is always possible. Yet, in spite of apparent failure, the career of Solon was a significant event in the history of civilization. Great and wise men had appeared long before Solon but their thinking was usually directed toward religious or moral questions; they were not political thinkers. Solon was the first individual to actually create a government, a government in which a number of the citizens took part. In fact, the very concept of citizenship was born at this time. Solon grasped the concept that the human community was a man-made device, not a divine institution ruled by a priest-king or an aristocracy of birth.

**Peisistratus.** There were those in Athens who did not find it to their interest to abide by the laws. The poor who had not gained all that they had wanted from Solon's reforms gathered around a military leader named *Peisistratus* (pie SIS truh tuhs). This man recognized their grievances and promised to help them if they would help him to take and retain power in the state. Peisistratus was not of noble birth, and he based his power on the support of the common people. In the year 546 B.C., he took over the government by force and held on to his power by giving land to the poor and by making Athens a powerful and respected state. He encouraged the founding of overseas settlements; these colonies not only eased the pressure of population but increased the military influence of Athens. Peisistratus also promoted the growing of olive trees by lending public money to those who wished to start an orchard. He encouraged artists, poets and musicians to come to Athens, and he constructed many public buildings.

*Tyrant* is the Greek word for a person who takes power in violation of the law and then rules by himself. Tyranny offended the Greek sense of order and balance, but it also represented the vigor and skill of an individual man. This particular tyrant, Peisistratus, did many things to improve the state, even though he used illegal means to do so. He broke the power of the nobility and favored the common people. However, the major difficulty with tyranny as a lasting form of government is its instability. A continual struggle for power surrounds a tyrant as others try to do what he has done, to seize the ruling power by force; tyranny sets a bad example. The success of tyranny depends entirely on the skill of the individual ruler; it is the man, not the office, which counts. Therefore, when Peisistratus' son was unable to command the same respect his father had, another revolution took place in Athens. The son was deposed in 510 B.C., and a new form of government had to be developed. Tyranny was not suited to the Athenian temperament.

Some of the once prominent Athenian families who had been exiled by Peisistratus returned to the city. However, the Athenian common man, be he farmer, merchant or artisan, had by this time increased his political and economic power. Even though some of the old noble families returned to power after the tyranny, it was no longer possible for them to reestablish a pure aristocracy. Too many changes had taken place, and the government which came after the rule of Peisistratus' family was more democratic than any political organization yet devised by man.

## Athenian Democracy

**Political Structure.** Under the new organization, Athens was divided into ten districts called *tribes*. Membership in a tribe depended on where one lived rather than on whom one's ancestors were. Each year, fifty men were chosen from each tribe to sit on the Council of Five Hundred. This council decided what issues were to be discussed by the assembly of all the citizens, which was called the *ekklesia* (ih KLEE zee uh). Ultimate power therefore rested with the entire citizen body of Athenians which met to decide upon public policy. Athenians did not elect representatives to speak for them; they spoke for themselves. Athens was now a *direct democracy* as opposed to a *representative democracy* in which one politician speaks for a large number of people. The Athenians were able to develop this direct form of democracy because their state was small and because all citizens could meet together in one place in the open air. We might even say that the mild climate of Greece made such a large assembly of people possible.

Members of the Council of Five Hundred were chosen by lot rather than by election. This procedure functions much as a lottery or raffle does today; names were drawn from a container. Therefore, every citizen had an opportunity to be in the government, and chance rather than popularity decided the choice. Election by lottery may seem a risky way to choose rulers as it leaves a great deal to chance. Yet, the members of the council changed each year, and each public official had to make an accounting to the people as a whole when he finished his term of office. These practices made it possible for a large number of people to serve in the government and encouraged honesty among public officials. A lottery system also made it possible for a person who was not a good "vote-getter" to serve his state.

The military leaders of Athens sat on a council of ten generals. These men were not chosen by lot but were elected by popular vote and could be reelected any number of times. Therefore, a good general could be chosen by the people.

**Ostracism.** * In order to prevent one man from gaining absolute power, the Athenians developed an interesting political device. Each year, the citizens had the opportunity of voting not only to remove someone from office but to banish him from the polis for a number of years. Citizens wrote the person's name on a piece of pottery called an *ostrakon*. This process, which required a vote of six thousand citizens against a particular man, was called *ostracism*. Needless to say, such an instrument could be misused and employed as a means for personal revenge. But the effectiveness of all political devices depends on the wisdom of the people who use them. Ostracism and exile, although not widely practiced today, have been used many times in the political history of man.

The most striking quality of Athenian political life was the fact that the people themselves shaped the policy of their community. For the first time in human history, rulers had to persuade the ruled to accept the laws which would govern them. Men, working together, shaped their own political environment. During the first 2,500 years since man had created civilization, his intellectual and moral energy was never extensively used to devise the best form of human cooperation. But in a relatively short time, Athens moved through many forms of government—aristocracy, oligarchy, tyranny and democracy. Men such as Herodotus, living in the democratic atmosphere of Athens, began to understand, perhaps for the first time, the dynamics of human society and the laws of politics.

*result in exile

## The Persian Threat

This creative Hellenic civilization with its new ideas about religion, nature and government existed in the small city-states of Greece, Athens in particular. The older civilization of the Near East had recently reached a kind of climax, and the entire area had been unified under the rule of the Persians. In the early fifth century, B.C., the Persians looked toward the west and moved across the Aegean Sea, beginning a series of battles known as the *Persian Wars*. Greek civilization was different from that of the Near East. If this difference was to continue, if the new ideas of the Greeks were to grow and expand, the domination by Persia and Eastern culture would have to be avoided.

**The Battle of Marathon.** In the year 490 B.C., the Persian emperor *Darius* (duh RI uhs) launched an invasion of Greece aimed at Athens, the city which had given aid to the Ionian cities when they attempted, unsuccessfully, to halt the Persian advance in Asia Minor. Darius crossed the Aegean Sea, and near the small village of Marathon, not far from Athens, the Persian army met the citizen army of Athens in a crucial battle. The Athenians won, demonstrating that a disciplined army of foot soldiers—the hoplites—could defeat a much larger army of Persian mounted warriors and infantry. This victory saved Greek civilization from extinction, for at this point, Greek culture could have been submerged under the culture of the Near East. The history of Western civilization, and perhaps the history of the world, might have been quite different had the outcome of this battle been reversed.

The Athenians won because of superior strategy; but perhaps an equally important element of the victory was the spirit and morale of the average Athenian soldier. Thanks to the reforms of Solon, the Athenian soldier was ruled by law and not by a king; thanks to Peisistratus, the soldier owned his own land, and thanks to the democratic constitution, he shared in the government of his state. In short, he was fighting to protect his own freedom—not to serve the glory of a king or nobleman. New ideas and new social forces had served to create loyalty and unity among the Athenians. The victory at Marathon confirmed and strengthened the leading Greek ideas. A state run by the people had proved capable of defending itself against a mighty empire. The glow of patriotism which swept over Athens as the runner from Marathon brought the news of victory convinced all Athenians that their way of life was superior to others.

Darius died before he could renew the struggle with the Greeks. His successor, *Xerxes* (ZURK seez), was truly the "King of Kings." The kings of Babylon and Assyria, the princes of Syria and Judah, the masters of the Phoenician fleets and the pharaohs of Egypt were all his subjects. Ruling an empire which spanned the Near East, Xerxes set out across the Hellespont to seek revenge for the defeat at Marathon and to bring the scattered Greek states under his rule. The Greeks were ill-prepared to meet this massive threat. Each polis was jealous and distrustful of the others, and within each city, there was violent disagreement. Many voices were raised in favor of coming to terms with the Persians and accepting their rule. Only Athens and Sparta finally agreed to resist the Persian advance, and even in these cities, there were voices which spoke out for surrender.

**The Battle of Thermopylae.** Because of the mountainous terrain of Greece, entry to the south could be gained only through narrow passes. It was at the pass at Thermopylae (thur MAHP uh lee), northwest of Athens, that a small band of Spartans threw themselves across the path of the Persians. The Spartans fought to the death, inflicting heavy losses on the enemy, but Xerxes had men to spare, and his navy was bearing down on Athens. Although Thermopylae was a defeat for the Greeks, the battle, described by Herodotus, stands for all times as a symbol of heroic defense. The monument erected to commemorate the Spartans who fell there expressed in the simplest of terms the strength of the Greek character.

> Go, stranger, and to Lacedaemon tell
> That here, obeying her behests, we fell.

**Victory at Salamis.** South of Thermopylae, the road to Athens was open; both the Persian army and navy were converging on the city. A leading statesman by the name of *Themistocles* (thuh MIHS tuh kleez) convinced the Athenians to leave the city and take to their ships, risking everything upon a naval battle. The Persians entered and destroyed the city, but in the Bay of Salamis, the Persian fleet, fighting in close quarters, was outmaneuvered and defeated by the Athenian fleet. The Athenians were saved by their knowledge of ships and of the sea, for Xerxes, without his navy, was stranded in Greece. The Persians withdrew from Greece and never again attempted an invasion.

After this victory, it was apparent that it had been the entire citizen body of Athens who had won the battle. The victory went to those who carried spears, rowed the ships and transported the equipment, as well as to Themistocles, who had devised the strategy. This had not been a victory of an oligarchy with peasants fighting for nobles; nor had it been a victory of a priest-king followed by devoted subjects. All of Athens acted as a unit, and when the citizens returned to the acropolis to rebuild what the Persians had destroyed, it was clear that no one class of people could rule the city. The democracy which had so recently been established had been emblazoned in the hearts of all Athenians by this common struggle. All of the ideas created by the Greeks would grow and expand in the now secure and vigorous environment of the democratic polis.

### Define

| polis | hoplites | ostracism |
| aristocracy | helots | direct democracy |
| oligarchy | tyranny | |

### Review and Answer

1. How did Hesiod help to expand Greek thought and values?
2. What were the possible solutions to the problem of the distribution of wealth and political power in the Greek states? Compare the Spartan and Athenian solution to this problem.
3. Show, in an interconnected essay, how each of the following men contributed to the development of Athenian politics: Hesiod, Solon, Peisistratus and Themistocles.
4. Why can it be said that the battles of Marathon and Salamis were extremely important battles in the history of the Western world?
5. What basic characteristics of Greek culture discussed in Chapter One can be seen influencing the development of the Athenian polis?

# Reading I
# The Hellenic Mind
## Selections from Herodotus

Herodotus, often called the "Father of History," was the first Greek historian. As a young man, he traveled widely, recording as he went the cultures and customs of the inhabitants of Greece, Asia Minor, the Middle East and North Africa. At the end of his travels, Herodotus compiled an account of what he had learned and recorded some of the important historical events of his time.

*The Laws of Nature*

For centuries, the Egyptians had believed that Egypt was the center of the universe and that the Nile was a divine force which came to nourish the land each year. On a visit to Egypt, Herodotus saw the Nile, a river unlike any he had ever seen, and he recorded some of his thoughts on this natural phenomenon. Through his thoughts, we can see the Greek mind working with the explanation of the Nile flood. The method Herodotus used is that of a scientist who looks at various theories and rejects all but the one which seems best to fit the facts as they are known at the time. The significance of this selection is not that Herodotus was right or wrong in his conclusion, but that he used a broad-minded and objective method in seeking the truth. In so doing, he not only denied the divinity of the river, but he saw the forces of nature acting in the same way in all lands. Herodotus grasped the concept of natural laws which could be understood by man.

Concerning the nature of the river, I was not able to gain any information either from the priests or from others. I was particularly anxious to learn from them why the Nile, at the commencement of the summer solstice, begins to rise, and continues to increase for a hundred days—and why, as soon as that number is past, it then retires and contracts its stream, continuing low during the whole of the winter until the summer solstice comes round again. On none of these points could I obtain any explanation from the inhabitants, though I made every inquiry, wishing to know what was commonly reported—they could neither tell me what special virtue the Nile has which makes it so opposite in its

---

George Rawlinson, trans., *History of Herodotus*, Vol. II (London: John Murry, 1875), pp. 28-36.

nature to all other streams, nor why unlike every other river, it gives forth no breezes from its surface.

Some of the Greeks, however, wishing to get a reputation for cleverness, have offered explanations of the phenomena of the river, for which they have accounted in three different ways. Two of these I do not think it worth while to speak of, further than simply to mention what they are. One pretends that the Etesian winds cause the rise of the river by preventing the Nile water from running off into the sea. But in the first place it has often happened, when the Etesian winds did not blow, that the Nile has risen according to its usual wont; and further, if the Etesian winds produced the effect, the other rivers which flow in a direction opposite to those winds ought to present the same phenomena as the Nile, and the more so as they are all smaller streams, and have a weaker current. But these rivers, of which there are many both in Syria and Libya, are entirely unlike the Nile in this respect.

The second opinion is even more unscientific than the one just mentioned, and also, if I may so say, more marvelous. It is that the Nile acts so strangely, because it flows from the ocean, and that the ocean flows all round the earth.

The third explanation, which is very much more plausible than either of the others, is positively the furthest from the truth; for there is really nothing in what it says, any more than in the other theories. It is, that the inundation of the Nile is caused by the melting of snows. Now, as the Nile flows out of Libya, through Ethiopia, into Egypt, how is it possible that it can be formed of melted snow, running, as it does, from the hottest regions of the world into cooler countries? Many are the proofs whereby any one capable of reasoning on the subject may be convinced that it is most unlikely this should be the case. The first and strongest argument is furnished by the winds, which always blow hot from these regions. The second is, that rain and frost are unknown there. Now whenever snow falls, it must of necessity rain within five days; so that, if there were snow, there must be rain also in those parts. Thirdly, it is certain that the natives of the country are black with the heat, that the kites and swallows remain there the whole year, and that the cranes, when they fly from the rigors of a Scythian winter, flock there to pass the cold season. If then, in the country where the Nile has its source, or in that through which it flows, there fell ever so little snow, it is absolutely impossible that any of these circumstances could take place.

As for the writer who attributes the phenomenon to the ocean, his account leads us into the unknown and it is impossible to disprove it by argument. For my part I know of no river called Ocean, and I think that Homer, or one of the earlier poets, invented the name, and introduced it into his poetry.

Perhaps, after censuring all the opinions that have been put forward on this obscure subject, one ought to propose some theory of one's own. I will therefore proceed to explain what I think to be the reason of the Nile's swelling in the summertime. During the winter, the sun is driven out of his usual course by the storms, and removes to the upper parts of

Libya. This is the whole secret in the fewest possible words; for it stands to reason that the country to which the Sun-god approaches the nearest, and which he passes most directly over, will be scantest of water, and that there the streams which feed the rivers will shrink the most.

To explain, however, more at length, the case is this. The sun, in his passage across the upper parts of Libya, affects them in the following way. As the air in those regions is constantly clear, and the country warm through the absence of cold winds, the sun in his passage across them acts upon them exactly as he is wont to act elsewhere in summer, when his path is in the middle of heaven—that is, he attracts the water. After attracting it, he again repels it into the upper regions, where the winds lay hold of it, scatter it, and reduce it to a vapor, where it naturally enough comes to pass that the winds which blow this quarter—the south and south-west—are of all winds the most rainy. And my own opinion is that the sun does not get rid of all the water which he draws year by year from the Nile, but retains some about him. When the winter begins to soften, the sun goes back again to his old place in the middle of the heaven, and proceeds to attract water equally from all countries. Till then the other rivers run big, from the quantity of rain water which they bring down from countries where so much moisture falls that all the land is cut into gullies; but in summer, when the showers fail, and the sun attracts their water, they become low. The Nile, on the contrary, not deriving any of its bulk from rains, and being in winter subject to the attraction of the sun, naturally runs at that season, unlike all other streams, with a less burden of water than in the summertime. For in summer it is exposed to attraction equally with all other rivers, but in winter it suffers alone. The sun, therefore, I regard as the sole cause of the phenomenon.

It is the sun also, in my opinion, which, by heating the space through which he passes, makes the air in Egypt so dry. There is thus perpetual summer in the upper parts of Libya. Were the position of the heavenly regions reversed, so that the place where now the north wind and the winter have their dwelling became the station of the south wind and of the noon-day, while, on the other hand, the station of the south wind became that of the north, the consequence would be that the sun, driven from the mid-heaven by the winter and the northern gales, would take himself to the upper parts of Europe, as he now does to those of Libya, and then I believe his passage across Europe would affect the Danube exactly as the Nile is affected at the present day.

### *The Laws of Politics*

In the second selection, Herodotus turns from physical nature to human nature and attempts to discover the laws of government. In the following account, three Persians are discussing the merits of three forms of government: *monarchy,* government by one man; *oligarchy* (sometimes called aristocracy), government by a few men; *democracy,* government by many men. This discussion never really took place. Herodotus placed the three theories in the mouths of three Persians in order to dramatize the issue.

The discussion seems to be a simple debate about various forms of government, but until the time of the Greeks, such a discussion would have been inconceivable. In this three-way argument, the principles of politics are presented in a logical and systematic manner, much in the way a group of scientists would present facts and theories. The debate is not about who would make a better ruler, but about *theories* of government. Its very existence shows that the Greeks were exposing questions of political organization to the light of human reason. Until this time, the structure of government had been taken for granted as having been established by the gods. The fact that we would feel at home in this discussion shows us how important the Greeks were in the shaping of our own civilization. They invented politics.

The first speaker was Otanes, and his theme was to recommend the establishment . . . of democratic government. "I think," he said, "that the time has passed for any one man amongst us to have absolute power. Monarchy is neither pleasant nor good. You know to what lengths the pride of power carried Cambyses, and you have personal experience of the effect of the same thing in the conduct of the Magi. How can one fit monarchy into any sound system of ethics, when it allows a man to do whatever he likes without any responsibility or control? Even the best of men raised to such a position would be bound to change for the worse—he could not possibly see things as he used to. The typical vices of a monarch are envy and pride; envy because it is a natural human weakness, and pride because excessive wealth and power lead to the delusion that he is something more than a man. These two vices are the root cause of all wickedness: both lead to acts of savage and unnatural violence. Absolute power ought, by rights, to preclude envy on the principle that the man who possesses it has also at command everything he could wish for; but in fact it is not so, as the behavior of kings to their subjects proves; they are jealous of the best of them merely for continuing to live, and take pleasure in the worst; and no one is readier than a king to listen to tale-bearers. A king, again, is the most inconsistent of men; show him reasonable respect, and he is angry because you do not abase yourself before his majesty; abase yourself, and he hates you for being a superserviceable rogue. But the worst of all remains to be said—he breaks up the structure of ancient tradition and law . . . and puts men to death without trial. Contrast with this the rule of the people [democracy]; first, it has the finest of all names

---

Herodotus, *The Histories*, trans. A. De Sélincourt (Harmondsworth, Middlesex, England: Penguin Books, 1955), pp. 209-211. Reprinted by permission.

to describe it—*isonomy*, or equality before the law; and secondly, the people in power do none of the things that monarchs do. Under a government of the people, a magistrate is appointed by lot and is held responsible for his conduct in office, and all questions are put up for open debate. For these reasons, I propose that we do away with the monarchy, and raise the people to power; for the state and the people are synonymous terms."

Otanes was followed by Megabyzus, who recommended the principle of oligarchy in the following words: "In so far as Otanes spoke in favor of abolishing monarchy, I agree with him; but he is wrong in asking us to transfer political power to the people The masses are a feckless lot—no where will you find more ignorance or irresponsibility or violence. It would be an intolerable thing to escape the murderous caprice of a king, only to be caught by the equally wanton brutality of the rabble. A king does at least act consciously and deliberately; but the mob does not. Indeed, how should it, when it has never been taught what is right and proper, and has no knowledge of its own about such things? The masses have not a thought in their heads; all they can do is rush blindly into politics and sweep all before them like a river in flood. As for the people, then, let them govern Persia's enemies, not Persia; and let us ourselves choose a certain number of the best men in the country, and give them political power . . . . it is only natural to suppose that the best men will produce the best policy."

Darius was the third to speak. "I support," he said, "all Megabyzus' remarks about the masses, but I do not agree with what he said of oligarchy. Take the three forms of government we are considering—democracy, oligarchy and monarchy—and suppose each of them to be the best of its kind. I maintain that the third is greatly preferable to the other two. One ruler: it is impossible to improve on that—provided he is the best man for the job. His judgement will be in keeping with his character; his control of the people will be beyond reproach; his measures against enemies and traitors will be kept secret more easily than under other forms of government. In an oligarchy, the fact that a number of men are competing for distinction in the public service cannot but lead to violent personal feuds; each of them wants to get to the top, and to see his own proposals carried; so they quarrel. Personal quarrels lead to open dissension, and then to bloodshed; and from that state of affairs the only way out is to return to monarchy—a clear proof that monarchy is best. Again, in a democracy, malpractices are bound to occur; in this case, however, corrupt dealings in government services lead not to private feuds, but to close personal associations, the men responsible for them putting their heads together and mutually supporting one another. And so it goes on, until somebody or other comes forward as the people's champion and breaks up the cliques which are out for their own interests. This wins him the admiration of the mob, and as a result he soon finds himself entrusted with absolute power—all of which is another proof that the best form of government is monarchy."

The defeat of Xerxes and the Persians in 480 B.C. saved the Greeks from falling under the rule of an Eastern monarchy and from seeing their distinctive ideas disappear under the impact of a then stronger culture. The major role played by Athens, especially in the naval victory at Salamis, gave the supporters of democracy a political victory. The citizens of Athens—soldiers and oarsmen—who had saved the city were now fully prepared to rule the city themselves. The Athenian gods had played no major role in this victory; in fact, some religious leaders claimed that the gods had favored the Persians. The common men of Athens had won the victory.

An Athenian of the post-Salamis era could well feel that men, unaided by the gods, had accomplished what had seemed to be an impossible feat. That same Athenian looked to the future, confident in the power of man not only to rule himself but to realize his fullest potential. The Hellenic spirit—the faith in man and his reason which we have seen developing in Homer and in the Ionian scientists—found in the triumphant city of Athens a setting in which to flourish.

In this unit, our focus will be on Athens in the fifth century B.C., for it was at this time and in this place that the Hellenic spirit, and perhaps the human spirit, attained its greatest power. The creations of this epoch became one of the strongest forces in the shaping of our own culture. It was a time in which the dynamic beliefs of the Greeks were put to the test; it was a time when humanity at its best and at its worst was exposed; it was a time of concentrated and incandescent brilliance.

# UNIT II
# The Flowering of Greek Civilization

# 3

# The Golden Age of Athens

That the Persian advance into Greece in the fifth century B.C. would be stopped was not a foregone conclusion. The Greek states had been fighting among themselves for centuries, and it was only with great difficulty that they had managed to come together to meet the army and navy of Xerxes. In fact, at the time of the first Persian invasion at Marathon in 490 B.C., the Spartans had not even arrived in time to meet the invading army. Yet, ten years later at Salamis, Athenians and Spartans worked together, and after this victory, other states joined with them to expel the Persians from Greece. Nonetheless, in the years after 480 B.C., the Persians still ruled some of the Greek islands and most of Ionia.

## The Delian League

In order to complete the expulsion of the Persians and to prevent another invasion, most of the Greek states in the Aegean area formed a league so that they could take joint action against a common enemy. The headquarters of this alliance of states was on the island of Delos, explaining why this organization is sometimes called the *Delian League*. In theory, each member state was required to contribute either ships or money, and all partners would have a share in the making of plans. In reality, the wealth, military power and prestige of Athens made this one city the most powerful member of the league. It was the Athenian navy which had delivered the decisive blow against the Persians, and it was the Athenian leaders who were most vigorous in pushing the enemy from the Aegean Sea.

**The Role of Athens.** Taking advantage of the control of the seas, Athens began to subdue nearby states who might rival her in trade. As the strongest city in the Delian League, Athens slowly began to dominate it. Some states preferred to contribute money rather than ships, and as a result, they had no means of protecting themselves against Athens. When the threat of a new Persian invasion subsided, some states wished to be free from contributing to the league, arguing that the reason for its existence had disappeared. In response to this, Athens compelled reluctant states to remain in the league and to continue their payments. In the year 462 B.C., the city of Thasos (THAY sohs) tried to leave the league but was reduced to submission by the Athenian navy. In 454 B.C., the treasury of the league was removed from the island of Delos to the city of Athens, and so after this date, the money was controlled by the Athenian government. The Delian League was slowly turning into an Athenian empire, and no Greek state was capable of resisting.

The Athenians justified the building of an empire by arguing that they had borne the brunt of the Persian invasion and that it was their fleet which was keeping the Persians at bay, as well as keeping the Aegean Sea free of pirates. All Greek states could join in the peace and security if they contributed money to Athens and let Athenian courts settle disputes between them. This line of reasoning ran in total opposition to the ingrained Greek belief that each polis should determine its own policy. However, the Athenian argument was backed up by superior military and financial resources.

The right of the stronger to rule the weaker was expressed by the Athenians when the city of Melos (MEE lohs) attempted to remove itself from the league and gain its independence. The historian *Thucydides* (thoo SIH dih deez) records the words of the Athenian generals which were spoken to the Melians just before they were attacked and destroyed.

> So far as right and wrong are concerned they [the Athenians] think that there is no difference between the two, that those who still preserve their independence do so because they are strong, and that if we fail to attack them it is because we are afraid. So that by conquering you we shall increase not only the size but the security of our empire. We rule the sea and you are islanders, and weaker islanders too than the others; it is therefore particularly important that you should not escape.
>
> You will see that there is nothing disgraceful in giving way to the greatest city in Hellas when she is offering you such reasonable terms—alliance on a tribute-paying basis and the liberty to enjoy your own property. And, when you are allowed to choose

between war and safety, you will not be so insensitively arrogant as to make the wrong choice. This is the safe rule—to stand up to one's equals, to behave with deference towards one's superiors, and to treat one's inferiors with moderation.

The logic of an empire—the rule over others—has never been more simply expressed.

**The Use of League Funds.** The money collected from the states in the Delian League was used by the Athenians to rebuild their city as well as to police the Aegean. Realizing the importance of sea power and the wealth to be gained by trade, the Athenians constructed a port city, Piraeus (pie REE uhs), about three miles from Athens itself. Between these two cities, a passage enclosed by two long walls was constructed so that Athens could have a protected route to the sea in the event that the city was ever attacked by land. Masters of the sea and secure on land, Athens seemed to be in a position to unify Greece under its rule.

Many of the temples and public buildings built in Athens during the years after Salamis were financed with league funds; many still stand as a record of Athenian wealth and artistic ability. The Parthenon, an architectural masterpiece dedicated to Athena, was built, in large part, with money collected from the members of the league. Skilled workers and artisans were paid from these funds, as were public officials, for their services to the government. It would seem that democracy and prosperity were possible because Athens had control over many other states. Democracy and empire seemed to go hand in hand.

To be an Athenian citizen in the mid-fifth century B.C. was to be in the most secure and powerful position that the average person had ever known in the history of mankind. Athenian citizenship was therefore a valuable possession, one which not many people could claim. After 450 B.C., only those born of Athenian parents were citizens. Here we see an interesting aspect of Greek democracy. The old idea of an aristocracy of birth, a system of society in which only those of noble birth were permitted to rule, remained the basic principle of democracy. Athenian democracy was a "democracy of birth"; strangers could not become citizens by moving to Athens and living there. Because of this restriction, the number of citizens remained small, and therefore direct democracy was still possible. It is estimated that the population of fifth-century B.C. Athens consisted of 168,000 citizens, 200,000 slaves and 30,000 resident foreigners.

This procession of horsemen is from a series of marble reliefs once on the Parthenon. The greatness of the sculpture can be seen in the sense of power and motion conveyed through motionless stone.

**Opposition to Athenian Power.** Why did the other Greek states permit Athens to gain so much power in Hellas? Most, of course, did not have the power to resist. Sparta, the second major city, was a landlocked state with no navy to speak of. The powerful Spartan army was unable to effectively attack the Athenians when they retired behind their city walls. Also, a revolt of the helots kept the Spartans busy at home, and as long as Athenian power did not touch them in the central Peloponnesus, there was no reason to go to war. However, the city of Corinth, located on an isthmus, soon felt the growing challenge of Athenian naval and commercial power. As the Athenians began to gain control of the land on the western side of Greece, the Corinthians sounded the alarm and managed to persuade some Greek cities to resist. There were sporadic wars between Athens and other Greek states during the middle of the fifth century B.C., and in 445 B.C., the Athenians realized that they could not master all of Greece and wage war against the Persians at the same time. A treaty, which lasted for thirty years, was then signed between Athens and the Peloponnesian states. With the end of hostilities, Athenians were free to enjoy the security and wealth which had come to them.

## The Athenian Empire

**Political Structure.** Perhaps the most significant accomplishment of the Greeks was the creation of the polis itself—a man-made organization in which people joined together not only to survive but to live "the good life," a human society in which the full potential of man could be realized. We have seen how the Athenian polis evolved over the years and, in the fifth century B.C., became a democracy. The key to this form of government was the direct involvement in some way of every citizen in the shaping of public policy. Every person had the opportunity to speak in the assembly of all the citizens. In addition, each citizen had a chance of being chosen to sit on the Council of Five Hundred or on a smaller committee which ruled the state for short periods. An Athenian served whether or not he wanted to run for office; he was chosen by lottery. Therefore, every Athenian was both a citizen and a politician. In Athens, *society* and the *state* became practically one and the same thing. Every Athenian was a public man.

**Pericles.** The man responsible for the building of the Athenian empire and the creation of the resplendent wealth of the city was *Pericles* (PAIR uh kleez). Pericles was an Athenian general who lived from about 495 to 429 B.C. He believed in the capabilities of free men and, in particular, in the right of Athenian men to rule both themselves and others. Pericles had seen the Athenians make their own defense against Persian despotism and go on to build a wealthy state. Like all Greeks, he worshipped the official gods, but his strongest religious feelings were enlisted in a faith in humanity and the worship of man.

One story about Pericles might be revealing. On one of his naval expeditions, his crew became terrified by an eclipse of the sun—supposedly an indication of the gods' disfavor. Pericles took the helmsman aside and threw his cloak over the man's eyes, asking him whether or not he was frightened by that kind of darkness. The maneuver calmed the fears of the crew. The story illustrates how much the Greeks, or at least Pericles, had been freed from some of the superstitions and beliefs which previous human cultures had created.

**Pericles and "Democracy."** The fifth century B.C. is often called the "Age of Pericles." Why, in what seems to be the most democratic of times, should one man's name be given to the era? Although the Athenian system of government was an extreme democracy, Pericles had great influence. He served on the council of generals, an *elected* position in Athenian government, for fifteen years. This meant that he was in a position to lead the democracy for a long uninterrupted period of time. All decisions had to be voted upon, and Pericles could lose an election or even be ostracized if his policy did not please the people. However, he chose to suggest measures which continually pleased the majority of the people. He conquered new lands for settlement and increased trade for merchants, as well as provided employment for artisans and laborers and payment for those who served in the government. He had great power, but his power sprung from the people, not from his role as either monarch or priest. Thucydides, who so often went directly to the heart of a political situation, said of Athens, "In what was nominally a democracy, power was really in the hands of the first citizen."

Although Pericles had a great deal of power, there had to be sensible and intelligent people in Athens because it was they, the people as a whole, who ultimately judged the wisdom of his decisions. How was it, then, that the average merchant, carpenter or stonemason could be capable of running a government and taking over, even if for a short time, the running of the state? Was the average Athenian more intelligent than the average American? Was every Athenian a statesman in disguise? Some people think that this indeed was the case, and in some ways, the Athenian may have possessed qualities which modern man lacks.

**The Ideal Athenian.** The ideal toward which everyone was educated was that of "the whole man," a man who could not only practice a trade, but who could also discuss public policy, engage in athletic contests and master intellectual problems. Greek plays, for example, were serious works of art dealing with complex philosophic problems. Yet, they were performed at a public function which most Athenians attended. Today, these plays are discussed by learned people in universities and schools, but in ancient Athens, they were written for the average man.

Although every Athenian did not sit around arguing about the fine points of philosophy, the training of the mind was undertaken with the same energy with which the body was trained to compete in sports. Intellectual pursuits were not regarded as frills, and physical training was not seen as being boorish—both had their proper place in a man's life. The average Athenian home was small and simple, and so the place where men met to discuss business, politics or philosophy was in the agora (the public marketplace). Life was lived in the open air; the outdoor gymnasium where physical training took place was also the place where intellectual discussion occurred. From the gymnasium to the public assembly was a short move, and the intellectual skill and political sense which was gained in one was carried over to the other. In such a manner was the Athenian secure in the belief that he was capable of self-government—he was a man of many skills.

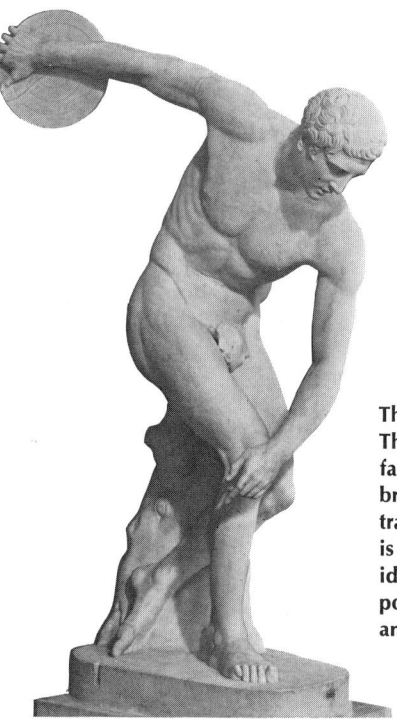

The fifth-century B.C. "Discus-Thrower," perhaps the most famous of Greek statues, breathes with vitality, illustrating many Hellenic traits. It is an example of the Greek ideal of the perfect human portrayed with dynamic energy and balance.

It is true that the possession of slaves who did menial work gave the Athenian more leisure time than modern man can have; also, the warm climate and clear skies of Greece enabled the Athenians to gather outside to exercise both mind and body. A combination of circumstances in fifth-century B.C. Athens created an atmosphere in which leisure time was used to the fullest.

**Man in Athenian Thought.** The emphasis placed upon man, which we have seen in Homer, grew in the fifth century B.C. to a worship of man. Arnold Toynbee, a well-known twentieth century historian, has said, "What distinguishes the Hellenic experiment in Humanism is that it was the most whole-hearted and uncompromising practice of man-worship that is on record up to date." Pericles had this faith in man, and the belief was also found in the writings of numerous Athenian philosophers of the period. *Protagoras* (pro TAG uh ruhs), for example, wrote that "man is the measure of all things." And, according to *Xenophanes* (zih NAHF uh neez):

> If oxen, or lions, or horses had hands like men, they too,
> If they could fashion pictures, or statues they could hew,
> They would shape in their own image each face and form divine—

Horses' gods like horses, like kine [cows] the gods of kine.
"Snub-nosed are the Immortals, and black," the Ethiops say;
But "No," the Thracians answer, "red-haired, with eyes of gray."

Even Greek drama expressed the Athenians' strong faith in humanity. In the words of the Athenian playwright *Sophocles* (SAHF uh kleez):

> Wonders are many on earth, and the greatest of these
> Is man, who rides the ocean and takes his way
> Through the deeps, through wind-swept valleys of
>     perilous seas
> That surge and sway.
> He is master of ageless Earth, to his own will bending
> The immortal mother of gods by the sweat of his brow,
> As year succeeds to year, with toil unending
>     Of mule and plough.
> He is lord of all things living; birds of the air,
> Beasts of the field, all creatures of sea and land
> He taketh, cunning to capture and ensnare
>     With sleight of hand.
> Hunting the savage beast from the upland rocks,
> Taming the mountain monarch in his lair,
> Teaching the wild horse and the roaming ox
>     His yoke to bear.
> The use of language, the wind-swift motion of brain
> He learnt; found out the laws of living together
> In cities, building him shelter against the rain
>     And wintry weather.
> There is nothing beyond his power. His sublety
> Meeteth all chance, all danger conquereth.
> For every ill he hath found its remedy,
>     Save only death.
> O wondrous sublety of man, that draws
> To good or evil ways! Great honour is given
> And power to him who upholdeth his country's laws
>     And the justice of heaven.

## Greek Drama

The characters and issues presented in each Greek play represented some of the values and beliefs which people held in fifth-century B.C. Athens. Drama is an art form in which individual actors impersonate other people and act out human situations. Drama was always closely connected with religion, and religious ceremonies themselves were really plays in which priests acted out certain set parts. In Egypt, for example, the events in the life of the god Osiris were acted out as a way of recreating these events and making the message of the myth known to the people.

Greek drama grew out of the worship of the god *Dionysus* (die uh NIE suhs), and religious plays were given as part of his worship. Thus, Greek drama in the fifth century B.C. retained a strong religious element; the performances were not regarded as entertainment but as the celebration of some serious theme. The fifth-century B.C. dramatists almost always used stories based on mythology, but they used these old stories as a means to express their own religious and ethical views. In Greek society, there was no body of fixed religious truth administered by a body of priests, and so the poets and playwrights served as religious thinkers.

The only way to fully grasp the beauty of Greek drama is to read, or better yet to see, the plays themselves. Here we can only make a few comments about the most important writers in the hope of encouraging further reading of the plays themselves.

**Aeschylus.** A playwright of Greek tragedy, *Aeschylus* (ES kuh luhs) lived from 525 to 456 B.C., during the early years of Athenian power and glory. His most famous work is a group of three plays, called the *Orestia* (or eh STEE uh), which was based on an incident related by Homer in the Odyssey. According to the plot, when King Agamemnon (ag ah MEHM nahn) returned from the Trojan War, he was killed by his wife Clytemnestra (klite ehm NEHS truh), who wanted to marry another man. The children of Agamemnon—Electra and Orestes (aw REHS teez)—then murdered their mother in revenge. This rather bloodthirsty tale of murder and revenge was merely related by Homer. Aeschylus, however, transformed the raw material of this tale and used it to express a new idea.

In the first of the three plays, the actual killing of Agamemnon was told with gripping dramatic power. The second play dealt with the murder of Clytemnestra by Orestes, her son. Since matricide was a deadly sin, Orestes was pursued by the *Furies*—minor gods whose job it was to avenge a crime. This pursuit was dramatized in the third play. Orestes ran to Athens for safety, and while he was there, the elders of Athens intervened, tamed the Furies and pardoned Orestes for his crime. Since his mother had committed the original deed, the elders decided that Orestes had been merely meting out punishment. The elders of Athens, acting as a court, decided upon the case and made it known that courts rather than individuals should mete out judgment.

What Aeschylus did in these plays was to depict, in dramatic form, the Athenian polis itself as an institution which substituted the *law of justice* for the older *law of revenge*. He portrayed on the stage the actual accomplishment of the polis—it had broken the power of the family feud by providing a form of law in which judges, chosen by the polis, took the place of personal revenge. If the elders of Athens had not intervened, as described in the final play, murder and revenge would have continued through an endless cycle. The *Orestia* dramatized the triumph of reason over instinct, and the public performance of this play in Athens served to reaffirm the Athenians' faith in their polis and in the power of human reason.

**Sophocles.** Coming after Aeschylus in the history of Athens was the famous playwright *Sophocles* (495-405 B.C.), whose plays usually presented a penetrating portrayal of man in search of self-knowledge. Sophocles retold the story of Oedipus (EH dih puhs), the mythical king of Thebes who unknowingly killed his father and married his mother. Oedipus, believing that his great mind and supreme reason could solve all problems, moved heaven and earth to discover the man who had committed the terrible crime, only to find that it was he, himself. Rather than dwelling on the sordid aspects of this story, Sophocles turned his play, *King Oedi-*

The Theater of Dionysus in Athens was the setting for the dramas described in this chapter. The exposed stage made scenery and settings unimportant compared with the human drama which was enacted in the open air before the citizen body.

*Alinari*

## HELLAS
(c. 5TH Century B.C.)

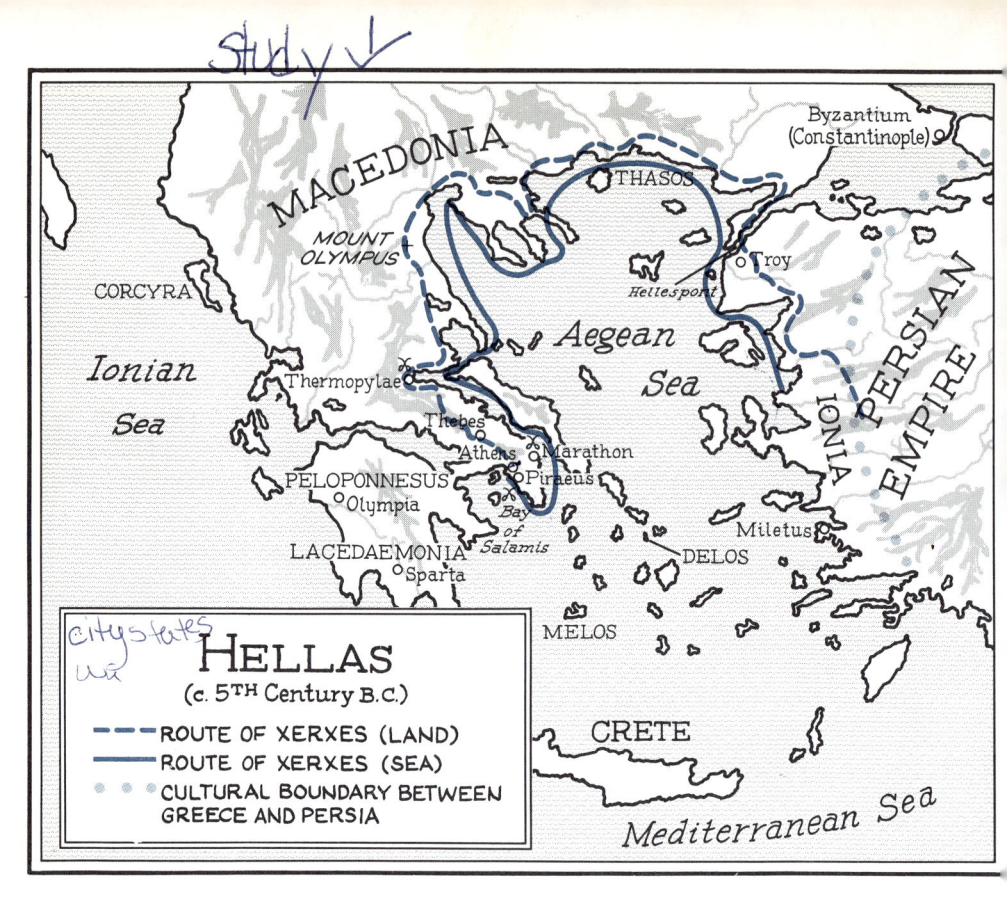

- - - ROUTE OF XERXES (LAND)
——— ROUTE OF XERXES (SEA)
• • • CULTURAL BOUNDARY BETWEEN GREECE AND PERSIA

With few inland cities, "Hellas" in the fifth century B.C. was a seaborne cultural entity that included many of the Mediterranean islands and nearby shores. The boundary that existed between Hellas and the Persian empire to the east was more cultural than physical.

pus, into an examination of the nature of man, his pride and his guilt. In the play *Antigone* (an TIH guh nee), Sophocles dealt with the problem of a conflict between an individual's conscience and the demands of the government, a conflict which is very much alive today.

Although the gods often appeared in Greek plays, the focus of the drama was always on man and the human condition. Playwrights portrayed man faced with some kind of problem so that members of the audience could identify with the main character and learn something about themselves from viewing the play.

**Euripides.** The tragedy-writer *Euripides* (yoo RIHP uh deez) lived in the late fifth century B.C., from 480 to 406, when Athens was engaged in a long and destructive war with Sparta. Euripides' characters were mythological, but yet they strike us as more human than the characters of the earlier writers. Euripides, having seen the breakdown of what was good in Athenian society, showed little faith in either the gods or the polis. His characters often stood alone, confronting impossible situations armed only with their own intelligence. The spectacle of man cut loose from all comfortable religious and ethical truths was presented in vivid terms in his plays. Euripides, in many ways, speaks most to our own age; in fact, one of his plays, *The Trojan Women,* recently enjoyed a long run in a modern theater.

**Aristophanes.** The last Greek playwright to be discussed is *Aristophanes* (air ihs TAHF uh neez), a comic writer who lived from 448 to 385 B.C. Aristophanes often presented a serious message in humorous form. He was a contemporary of Euripides, but Aristophanes chose laughter rather than tragedy as his method. His plays often dealt with living people, philosophers and statesmen, and most of his writing was critical of these public figures. His plays are often difficult for us to fully understand, because we do not know all the people referred to. It is remarkable that he could criticize the government so openly during a war, a fact which might well show that for the Greeks, freedom of expression was a reality.

The Greek playwrights were much like the Hebrew prophets in that they were individual thinkers who reflected and wrote about basic religious and ethical problems. Unlike many of the thinkers of the ancient world, they have a message for all times. Much of Greek thought deals with issues of man and the gods, good and evil, right and wrong—basic problems which face people of all ages. On the Greek stage, man, in both his dignity and degradation, is displayed in a clear light, thus serving as a mirror in which every man can see himself and learn of his own nature.

## The Unity of Athenian Culture

It is not only the content or message of Greek literature which is worthy of study. The Greek plays themselves have a beauty in the poetry and in the balanced structure of the action, which, in turn, has a sense of unity and basic harmony. While using their minds to probe the meaning of life and the nature of man, the Greeks developed a remarkable sense of beauty. This desire for beauty can be seen in many elements of Greek life and culture. For example, Athenian vases and cups were made to be more than practical, everyday utensils; they were at the same time works of art. The beauty and variety of Greek vases can be quickly grasped by looking at them in a museum. Each one is striking in its color and design, but no one vase is like the other.

The major characteristic of Greek culture was this sense of form or symmetry in which each vase, play, poem, statue or temple was appropriate to its function. The Parthenon, a building which is the embodiment of the Greek spirit, is a perfect building, balanced and restrained, yet containing sculpture which breathes vitality and action. Just as Greek plays must be read, so Greek sculpture and architecture must be seen. It is perhaps in the Greeks' portrayal of the human form that their worship of man, their intense humanism, can best be seen. Man in his perfect form confronts us in a Greek statue and represents the ideal toward which all of Greek culture strived. Greek statues were not copies of men but rather were images of an idealized man, a perfect model which natural man was to strive to imitate.

The Age of Pericles is called a Golden Age because men reached a kind of perfection, and they established standards and goals by which men of later ages have measured themselves and their culture. The direct encounter of modern man with the poets, playwrights, statesmen and artists of Athens can be an invigorating and ennobling experience.

## Define

Delian League      Sophocles       Euripides
Piraeus            Dionysus        Aristophanes
Pericles           Aeschylus

## Review and Answer

1. Describe the forces and circumstances which led to the development of the Athenian empire.
2. What were the economic bases of Athenian greatness in the fifth century B.C.?
3. What does it mean to say that *society* and *the state* became the same thing in fifth-century B.C. Athens?
4. What was the purpose of Greek drama, and what issues did Greek plays present?
5. In what ways was Athenian democracy different from modern democratic governments?

# 4

# The Agony of Hellas

Many people have the misconception that the Greeks were perfect people, living in the midst of continual beauty in a cozy family, governing themselves, philosophizing and relaxing. Art, however, is not reality, and perhaps the greatness of the Greek achievement stems from the fact that life was not perfect and easy for them. The educated Athenian might ponder the meaning of Sophocles' plays, delight in the order and dignity of the Parthenon, and realize that an eclipse of the sun was no different than a cloak thrown over his eyes. Yet, the majority of Greeks continued in their old ways, preferred the rough humor of Aristophanes, saw the Parthenon as a status symbol or as a source of employment for sculptors, stonemasons, and laborers and lived in constant fear of the wrath of the gods.

It was not only the uneducated and superstitious who made the ideal of a perfect society impossible to attain. Differences of opinion, greed for money and the desire for fame or power can influence the most intelligent and cultured person. The Athenians' treatment of the smaller allied states shows clearly both the disdain felt toward non-Athenians and the brutality which this disdain produced. Such arrogance existed within, as well as without, the walls of Athens. The Roman biographer *Plutarch* (PLOO tark) described fifth-century B.C. Athens by saying, "Below the surface of affairs in Athens, there had existed from the very beginning, a kind of flaw or seam, such as one finds in a piece of iron, which gave a hint of the rift that divided the aims of the popular and the aristocratic parties."

## The Peloponnesian War

The old struggle between those who favored a government by a few and those who favored a government by many was still going on. As long as Athens was wealthy, secure from attack and had a strong leader, democracy seemed to work well. However, in the late fifth century B.C., the Greeks fought a major war, filled with death, destruction and the loss of wealth, plus the loss of Pericles, who died in 429 B.C. The unity of the polis was broken, and the Athenians faced severe social and political problems. The war which was to test the strength of Greek society and culture began in 431 B.C. and was fought between Athens and Sparta, each aided by allies. The conflict ended in 404 B.C. with the defeat of Athens. The significance of the *Peloponnesian War* lies in the fact that just as the Greeks seemed to be attaining the realization of human perfection, a war among Greeks themselves broke out; the war not only reduced the material power of all of Greece but brought out the worst aspects of man's nature.

**The Greek Mind in Turmoil.** By freeing man from the ties of tradition-bound society and age-old religions, the Greeks had unleashed the power of man, with his potential for endless development. Yet, this very release had set loose equally strong and equally human powers of self-destruction. The godlike man whom Homer had caught a glimpse of, whom Sophocles had praised, and whom the arts had depicted turned against himself at the very moment he had freed himself from the old shackles of life and thought. He could not go back, and he had not yet worked out the way to go forward. Just as the wisdom of Oedipus had been the instrument of his downfall, the triumph of the Greek mind seemed to cause its own degradation. The Greeks of the late fifth century B.C., during the dreadful war, gazed on this paradox in all the clarity that their thinkers could produce. It is this vision which makes their experience so important to us.

In studying this paradox of the Greek mind, we will look briefly at the Peloponnesian War and at the late fifth century B.C. Our focus will be on two men—one a general and historian, the other a teacher and philosopher. *Thucydides,* the historian, realized the tremendous consequences of the war and decided to record the events in detail, having experienced the war firsthand. His analysis of the causes of the war and its effects on both men and ideas makes him a most valuable person for us to study. *Socrates* (SAHK ruh teez), a teacher and philosopher, attempted to seek the truth and to provide a philosophy of life for his fellow-citizens in an age when the certainties of Pericles' time were no longer accepted and when the gods seemed to have deserted Athens. His desire to teach both himself and others to distinguish truth from falsehood, knowledge from mere opinion, shows the Greek spirit in its purest form. The fact that he was put to death by the Athenian people themselves is a brutal example of the complexity of human nature.

**The Early War Years.** As Thucydides relates, the war began when the states in the Peloponnesus, especially Corinth, believed that Athens was about to dominate the whole of Hellas. The Corinthians prodded the conservative Spartans to rouse themselves and to defend the liberty of the Greek states. In the war, the Peloponnesian states, along with Thebes, fought against Athens and its empire. The Athenians had control of the sea, a rich treasury and the support of the island states within their empire. The Peloponnesians had better land forces and were able to gather a large number of allies from the mainland of Greece itself.

**Disunity in Athens.** In many states, people took different views on the war, depending on their position in society. Democrats tended to favor Athens, whereas oligarchs leaned toward Sparta. The Peloponnesian War, therefore, was a war between classes of men, a civil war, as well as a war between separate states. In Athens, the oligarchs were not fully in favor of the war, and when it continued year after year, Athenian society became more and more divided. Pericles, representing the democratic group, decided that all Athenians should move within the walls of the city. He wanted not to engage the Spartans on the land but rather to

This sculpture of a Greek archer shows the quality of controlled brutality which, in Greek culture, coexisted with an admiration of human beauty and grace. Both qualities are not lacking in this statue.

*German Archaeological Institute*

use power where Athens had it—on the sea. This policy was opposed by the land-holding oligarchy, whose lands would be destroyed by the Spartan army; city people favored it. At the outset of the war, crowded conditions in the city had led to a severe plague which killed one-third of the population. The strain of the war and the increasing division between the classes within Athens eventually led to violence.

After Pericles' death in 429 B.C., no leader emerged who could unify the people. One leader, *Cleon*, argued for a vigorous prosecution of the war; another statesman, *Nicias* (NISH ee uhs), a leader of the oligarchical class, wished to arrange a negotiated peace with Sparta. After ten years of fighting, Nicias' truce was signed, but it lasted for only a few years.

**The War and the Democratic System.** The war exposed the shortcomings of a democracy, for open discussion of issues could often lead to a confusion of goals and a lack of firm decision. The oligarchical party became more and more distrustful of the ability of the average citizen to handle political power.

Cleon himself was outspokenly critical of Athenian democracy —a fact which is apparent in the following speech made by Cleon to the citizens of Athens and recorded by Thucydides.

> The blame is yours for stupidly instituting these competitive displays [debates]. You have become regular speech goers, and as for action you merely listen to accounts of it; if something is to be done in the future, you estimate the possibilities by hearing a good speech on the subject, and as for the past you rely not so much on the facts which you have seen with your own eyes as on what you have heard about them in some clever piece of verbal criticism. Any novelty in an argument deceives you at once, but when the argument is tried and proved you become unwilling to follow it; you look with suspicion on what is normal and are the slaves of every paradox that comes your way. The chief wish of one of you is to be able to make a speech himself, and, if you cannot do that, the next best thing is to compete with those who can make this sort of speech by not looking as though you were at all out of your depth while you listen to the views put forward, by applauding a good point even before it is made, and by being as quick at seeing how an argument is going to be developed as you are slow at understanding what in the end it will lead to. You are simply victims of your own pleasure in listening, and are more like an audience sitting at the feet of a professional lecturer than a parliament discussing matters of state.

**Alcibiades.** The truce arranged by Nicias was broken when Athens decided to attack Syracuse, a Greek city on the island of

Sicily. This wealthy city in the West had once been a colony of Corinth and was thought to be friendly to the Peloponnesian cause. The statesman who persuaded the Athenian assembly to make the invasion was the young and brilliant *Alcibiades* (al suh BI uh deez). This man appeared to be the ideal Greek. He was near perfect in bodily form and physical strength, and as a pupil of Socrates, he had a razor-sharp mind. He looked like a statue of the perfect man; he was proud of his accomplishments, paid little or no attention to the gods, and sought to live as full a life as possible. He was all that was admired by the Greeks of his day. Read the following fragment from one of Alcibiades' speeches (as recorded by Thucydides) in which he urged the Athenians to intervene once again in the war.

> Do not be put off by Nicias' argument for non-intervention and his distinction between the young and old. Let us instead keep to the old system of our fathers who joined together in counsel, young and old alike, and raised our state to the position it now holds. So now in the same way make it your endeavour to raise this city to even greater heights, realizing that neither youth nor age can do anything, one without the other, but that the greatest strength is developed when one has a combination where all sorts are represented—the inferior types, the ordinary types, and the profoundly calculating types, all together. Remember, too, that the city like everything else will wear out of its own accord if it remains at rest, and its skill in everything will grow out of date; but in conflict it will constantly be gaining new experience and growing more used to defend itself not by speeches, but in action. In general, my view is that a city which is active by nature will soon ruin itself if it changes its nature and becomes idle, and that the way that men find their greatest security is in accepting the character of the institutions which they actually have, even if they are not perfect, and living as nearly as possible in accordance with them.

It was, therefore, the vigorous and good qualities of the Greeks which served to lead the Athenians to extend a war which was to become so destructive to their culture.

The Athenian expedition left for Syracuse with Alcibiades in command, but Alcibiades was accused of having committed an irreligious act before leaving, and he was asked to return to stand trial. The brilliant general took this request as an insult to his genius, and he went over to the Spartan side to offer his services to them. The expedition against Syracuse resulted in a disaster for Athens; its army was cut to pieces, and the survivors were taken into slavery. In 404 B.C., the Spartans gained control of the Helles-

Alinari—Art Reference Bureau

This statue of the Greek god Hermes is an example of the ultimate in the Greek quest for the perfect human. Here is a figure whose face and form are perfect in their beauty. The statue is a powerful illustration of the Greek worship of the human form.

pont and, with Persian assistance, forced Athens to surrender. The long walls between Athens and Piraeus were torn down, and Sparta became the most powerful state in Greece. The deeper result of the war, however, was the damage the Greeks did to each other.

**The Late War Years.** This damage was even more tragic when citizens within a state fought against each other in a civil war. Even in Athens, where democracy had seemed to be the most established, people turned against each other and were willing to seek aid from outside the polis. The Athenian aristocrats called in the Spartan army to help them get rid of a democratic government. In other states, those who believed in democracy were willing to enlist the aid of Athens even though the Athenians might officially be their enemy. A government ruled by a few men, called the *Thirty Tyrants,* was established in Athens, and many people were put to death in the process. In time, democracy was reestablished with equal violence. The following words carved on a monument attest to the anger aroused by these class conflicts: "Here lie the brave men who checked for a time the arrogance of the damned democracy of Athens."

## Socrates

Socrates, who lived most of his mature life during the war and social upheavals, was keenly aware of man's potential and of his problems. He was a loyal Athenian citizen, but he attempted to stay out of politics. In Athens, however, a brilliant man could not retain a private existence. Alcibiades, one of Socrates' pupils, had defected to Sparta and eventually ended his life in Persia. Socrates remained in Athens but was put to death in 399 B.C. for his teachings—not, as we might expect, by the Thirty Tyrants, but by the people themselves soon after democracy returned to Athens.

**Education in Athens.** In a city such as Athens, where every citizen participated in public affairs, education was very important. Although education was not invented by the Greeks, the kind of training necessary for an Athenian citizen was quite different from that required by an Egyptian or Sumerian. An Athenian had to be able to handle political issues. His life was more demanding than that of his ancestor of Homeric times, when courage and military skills were all that were required. In addition to politics, the Athenian of the fifth century B.C. had to develop the intellectual equipment to work out his own philosophy of life.

The glory of the Age of Pericles rested on the belief that man was the measure of all things. For the wealthy, confident and secure man of Athens, the superstitions and beliefs of the past were deemed no longer necessary. However, the brutal Peloponnesian War had shown man to be capable of violence, evil and inhuman actions. In response to this realization about man, the Greek thinkers could go in one of two directions: they could either fall back on old traditions and assume that man was weak and dependent on the gods; or they could work to train the mind of man to grasp the unchanging truth in a rapidly changing world and so to make man's "measure" both firm and rational. The basic humanism of the Greeks, severely tested by the war, had to be supported by a man-made system of values developed without reliance on the traditional beliefs of a simpler age. Through proper education, man could be made perfect.

Organized schools such as we know today did not exist. Rather, there were professional teachers who moved through the city offering for sale their skill in training young people. Such wandering teachers were called *sophists* (SAHF uhsts). What they taught was called *rhetoric,* a word which we use today to describe the ability to write and speak correctly. In view of the fact that Athens was a direct democracy, the ability to make a proper speech was an essential skill and of far greater importance than it is to us. However, for the Greeks, rhetoric carried with it a broader meaning than merely the ability to make a good public speech. To them, rhetoric meant proper thinking, the necessary prelude to proper speaking. Sophists filled the educational needs of the democratic polis of Athens. They, themselves, were a product of the polis.

**The Sophists.** The sophists claimed that through their teaching, they developed in their pupils a quality which, in Greek, is called *arete*. This word is usually translated into English as "virtue," but as is always the case with translations, *arete* meant more to the Greeks than "virtue" means to us. To them, *arete* was excellence of some sort. For example, the *arete* of a warrior as portrayed by Homer was the full development of qualities such as courage, honor and personal loyalty. The *arete* of a craftsman was the perfect use of his hands to achieve excellence in his particular craft. The sophists' *arete* dealt with the perfection of skills and attitudes needed by citizens, the ability to make wise decisions and to express them well.

Socrates, a teacher whose interests went beyond those of the sophists, had a sense of *arete* which was both broad and deep. He sought to develop the *arete,* or excellence, of the individual man, to bring about the full realization of his humanity and a complete understanding of his own nature. The quest for this kind of virtue was embodied in the Greek motto, "Know thyself," a quest which every person at every time in history must make. Hence, Socrates focused his attention on man and became one of the major proponents of *humanism*. As he himself put it:

> . . . so long as I draw breath and have my faculties, I shall never stop practicing philosophy and exhorting you and elucidating the truth for everyone that I meet. I shall go on saying in my usual way, "My very good friend, you are an Athenian and belong

to a city which is the greatest and most famous in the world for its wisdom and strength. Are you not ashamed that you give your attention to acquiring as much money as possible, and similarly with reputation and honor, and give no attention or thought to truth and understanding and the perfection of your soul?"

Socrates took issue with most of the sophists because they gained money and prestige by teaching people how to argue cleverly for any cause, good or bad. The fascination with clever mental and verbal gymnastics was one result of the sophists' teaching. Socrates, living in a troubled time when old values were no longer valid, was more interested in teaching wisdom than clever word-play. He took no money from those who learned from him; he was not a seller of intellectual skills. He wanted to see the human mind, that powerful instrument which the Greeks had discovered, used to create a perfect man and a perfect society.

**The Socratic Method.** Socrates' search for knowledge came through conversation, or *dialogue,* with other men. According to him, wisdom could not be gained from relying on the sayings of wise men in the past, or even from listening to a living wise man lecture. Knowledge came from the give and take of discussion, the informed conversation of living men. This *Socratic method,* a new means of extracting knowledge from within men themselves, is recorded in the many *Socratic Dialogues,* which were written down by *Plato* (PLAY toe), a pupil of Socrates. In one of these Dialogues, the group is attempting to analyze the meaning of a poem. Socrates breaks in and says:

> The best people avoid such discussions, and entertain each other from their own resources, testing one another's mettle in what they had to say themselves. These are the people, in my opinion, whom you and I should follow, setting the poets aside and conducting the conversation on the basis of our own ideas. It is the truth, and our own minds, that we should be testing. If you want to go on with your questions, I am ready to offer myself as an answerer; or if you prefer, be my respondent, to bring to its conclusion the discussion which we broke off in the middle.

In using conversation to "test each other's mettle," Socrates was using the old Homeric concept of conflict. However, for Socrates, this conflict led to a strengthening of the mind rather than a toughening of the body. His deep concern with man's mind and soul, and his awareness of the effects which ideas have on a human being, can be seen in the following conversation. Socrates saw a young man, Hippocrates (hih PAHK ruh teez), who was on his way to listen to the great sophist, Protagoras. Socrates detained him to give him some advice.

> "Can we say then, Hippocrates, that a Sophist is really a merchant or a peddler of the goods by which a soul is nourished? To me he appears to be something like that."
> "But what is that which nourishes a soul?" asked Hippocrates.
> "What it learns, presumably," I said, "and we must see that the Sophist in commending his wares does not deceive us like the wholesaler and the retailer who deal in food for the body. These people do not know themselves which of the wares they offer is good or bad for the body, but in selling them praise all alike; and those who buy from them don't know either, unless one of them happens to be a trainer or a doctor. So too those who take the various subjects of knowledge from city to city and offer them for sale, retail to whoever wants them, commending everything that they have for sale; but it may be, my dear Hippocrates, that some of these men also are ignorant of the beneficial or harmful effects on the soul of what they have for sale, and so too are those who buy from them, unless one of them happens to be a physician of the soul. If then you chance to be an expert in discerning which of them is good or bad, it is sage for you to buy knowledge from Protagoras or anyone else; but if not, take care you don't find yourself gambling dangerously with all of you that is dear to you. Indeed the risk you run in purchasing knowledge is much greater than that in buying provisions. When you buy food and drink, you can carry it away from the shop or warehouse in a receptacle, and before you receive it into your body by eating or drinking you can store it away at home and take the advice of an expert as to what you should eat and drink and what not, and how much you should consume and when; so there is not much risk in the actual purchase. But knowledge cannot be taken away in a parcel. When you have paid for it you must receive it straight into the soul; you go away having learned it, and are benefited or harmed accordingly."

For Socrates, therefore, knowledge was a real substance capable of doing great harm or great good.

**The Search for Truth.** Socrates never wrote down any of his teachings because, in a sense, he had no system or doctrine which could be memorized by his followers. Unlike the Hebrews, the Greeks were not "a people of the book" who based their culture upon a sacred scripture. Their thinkers were the poets, philosophers and dramatists. Truth was the great goal, but the "truth" of any one time, of any one thinker, was always in the process of changing. Even the "truth" of Homer was challenged by later thinkers, Socrates included. Socrates, whose entire life was a

## THE AGONY OF HELLAS 61

search for truth, could never say with finality that he had reached absolute truth. His thoughts and ideas came as the result of the dynamic interaction of individuals in the process of conversation. To our own age, which seems to have lost the art of conversation, the experience of Socrates, gaining insights and wisdom like sparks shooting off from the friction of two minds in a dialogue, might well lead us back to genuine conversation. For any student, a reading of the Socratic Dialogues should be the introduction to genuine learning. As Socrates said:

> I am one of those who are very willing to be refuted if I say anything which is not true, and very willing to refute anyone else who says what is not true, and quite as ready to be refuted as to refute; for I hold that this is the greatest gain of the two, just as the gain is greater of being cured of a very great evil than of curing another. For I imagine that there is no evil which a man can endure so great as an erroneous opinion.

As a means of coming closer to grasping the differences between the Greek and Egyptian cultures, we should compare Socrates' statement with the Egyptian saying about a wise man: "Truth comes to him (fully) brewed, in accordance with the sayings of the ancestors.*

**Good and Evil Explained.** Socrates believed that he was wise only because he realized that he did not possess true wisdom. His way of seeking true wisdom was to clear away old ideas and beliefs so that the mind could start afresh. By using this method, Socrates proclaimed a faith in the ability of man to form his own values without the aid of traditional beliefs. Old restraints were taken away, and man was left on his own. Virtue would come through knowledge, and for Socrates, evil was merely a lack of knowledge. No one did evil while knowing that it was evil. A man might mistake an evil action for a good one, but this choice was only the result of cloudy thinking. The aim of Socratic education was to clear the mind of the clouds which brought about evil actions. Such optimistic faith in man's rationality has never been more strongly expressed than by Socrates and his followers. In the midst of the Peloponnesian War and the evil caused by it, Socrates clung to the hope that clear thinking was possible and that through it, society could be made perfect.

While Socrates was clearing the minds of people, he, of course, became unpopular. As he said, "It is literally true (even if it

---

* In this quotation, the parentheses indicate a conjecture made by the translator since the meaning in the original was unclear.

sounds rather comical) that God has specially appointed me to this city as though it were a large thoroughbred horse which because of its great size is inclined to be lazy and needs the stimulation of some stinging fly." A stinging fly, a disturber of accepted beliefs, is never well-liked, especially if one of his pupils (namely, Alcibiades) becomes a traitor. Socrates loved Athens and remained faithful to the end, but he had little faith in democracy as an absolute system. According to him, "A good decision is based on knowledge and not on numbers." The oligarchs used his arguments to put themselves in power, but Socrates did not favor them; excellence came from true intelligence, not from noble birth.

**The Death of Socrates.** When the democratic group was restored to power, the people condemned Socrates to death for leading the young astray and for criticizing old ideals. When offered a chance to escape, Socrates refused; he showed the ultimate courage by not going back on his views but still accepting the judgment of his fellow citizens. The logic of this position led to death, but even this prospect did not fill him with fear.

> For let me tell you something, gentlemen, that to be afraid of death is only another form of thinking that one is wise when one is not; it is to think that one knows what one does not know. No one knows with regard to death whether it is not really the greatest blessing that can happen to a man; but people dread it as though they were certain that it is the greatest evil; and this ignorance, which thinks that it knows what it does not, must be ignorance most culpable. This I take it, gentlemen, is the degree and this the nature of my advantage over the rest of mankind; and if I were to claim to be wiser than my neighbor in any respect it would be in this: that not possessing any real knowledge of what comes after death, I am also conscious that I do not possess it.

Here we see Socrates being consistent to his philosophy and being armed to face death with courage and even grandeur. He realized the debt which he owed to the polis, to Athens, which had nourished him throughout his life, and so he would not tarnish his loyalty by running away at the end. In so doing, he affirmed the commitment to the polis. In the following passage, Socrates expressed his deep sense of obligation and the almost religious bond of unity which existed in the polis.

> Suppose that while we were preparing to run away from here (or however one should describe it) the Laws and Constitution of Athens were to come and confront us and ask this question: "Now Socrates what are you going to do? Can you deny that by

"The Death of Socrates," which was painted by the French artist Jacques Louis David in the late eighteenth century, shows the continuing impact of Greek themes and styles. Socrates is about to drink the poison, confident and without fear in spite of the grief and confusion around him. Hellenic clarity and reason can be clearly seen.

this act which you are contemplating you intend, so far as you have the power, to destroy us; the Laws and the whole State as well? Do you imagine that a city can continue to exist and not be turned upside down if the legal judgements which are pronounced in it have no force but are nullified and destroyed by private persons? . . . Did we not give you life in the first place? Was it not through us that your father married your mother and begot you? . . . Are you not grateful to those of us Laws which were instituted for . . . requiring your father to give you a cultural and physical education? . . . Can you deny . . . that you were our child and servant, both you and your ancestors?"

In accepting the judgment of the laws and in accepting death, Socrates not only affirmed a loyalty to the polis, but he showed his belief in the immortality of truth. The taking of a life cannot destroy the progress of truth. Socrates did not die quietly; his death has disturbed the ages.

I tell you, my executioners, that as soon as I am dead, vengeance shall fall upon you with a punishment far more painful than your killing of me. You have brought about my death in the belief that through it you will be delivered from submitting your conduct to criticism; but I say that the result will be the opposite. You will have more critics, who up 'til now I have restrained without your knowing it; and being younger they will be harsher to you and will cause you more annoyance. If you expect to stop denunciation of your wrong way of life by putting people to death, there is something amiss with your reasoning. This way of escape is neither possible nor creditable; the best and easiest way is not to stop the mouths of others, but to make yourselves as good men as you can. This is my last message to you who voted for my condemnation.

Perhaps Socrates had Alcibiades in mind as an example of a younger and more violent critic. In any event, the Peloponnesian War, with its suicidal warfare among the Greek states and the violence it caused within the polis, violence which culminated in the execution of a great thinker, raised basic questions about the nature of man. The questions posed by the Greeks have yet to be answered.

Perhaps it was better for all of us that Greek culture was not permitted to grow in a peaceful and secure society but rather was forced to come to grips with the full range of man's potential—cruelty as well as kindness, ignorance as well as wisdom, ugliness as well as beauy. The experience of the Greeks as recorded by their artists, playwrights, philosophers and historians has become and remains, in the words of Thucydides, "a possession for all times."

## Define

| Thucydides | Nicias | rhetoric |
| Socrates | Alcibiades | dialogue |
| Cleon | sophists | |

## Review and Answer

1. What were some of the weaknesses of democracy as a form of government which Cleon pointed out in his speech (page 54)?

2. How can both the words (page 55) and the career of Alcibiades be seen as a symbol of the paradox of Greek culture?

3. What were the full consequences of the Peloponnesian War, and why was this war particularly disturbing to Greek culture and society?

4. What was Socrates' mission in life, and what methods did he use in the pursuit of his goal?
5. How can the issues raised by Socrates, as well as his political reasoning and the circumstances of his death, be related to questions raised by political dissent today?

## Reading II
# Greek Society: Unity and Disunity
### Selections from Thucydides

The Greek polis was the setting for the creation of Hellenic culture. This social unit symbolized the unity of citizens and the concentration of creative energy. At the same time, the very intensity which had created and sustained the independent polis was capable of destroying that very unity. A vigorous people, the Greeks were capable of both grandeur and degradation. The two documents which follow, drawn from the writings of Thucydides, illustrate the best and the worst of Greek political experience.

*The Funeral Oration of Pericles*

It was a practice in Athens to have a public funeral for men who had died in combat. At these services, which were attended by the entire citizen body, a leading statesman was chosen to give a speech or oration. Pericles' *Funeral Oration,* as recorded by Thucydides, stands as a clear and passionate statement of the ideals of Athenian democracy. From this document, we can not only learn some facts about Athenian society and values, but we can grasp the sense of unity and involvement created by the Greek polis.

To what extent Pericles' words represent the realities of Athenian politics and society is difficult to say. As with most politicians, Pericles presents his nation in a favorable light. Yet, the ideals expressed by him did represent what Athenians believed their city could be. His is the classic definition of the perfect society.

Let me say that our system of government does not copy the institutions of our neighbours. It is more the case of our being a model to others, than of our imitating anyone else. Our constitution is called a democracy because power is in the hands not of a minority but of the whole people. When it is a question of settling private disputes, everyone is equal before the law; when it is a question of putting one person before another in positions of public responsibility, what counts is not membership of a particular class, but the actual ability which the man possesses. No one, so long as he has it in him to be of service to the state, is kept in political obscurity because of poverty. And, just as our political

---

Thucydides, *The Peloponnesian War,* trans. Rex Warner (Harmondsworth, Middlesex, England: Penguin Books, 1954), pp. 116-121. Reprinted by permission.

life is free and open, so is our day-to-day life in our relations with each other. We do not get into a state with our next-door neighbour if he enjoys himself in his own way, nor do we give him the kind of black looks which, though they do no real harm, still do hurt people's feelings. We are free and tolerant in our private lives; but in public affairs we keep to the law. This is because it commands our deep respect.

We give our obedience to those whom we put in positions of authority, and we obey the laws themselves, especially those which are for the protection of the oppressed, and those unwritten laws which it is an acknowledged shame to break.

And here is another point. When our work is over, we are in a position to enjoy all kinds of recreation for our spirits. There are various kinds of contests and sacifices regularly throughout the year; in our own homes we find a beauty and a good taste which delight us every day and which drive away our cares. Then the greatness of our city brings it about that all the good things from all over the world flow in to us, so that to us it seems just as natural to enjoy foreign goods as our own local products.

Then there is a great difference between us and our opponents, in our attitude towards military security. Here are some examples: Our city is open to the world, and we have no periodical deportations in order to prevent people observing or finding out secrets which might be of military advantage to the enemy. This is because we rely, not on secret weapons, but on our own real courage and loyalty. There is a difference, too, in our educational systems. The Spartans, from their earliest boyhood, are submitted to the most laborious training in courage; we pass our lives without all these restrictions, and yet are just as ready to face the same dangers as they are. Here is a proof of this: When the Spartans invade our land, they do not come by themselves, but bring all their allies with them; whereas we, when we launch an attack abroad, do the job by ourselves, and, though fighting on foreign soil, do not often fail to defeat opponents who are fighting for their own hearths and homes.

. . . . . . . . . .

Our love of what is beautiful does not lead to extravagance; our love of the things of the mind does not make us soft. We regard wealth as something to be properly used, rather than as something to boast about. As for poverty, no one need be ashamed to admit it: the real shame is in not taking practical measures to escape from it. Here each individual is interested not only in his own affairs but in the affairs of the state as well: even those who are mostly occupied with their own business are extremely well-informed on general politics—this is a peculiarity of ours: we do not say that a man who takes no interest in politics is a man who minds his own business; we say that he has no business here at all. We Athenians, in our own persons, take our decisions on policy or submit them to proper discussions: for we do not think that there is an incompatibility between words and deeds; the worst thing is to rush into action before the consequences have been properly debated. And this is another point where we differ from other people. We are capable at the same time of taking risks and of estimating them beforehand. Others are brave out of ignorance; and, when they stop to think, they begin to fear. But the man who can most truly be accounted brave is he who best knows the meaning of what is sweet in life and what is terrible, and then goes out undeterred to meet what is to come.

Again, in questions of general good feeling there is a great contrast between us and most other people. We make friends by doing good to others, not by receiving good from them. This makes our friendship all the more reliable, since we want to keep alive the gratitude of those who are in our debt by showing continued goodwill to them: whereas the feelings of one who owes us something lack the same enthusiasm, since he knows that, when he repays our kindness, it will be more like paying back a debt than giving something spontaneously. We are unique in this. When we do kindnesses to others, we do not do them out of any calculations of profit or loss: we do them without afterthought, relying on our free liberality. Taking everything together then, I declare that our city is an education to Greece, and I declare that in my opinion each single one of our citizens, in all the manifold aspects of life, is able to show himself the rightful lord and owner of his own person, and do this, moreover, with exceptional grace and exceptional versatility. And to show that this is no empty boasting for the present occasion, but real tangible fact, you have only to consider the power which our city possesses and which has been won by those very qualities which I have mentioned. Athens, alone of the states we know, comes to her testing time in a greatness that surpasses what was imagined of her. In her case, and in her case alone, no invading enemy is ashamed at being defeated, and no subject can complain of being governed by people unfit for their responsibilities. Mighty indeed are the marks and monuments of our empire which we have left. Future ages will wonder at us, as the present age wonders at us now. We do not need the praises of a Homer, or of anyone else whose words may delight us for the moment, but whose estimation of facts will fall short of what is really true. For our adventurous spirit has forced an entry into every sea and into every land; and everywhere we have left behind us everlasting memorials of good done to our friends or suffering inflicted on our enemies.

. . . . . . . . . . . . .

So and such they were, these men—worthy of their city. We who remain behind may hope to be spared their fate, but must resolve to keep the same daring spirit against the foe. It is not simply a question of estimating the advantages in theory. I could tell you a long story (and you know it as well as I do) about what is to be gained by beating the enemy back. What I would prefer is that you should fix your eyes every day on the greatness of Athens as she really is, and should fall in love with her. When you realize her greatness, then reflect that what made her great was men with a spirit of adventure, men who knew their duty, men who were ashamed to fall below a certain standard. If they ever failed in an enterprise, they made up their minds that at any rate the city should not find their courage lacking to her, and they gave to her the best contributions that they could. They gave her their lives, to her and to all of us, and for their own selves they won praises that never grow old, the most splendid of sepulchres—not the sepulchre in which their bodies are laid, but where their glory remains eternal in men's minds, always there on the right occasion to stir others to speech or to action. For famous men have the whole earth as their memorial: it is not only the inscriptions on their graves in their own country that mark them out; no, in foreign lands also, not in any visible form but in people's hearts, their memory abides and grows. It is for you to try to be like them. Make up your minds that happiness depends on being free, and freedom depends on being courageous. Let there be no relaxation in face of the perils of the war. The people who have most excuse for despising death are not the wretched and unfortunate, who have no hope of doing well for themselves, but those who run the risk of a complete reversal in their lives, and who would feel the difference most intensely, if things went wrong for them. Any intelligent man would find a humiliation caused by his own slackness more painful to bear than death, when death comes to him unperceived, in battle, and in the confidence of his patriotism.

## Civil War in Greece

In the following document, Thucydides shows the other side of Greek politics and presents a penetrating description of the struggle between groups of citizens within the polis during the Peloponnesian War. This account of the Greek civil wars remains to this day a classic account of political passions. It can be used to understand the basic pattern of social discord at any period in man's history.

So revolutions broke out in city after city, and in places where the revolutions occurred late the knowledge of what had happened previously in other places caused still new extravagances of revolutionary zeal, expressed by an elaboration in the methods of seizing power and of unheard of atrocities in revenge. To fit in with the change of events, words, too, had to change their usual meanings. What used to be described as a thoughtless act of aggression was now regarded as the courage one would expect to find in a party member; to think of the future and wait was merely another way of saying one was a coward; any idea of moderation was just an attempt to disguise one's unmanly

---

Thucydides, *The Peloponnesian War*, trans. Rex Warner (Harmondsworth, Middlesex, England: Penguin Books, 1954), pp. 208-211. Reprinted by permission.

character; ability to understand a question from all sides meant that one was totally unfitted for action. Fanatical enthusiasm was the mark of a real man, and to plot against an enemy behind his back was perfectly legitimate self-defense. Anyone who held violent opinions could always be trusted, and anyone who objected to them became a suspect. To plot successfully was a sign of intelligence, but it was still cleverer to see that a plot was hatching. If one attempted to provide against having to do either, one was disrupting the unity of the party and acting out of fear of the opposition. In short, it was equally praiseworthy to get one's blow in first against someone who was going to do any wrong at all. Family relations were a weaker tie than party membership, since party members were more ready to go to any extreme for any reason whatever. These parties were not formed to enjoy the benefits of the established laws, but to acquire power by overthrowing the existing regime; and the members of these parties felt confidence in each other not because of any fellowship in a religious communion, but because they were partners in crime. If an opponent made a reasonable speech, the party in power, so far from giving it a generous reception, took every precaution to see that it had no practical effect.

Revenge was more important than self-preservation. And if pacts of mutual security were made, they were entered into by the two parties only in order to meet some temporary difficulty, and remained in force only so long as there was no other weapon available. When the chance came, the one who first seized it boldly, catching his enemy off his guard, enjoyed a revenge that was all the sweeter from having been taken, not openly, but because of a breach of faith. It was safer that way, it was considered, and at the same time a victory won by treachery gave one a title for superior intelligence. And indeed most people are more ready to call villainy cleverness than simple-mindedness honesty. They are proud of the first quality and ashamed of the second.

Love of power, operating through greed and through personal ambition, was the cause of all these evils. To this must be added the violent fanaticism which came into play once the struggle had broken out. Leaders of parties in the cities had programs which appeared admirable—on one side political equality for the masses, on the other, the safe and sound government of the aristocracy—but in professing to serve the public interest they were seeking to win the prizes for themselves. In their struggles for ascendancy nothing was barred; terrible indeed were the actions to which they committed themselves, and in taking revenge they went farther still. Here they were deterred neither by the claims of justice nor by the interests of the state; their one standard was the pleasure of their own party at that particular moment, and so, either by means of condemning their enemies on an illegal vote or by violently usurping power over them, they were always ready to satisfy the hatreds of the hour. Thus neither side had any use for conscientious motives; more interest was shown in those who could produce attractive arguments to justify some disgraceful action. As for the citizens who held moderate views, they were destroyed by both the extreme parties, either for not taking part in the struggle or in envy at the possibility that they might survive.

As the result of these revolutions, there was a general deterioration of character throughout the Greek world. The simple way of looking at things, which is so much the mark of a noble nature, was regarded as a ridiculous quality and soon ceased to exist. Society had become divided into two ideologically hostile camps, and each side viewed the other with suspicion. As for ending this state of affairs, no guarantee could be given that would be trusted, no oath sworn that people would fear to break; everyone had come to the conclusion that it was hopeless to expect a permanent settlement and so, instead of being able to feel confident in others, they devoted their energies to providing against being injured themselves. As a rule those who were least remarkable for intelligence showed the greater powers of survival. Such people recognized their own deficiencies and the superior intelligence of their opponents; fearing that they might lose a debate or find themselves out-maneuvered in intrigue by their quick-witted enemies, they boldly launched straight into action; while their opponents, over-confident in the belief that they would see what was happening in advance, and not thinking it necessary to seize by force what they could secure by policy, were the more easily destroyed because they were off their guard.

Hellenic culture was created in the polis, that compact social unit developed by the Greeks, a vibrant social organism which reached its full growth in the wonderful and terrible fifth century B.C. In the years which followed the Peloponnesian War, Hellenic patterns of life and thought spread beyond Greece and expanded beyond the confines of the polis until the entire Mediterranean area was permeated by Greek cultural forms. In this diffusion of men and ideas, new forms of thought and social organization were developed, forms which represent basic elements of Mediterranean civilization.

This unit presents both the spread of Greek culture and the changes it underwent after the Athenian Golden Age. The powerful and timeless ideas of Plato, perhaps the most famous Greek thinker, are presented in Reading III. In Chapter Five, the career of a most remarkable individual, Alexander the Great, is traced, and in Chapter Six, the prevailing culture of the Mediterranean world on the eve of the Roman conquest is described. During the two hundred years covered in this unit, the ancient centers of civilization attained a kind of cultural unity, with Greek forms as the binding element.

# UNIT III
# Greek Civilization and the Mediterranean World

# 5

# The Growth of a Universal Culture

The Peloponnesian War, which ended in 404 B.C., was one of the most tragic wars in human history. The destruction which it caused came at a time when the Greeks had erected great monuments to human reason and beauty and had developed the most noble and optimistic ideal of man. At this very time, a time of greatness, the Greeks fell upon each other in a suicidal war.

The physical destruction was immense. Farms were ruined, property destroyed and human life wasted on a huge scale. In the end, no one triumphed, for the Spartan victors were as exhausted as the defeated Athenians. All of Greece was ravaged, but the destruction was more than a physical one. Within the cities themselves, war broke out between the classes, and the spirit of freedom died. The class wars, climaxed by the execution of Socrates, were symbols of deep discontent in the polis. In fact, the unity of the polis had failed; the brilliant cultural creations, born of this union of men and ideas, could not be restored. The career of the traitor Alcibiades showed that the Greeks had outgrown the polis and that they were seeking a wider form of social organization, wider than Pericles or Socrates would have dreamed possible.

## An Expanding Outlook in Greece

Unity among the Greek states seemed farther away than ever. The war itself represented the inability of states with a common culture to produce any kind of unity. The Greeks saw unity only in the form of domination by one state over others. In the early fifth century B.C., after the Persian Wars, Athens had attempted to gain the leadership of Greece through the Delian League. The Spartans attempted the same thing after the Pelopennesian War, but they were unable to carry their unique ideas of government over a large area. The Greek states seemed to be so evenly matched that no one state could unify the entire land. Later in the fourth century B.C., the city of Thebes rose to power and for a while came close to unifying Greece, but other states allied together and defeated the Thebans. In all of these wars, various Greek states were willing to seek the aid of the Persians for their own ends, and in such a way, the Persian kings gained a degree of influence in Greece which they had not had since the days of Marathon and Salamis.

**The Spread of Hellas.** But, as we have seen, Hellenic culture was not confined to Greece itself. For centuries, Greeks had been founding cities throughout the Mediterranean area, especially in the West. These western Greek cities, of which Syracuse was the most important, were now as wealthy and as powerful as the cities of Greece itself. They were producing olive oil, wine and manufactured items in abundance, so much so that cities such as Athens and Corinth were no longer the primary centers of commerce. The vineyards and olive groves of Greece lost their control over the production of valuable commodities, and the economic level of Greece declined.

The broadening of the Greek world can be seen in the fact that many important Greeks traveled more than they had in the past. Socrates had never left Athens; the polis was his spiritual home even when it had condemned him to death. Alcibiades, however, saw the entire world as his home. Another well-known pupil of Socrates, the philosopher Plato, did not involve himself in the democratic life of Athens. Rather, he retired from active life and lived in a world of ideas. When he did become involved in politics, it was at Syracuse, where he was advisor to the tyrant Dionysius (die uh NISH ee uhs). Aristotle, a pupil of Plato, was content to serve as tutor in the court of the king of Macedonia.

Macedonia was a semicivilized state in the north of Greece and had a monarchical form of government. It was a Greek-speaking state, but it was not a closely-knit, democratic polis as the Athens of Pericles had been. The lack of involvement in the political life of just one polis was an indication of the restlessness and rootlessness of Greek life in the fourth century B.C. Greek culture was taking on a new shape.

**Xenophon.** This new trend in Greek culture can be illustrated clearly in the career of a soldier named *Xenophon* (ZEH nuh fuhn). Xenophon was a Spartan general who led a group of Greek soldiers in a series of battles on behalf of the Persian prince Cyrus. Cyrus was attempting to make good his claim to the Persian throne, and he therefore needed good soldiers. He hired an army of Greeks who served him well, even though he himself was killed in the civil war. Once Cyrus had been killed, the Greeks were on their own, deep in the heart of the Persian empire and far from the sea. As they marched to the sea, Xenophon showed his strength as a leader, and his troops displayed the disciplined power of the Greeks. The story of this military expedition is told by Xenophon in his famous book, *The March Up Country*.

Xenophon's expedition into Persia illustrated several things. First of all, it showed that the Greeks were no longer citizen-soldiers fighting only on behalf of their own polis. Xenophon's men were drawn from several Greek city-states, and they fought for pay; they were professional soldiers hired by a Persian prince. The polis, although it was still the basic political unit in Greece, was no longer the commanding force it had been; it was becoming out of date. Second, this military venture showed the continued strength and value of the Greek military system. Politically, Greece was divided, but individual Greeks continued to be confident, aggressive and effective. Even the Persians were using them.

**The Rise of Individualism.** In the careers of Alcibiades, Plato, Aristotle and Xenophon, we see Greeks as individuals and not as members of a given polis. This individualism of Greek culture in the fourth century B.C. can also be seen in art. Statues of men from this period were visual representations of distinct individuals, not idealized portraits of human perfection. The plays of the fourth century B.C. dealt with individuals rather than with characters who represented ideals. The last of the great playwrights, Euripides, sounded the note of freedom from the old ideas of the polis. Unlike earlier drama, the characters of his plays seemed to stand alone, unprotected by group values. Euripides, like Aristotle, ended his life in the Macedonian court far from the tight Athenian polis.

It would be wrong to assume that the vigor of Greek civilization had been diminished in the fourth century B.C. The flourishing of Greek cities in the West, the march of Xenophon and the powerful ideas of Plato and Aristotle all indicate that Greek civilization was just coming into its own. But the fact that some of these thinkers left Greece, and the fact that the Greek states were locked in endless warfare among themselves, seemed to indicate a weakness in

Greek culture. The rampant individualism of men and of separate city-states made any kind of unity or stability impossible.

## The Struggle for Political Unity

Both Plato and Aristotle turned their minds to questions of political organization and attempted to find some firm basis for group living. As thinkers, they opened wide vistas of the mind and provided ideas and insights for future generations; as practical statesmen, they were failures. Practical politics do not seem to have been a gift of the Greeks. The very power which Greek thought unleashed was, and still is, incapable of being disciplined. The Greeks left a disturbing legacy, one which excites the mind and constantly urges change and growth.

**Objections to the Nation-state.** From our vantage point in history, the solution to the problems of Greek politics seems simple. In Greece, there were many separate states with a common language and cultural heritage, yet they were continually at war with each other. Why, we might ask, did they not join into a Greek nation, just as the thirteen American colonies joined into one nation? All of Greece is no larger than New York State! However, before answering this question, we should consider a few facts. The small, independent polis was the birthplace of Greek greatness. It was in this environment that democracy was invented and the intellectual vision of man expanded. To Plato and Aristotle, the polis was the only conceivable form of human cooperation. It was a state small enough to permit every citizen to take part in the shaping of policy and in the enjoyment of freedom. To give up the independent polis would be to give up all that seemed good in Greek life. Who would control the new Greek nation? Would not one state or another end up dominating the union? The Greek mind did not produce the kind of practical, down-to-earth political thinking which could have devised a federation of states in which both freedom and unity could be attained. To the Greek mind, the only alternative to independence was tyranny.

But are we any different today? Do we not believe that the greatness and freedom in the United States is bound up in the independence of our nation? Are there many Americans who would willingly permit important decisions to be made by non-Americans? For us, the nation-state seems to be the only possible form of government. We might approve of membership in the

United Nations, an organization in which representatives from all nations can meet to discuss common problems, but would we want to give the United Nations power to determine policy within our nation? Would many of us run the risk of being outvoted by other nations on an issue which would affect our personal lives?

Yet people living centuries from now, at a time in which world government may well exist, might look at the twentieth century A.D. and marvel at our willingness to fight with people for the sake of national independence. Today's conditions seem to require a new form of government, a government broader than the nation-state, but we find such a government difficult to conceive. The realities of the fourth century B.C. seemed to require a broader form of government, broader than the city-state, but the Greeks of that time found such a government difficult to conceive. Like us in many respects, they believed that a union of many states would bring about a loss of freedom.

**Isocrates.** In the fourth century B.C., the issue of polis independence, as opposed to some kind of Greek union, was debated in many states. Once again, Athens provides us with evidence of this dispute. The Athenian orator *Isocrates* (ie SAHK ruh teez), who lived from 436 to 338 B.C., looked forward to a unified Greece under vigorous leadership. Isocrates believed that Greek culture was the greatest blessing ever given to mankind, and he saw the Greek mission to be the spreading of this culture throughout the world. He wanted to create a union of the Greek states, and in so doing, create the combined power needed to accomplish his goal of spreading Greek culture. He particularly wanted to see the Greeks destroy the Persian empire and spread Greek ideas and institutions throughout the Near East. He, like most Greeks, regarded those living under a different cultural heritage as barbarians.

Athletic contests held each year at Olympia brought Greeks from all cities together. At one of these "Panhellenic" (from *Pan*, meaning all, and *Hellenic*) games, Isocrates gave an oration urging the Greeks to unite and spread the gospel of Hellenism. At times such as these, when enthusiasm was running high, Greek unity was a goal desired by all. However, as the Greeks returned to their cities, the idealism of the games gave way to the realities of politics. Even Isocrates assumed that Athens should be the leader of a united Greece; national unity and city-state freedom seemed to be incompatible goals.

**King Philip of Macedonia.** In time, the power of King Philip of Macedonia made the possibility of Greek unity more than just an ideal of orators. Philip, a rude, semiliterate ruler, had welded the tribes of Macedonia into a powerful nation. He had no use for democracy or the fine ideals of Greek philosophers, but he knew the value of Greek military organization. Also, he invited prominent Athenians such as the philosopher Aristotle and the playwright Euripides to his court in order to give his kingdom the appearance of being a cultured state. Philip slowly began subduing the states south of him, and by the middle of the fourth century B.C., it was apparent that he was in a position to conquer the whole of Greece. The unity of Greece was to be attained through submission to the rule of a warrior king, possessing only the veneer of those traits which the Greeks admired.

Philip not only played one small state off against the other, but he gained the support of many Greeks who saw in him the hope for unity and a crusade against the Persians. Isocrates openly urged Philip to form a Hellenic League and lead it across the Aegean Sea; public opinion in all Greek states was divided on the question of accepting Philip and the Macedonians as the unifiers of Greece.

The Athenian orator *Demosthenes* (dih MAHS thuh neez), who lived from 385 to 322 B.C., rose up as the leader of the anti-Macedo-

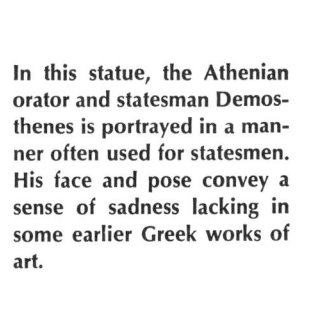

In this statue, the Athenian orator and statesman Demosthenes is portrayed in a manner often used for statesmen. His face and pose convey a sense of sadness lacking in some earlier Greek works of art.

nian group in Athens and spoke out eloquently on behalf of the freedom and independence of his city-state. He believed that the Greek way of life was tied to the fate of the small independent polis. Demosthenes saw in Philip's one-man rule and uncivilized warriors the forces of brute power, unredeemed by the finer aspects of Greek culture. To him, Philip was a barbarian, no better than the king of Persia. His speeches against Philip, called *Philippics*, remain to this day stirring statements on behalf of human freedom.

Demosthenes convinced Thebes to forget grievances against Athens and to join in a stand against Philip. However, after the Macedonian victory in the battle of Chaeronea (kehr uh NEE uh) in 338 B.C., Philip became the undisputed master of Greece. The age of polis independence was over, and the consolidation of Greece was begun. Philip left Athens free of Macedonian troops, but that city now had no choice but to accept the logic of the facts; resistance to Macedonian rule was out of the question.

In the year 336 B.C., Philip was killed and his son Alexander, a pupil of Aristotle, assumed the throne. In the years which followed, Alexander used the circumstances which previous events had placed before him and became one of the most significant men in the history of the world.

**Explaining the Macedonian Success.** Before we look at the career of the man who came to be called "Alexander the Great," it would be well to reflect on what had actually happened to Greece since the days of Pericles. During these years, a nation on the fringes of a civilized area borrowed some ideas which had been created in the central area. These ideas were grafted on to a relatively simple but vigorous society, thereby producing a military and political unit more aggressive and unified than the states in the heartland of civilization. The heartland, weakened by class struggles and disastrous wars, eventually fell under the rule of the upstart nation on the fringes. In general terms, this was the relationship which developed between Macedonia and Greece during the fourth century B.C.

Can this description serve equally well to explain events during other periods of man's history? The Assyrians once lived on the fringes of Mesopotamian culture and borrowed many ideas from Babylonia and Sumer. They went on to conquer Mesopotamia and become the dominant power in the land between the rivers. As we shall soon see, a similar pattern emerged in the case of the

Romans, who developed on the edges of Mediterranean civilization and eventually conquered that world. The Assyrians did what the Macedonians did, and the Romans repeated the Macedonian accomplishment on a larger scale.

Perhaps even the history of the United States has followed this pattern. America is clearly an offshoot of European civilization, existing for years on the fringes of that civilization and borrowing many of its ideas. Americans regarded Europe as their cultural home, often sending their sons to be educated in Paris or London and encouraging European scholars to come to America. Out of the heritage of Europe, America forged a powerful nation, rich in natural and human resources. After the First and Second World Wars, wars in which the European states exhausted each other, America assumed the predominant role in Europe. The fact that many Europeans resent American wealth and power should serve to illustrate the way cultivated Athenians may have felt about the Macedonians after the battle of Chaeronea.

## Alexander the Great

After the death of Philip, the Greeks once again attempted to push back the Macedonians. However, Alexander struck with lightning speed. He destroyed completely the city of Thebes, sparing only the house of Pindar (PIN duhr), a famous lyric poet of ages past. By this gesture, Alexander hoped to show that although he meant to rule Greece, he had respect for its culture. Some of those who supported this young Macedonian saw in him the savior of Greece, a man who could be both statesman and warrior, both philosopher and king. Whatever he was—and the debate about Alexander is still going on—he quickly led his army of Greeks and Macedonians to the Hellespont. On the other side stood not only the Persian empire but the centers of ancient civilization itself, cities which represented three thousand years of human culture. The Greeks were poised to plunge into the breadth and depth of the Near East, not as hired soldiers but as conquerors, bringing both the sword and the heritage of their culture. The history of civilization was about to enter a new phase.

**The Conquest of Persia.** The Persian empire rose to meet the challenge from the West, and King Darius chose to engage the Macedonian army in open battle soon after it entered Asia. Some of the king's advisors were fearful of Alexander and urged the king

Alinari

Shown here is a detail from a large mosaic depicting Alexander in battle against the Persian King Darius. It is thought to be a fairly accurate representation of how the young Macedonian really looked.

to retreat, burning the fields as he went. This kind of "scorched earth" tactic would have drawn Alexander deep into Persian territory, far from his home base; cut off from reinforcements, he perhaps could be easily defeated. However, Darius chose to meet the Macedonians at the Granicus River in Asia Minor, only to be soundly defeated. Alexander kept a copy of the *Iliad* with him and thought of himself as a Homeric hero. To him, this victory was a reenactment of the Trojan War.

One of the reasons for the military success of the Macedonians was their development of a new military technique. Their basic fighting unit was a large group of men standing side by side and armed with long spears. This group, called a *phalanx* (FAY lanks), was trained to move as one man, and when it bore down upon the enemy, it was unstoppable. The "Macedonian phalanx" was Alexander's secret weapon, and it served as the basic military technique for several hundred years until the time of the Romans.

Moving into Syria, Alexander's army clashed with the Persians at Issus, and after this second Persian defeat, Darius offered to give up all of his holdings west of the Euphrates River. Alexander, who by now believed that destiny was on his side, refused the offer and swept through Syria on his way to Egypt. In order to see that his communications with Greece were kept open, he laid siege to the Phoenician coastal cities. After the fall of Tyre, he gained the needed seaports and control of the sea. Egypt had never been a secure part of the Persian empire, and so Alexander's entry into the Nile valley was not strongly opposed.

**The Fall of Egypt.** While in Egypt, the young conqueror traveled to the shrine of Amon (AH muhn), the place of worship for the major Egyptian god. After a meeting with the priests of Amon, Alexander claimed that they saw him as a god, the son of Amon. Such a title gave him the right to become the pharaoh of Egypt. Alexander's claim to be divine angered some of his Greek followers, but it strengthened his position in the eyes of his new subjects in Egypt, who were accustomed to the idea of divine kingship.

By the year 331 B.C., Alexander ruled a large portion of the Near East, although the main body of the Persian army was still intact. Leaving Egypt, he moved to the east, crossed the Euphrates and delivered the final blow to the Persian army. Darius himself fled to the plains of Iran but was murdered by some of his followers who no doubt realized that the future of the Persian empire rested with Alexander. With the death of Darius, Alexander became both king of Persia and pharaoh of Egypt. With increasing confidence, he pushed his army farther to the east. In 327 B.C., he reached the Indus River and entered India. He returned to Babylon in 323 B.C. and there contracted a fever and died. He was thirty-three years old.

In eleven years of military activity, Alexander had accomplished more than anyone to that time had ever done in a single lifetime. With the exception of the western Mediterranean, the entire civilized world was under his rule. He had marched his men thousands of miles, founded twenty-five cities and spread Greek culture to what then appeared to be the ends of the world. Alexander was one of those revolutionary figures after whom the world is radically changed.

**Alexander as Conqueror.** Although this Macedonian came to the Near East as a conqueror, he lost some of the exclusiveness which was characteristic of Greek culture. He acquired a respect for the Persian, Egyptian and Babylonian cultures. He married a Persian princess, adopted Persian dress and attempted to break

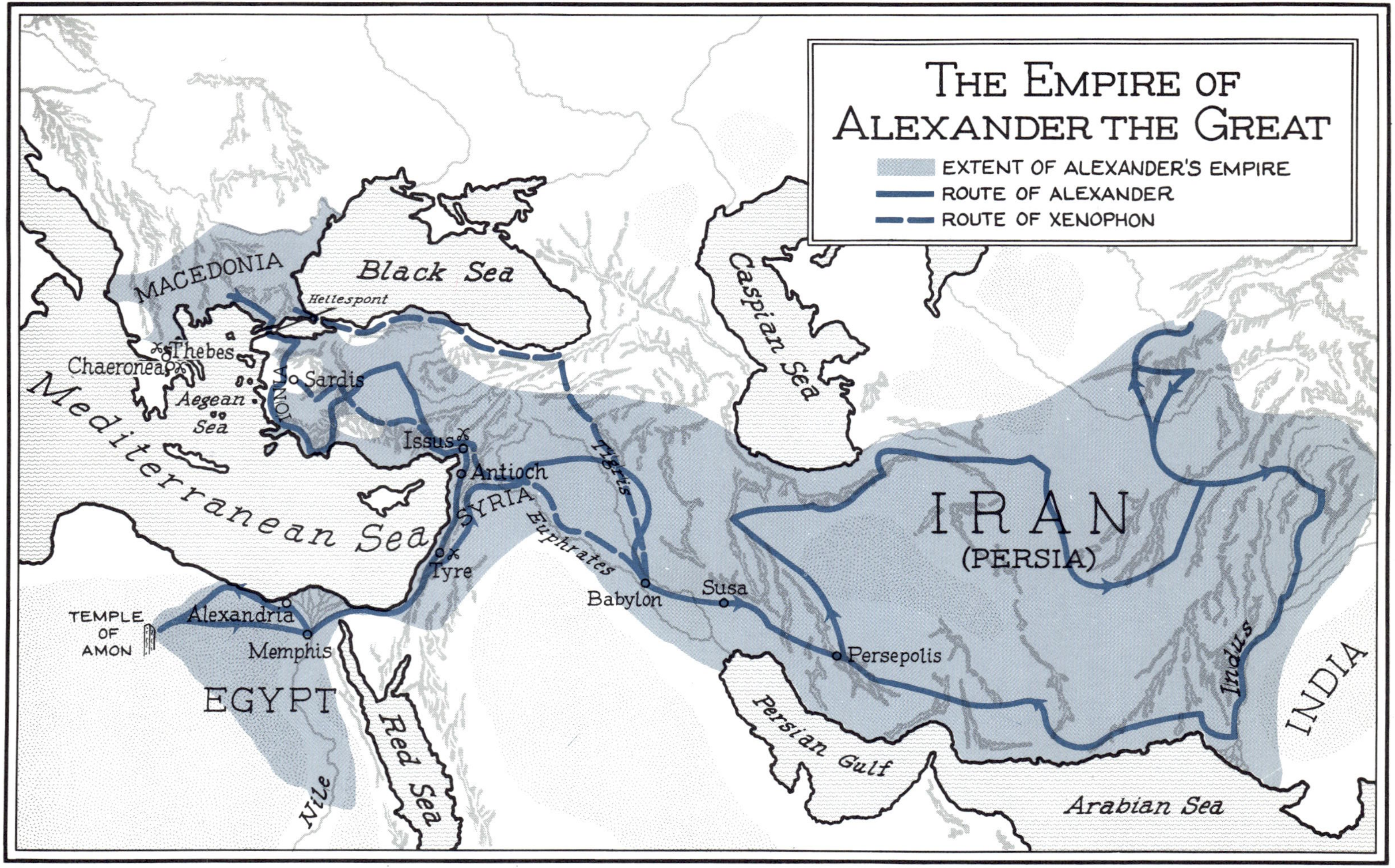
THE EMPIRE OF ALEXANDER THE GREAT
EXTENT OF ALEXANDER'S EMPIRE
ROUTE OF ALEXANDER
ROUTE OF XENOPHON
MACEDONIA
Black Sea
Hellespont
Caspian Sea
Thebes
Chaeronea
Sardis
IONIA
Aegean Sea
Mediterranean Sea
Issus
Antioch
SYRIA
Tyre
Tigris
Euphrates
Babylon
Susa
Persepolis
IRAN
(PERSIA)
Indus
INDIA
Persian Gulf
Arabian Sea
TEMPLE OF AMON
Alexandria
Memphis
EGYPT
Nile
Red Sea

down the once iron-clad division between Greeks and barbarians. Waves of Greek immigrants flocked to his new cities, the most important of which was *Alexandria,* at the mouth of the Nile. Greeks mingled with non-Greeks, and new cultural forms had to be devised to cope with this changed situation. The patterns of life which had been developed by both Greeks and non-Greeks had to change in the face of this kind of mixing. To what extent Alexander had wanted to create world unity—a human society in which national and cultural distinctions would no longer separate people—is difficult to say. To create such a society, Alexander would have had to consolidate his conquests and build a lasting empire. But like the heroes of *Iliad,* he lived a full but short life.

Regardless of what Alexander's ideals might have been, it was clear that Macedonian troops and Greek culture were in a favored position. Greek became the prevailing language of the Near East and was used for commerce, learning and government. The leaders who came to power after Alexander were his Macedonian officers, and the Near East had to come to terms with Greek civilization. The Near East became Hellenized, but in the process, the shape of Greek culture itself underwent substantial changes.

**Alexander the Great in Retrospect.** To what extent Alexander himself is responsible for these momentous changes in the shape of human history is an interesting question. To those who see history as the action of great individuals, the events of this period can be interpreted as the consequences of Alexander's own personality. On the other hand, to those who believe that circumstances and conditions, rather than individuals, are responsible for historical changes, Alexander appears as a man who merely used existing conditions and forces. According to this second theory, Alexander hastened a trend which was already in progress. The Persian empire had been weak for some time, and the Greeks had penetrated into Persia before Alexander had even been born. Whether Greek culture would have become the dominant culture of the Mediterranean world if Alexander had not lived is an unanswerable question. But attempting to answer it is not a wasted

**In the year 334 B.C., Alexander of Macedonia began a meteoric conquest of the area that two hundred years earlier had been conquered in part by the Persians and forged into a stable empire. The lands he subdued extended from Greece to India—an area wider than the continental United States. Alexander's route is shown on the map on page 84.**

effort. What we are asking here is to what extent are individual men capable of shaping events, and to what extent are events beyond the control of individuals? We can apply this kind of thinking to the course of our own lives.

Alexander's early death raised an immediate political problem. Who would be his successor? In spite of his remarkable career, the empire he created was an empire in name only; it rested on his personal conquests. He had not been able to develop permanent institutions adequate to govern a political unit of this size. It is said that when asked the question as to whom he would leave his empire, Alexander answered, "to the strongest." Such a solution to the problem of succession led to a struggle between his strongest generals. In a short time, it became apparent that no one of these military men would be capable of ruling all of Alexander's conquests. The empire dissolved into three major parts, three "successor states," and several smaller divisions. General *Ptolemy* (TAHL uh mee) became ruler of Egypt; General *Seleucus* (suh LOO kuhs) became the ruler of the Syrian and Mesopotamian part of the empire; and General *Antigonus* (an TIH guh nuhs) retained Macedonia and Greece. In Asia Minor, a few smaller states and independent cities remained.

The sheer scope and speed of Alexander's conquests, the disruption of long established states and empires and the creation of new cities is almost without parallel in the history of the world. Compared with the issues of Alexander's time, the problems which confronted men like Pericles and Demosthenes—problems of city-state politics—appear dwarfed. The sequence of events culminating in Alexander's brief but expansive empire changed the shape of the Mediterranean world. Greek culture was in no way diminished—the issues raised by Greek thinkers still were relevant—but it was forced into new lines of development. Greek culture was no longer a product of the polis; it had the entire known world for its area of expression.

### Define

Xenophon
Isocrates
Philip of Macedonia
Demosthenes

*Philippics*
battle of Chaeronea
Alexander of Macedonia
phalanx

Alexandria
Ptolemy
Seleucus
Antigonus

## Review and Answer

1. What evidence can be given to show that Greek culture was spreading beyond the polis and beyond Greece during the fourth century B.C.?
2. Why were the Greeks both unwilling and unable to develop a political system broad enough to accommodate the spread of their culture?
3. What was the fundamental issue which separated Isocrates and Demosthenes?
4. Why was it that a backward state, Macedonia, provided the leadership to unify Hellas?
5. To what extent can the widespread geographical expansion of Greek culture be attributed to Alexander? Why is this an important question?

# 6

# The Hellenistic World

The period of time from the death of Alexander to the Roman conquest three centuries later is called the *Hellenistic period*. The important cities of this period were *Alexandria,* the capital of the Ptolemaic state; *Antioch,* the capital of the Selucid monarchy; *Carthage,* a major power in the West and a former Phoenician colony; and *Rome,* a Western city which eventually was to become the capital of the entire Mediterranean area. The political and military events of this period need not concern us in this chapter. Rather, we will focus attention on some of the basic patterns of life and thought which were constructed during the Hellenistic age, patterns which were to exist until the end of ancient civilization itself.

## Patterns of Culture in the Hellenistic Period

The basic political unit was the large, monarchical state, a fact which represented a return to an older form of government. In the development of divine monarchy as the standard form of government, we can perhaps see the spirit of the East overcoming Greek political ideas. Of the three major states, the kingdom of the Ptolemys was the most stable. It had the almost three-thousand-year-old Egyptian monarchy and bureaucracy on which to build. To the people of Egypt, life under the Ptolemys was much the same as it had been under the pharaohs. Even under Greek rule, bodies continued to be mummified.

The Selucid kingdom was a less defined area covering Syria, Mesopotamia, Persia and, at times, parts of Asia Minor. This kingdom encompassed many different kinds of people, and the Selucid kings were often called upon to put down revolutions. The implanting of Greek ideas and institutions was carried on with vigor and often met stiff resistance from the native population. In Greece itself, the city-states continued to exist as separate units, but effective power was in the hands of the kings who ruled from Macedonia. In the West, a balance of power existed for a time between Carthage, the Greek cities in Sicily and Italy and the growing power of Rome.

**Urban Life.** Cities remained the basic centers of social and intellectual life, but few of them were independent political units. In Greece, the citizens no longer took an active part in public affairs as they had done in the time of Pericles. Cities were units within large monarchies, and political power was in the hands of kings. Political life declined, and individuals directed their energies and wealth to the service of private ends. Merchants built elaborate homes, hired artists to decorate them and often enjoyed the pleasures of literature and the arts. An individual might join different groups for pleasure, profit or spiritual solace, but he was not an active citizen sharing in the public life of his city. It is significant that artistic treasures of this period were usually found in private homes and not in public buildings.

**Cosmopolitan Attitudes.** Once a man had mastered the Greek language, he became a citizen of the world and not a citizen of the city of his birth. The word *cosmopolitan,* meaning citizen of the world, described the political realities of this age. Merchants traveled widely and often had branch offices in many cities. Local loyalty was no longer a powerful force, and the individual man stood alone in an enlarged world. Although a man might be a "citizen of the world," this was not an effective or meaningful citizenship, and the individual had no established group in which to focus his energies. Individualism, therefore, was the dominant trend which we can see reflected in the Greek art of the period.

Hellenistic sculpture portrayed man in a thoroughly realistic manner, with all the irregularities and imperfections of humanity. Statues of kings, on the other hand, were perfect and almost godlike. The older style of portraying men as gods and gods as men no longer existed; divinity and humanity were no longer joined in a single work of art. This fracturing of the unity of Greek art could be taken as symbolic of the breaking of the unity which once existed in the Greek polis.

This was an age of bigness. The monarchs commanded large armies and navies, employed many civil servants and presided over a volume of trade, manufacturing and agriculture which was greater than it had ever been. Cities such as Alexandria and Antioch were larger and wealthier than Athens or Sparta had been even at the height of their power. One of the jewels of the Hellenistic age was the Temple of the Muses in Alexandria, a combination university, library and museum. Here, artists, scholars and inventors continued to turn their minds to the understanding of nature and the creation of beauty.

**Achievements in Science and Thought.** Around 300 B.C., the mathematician *Euclid* established many of the principles of geometry, thereby enabling men to understand spatial relationships. The scientist *Archimedes* (ark uh MEE deez), who lived from 287 to 212 B.C., discovered the principle of specific gravity and estimated the circumference of the earth. The astronomer *Ptolemy* developed a theory which accounted for the movement of the sun and planets around the earth. This theory satisfied men for many centuries. Even the concept of steam power was known to scientists in Alexandria. Clearly the power of the human mind which the Greeks had unleashed had not diminished. There were, however, fewer first-rate poets, historians and playwrights than there had been in the past.

The fact that the Hellenistic Greeks did not invent a workable steam engine is one of the intriguing facts in the history of human thought. The Greeks knew that the steam from boiling water was a source of energy, but they saw no need to apply this principle to large machines. The failure to use this knowledge is not due to a lack of intelligence. Rather, it is because ancient society had adequate energy in the form of slaves. It was only when widespread slavery no longer existed and labor was in short supply that man felt the need to use his intelligence to create another form of power. In such a way does the structure of society determine the use to which man puts his intelligence.

**The Average Citizen.** Life for the average person was probably no different in the third and second centuries B.C. than it had been for hundreds of centuries. The big issues of war and diplomacy were of little concern to him unless soldiers happened to tramp through his garden. The world of scholars and thinkers was not his world. The ideas which shaped the values of this period were the ideas of a small number of people. The social vision of the best thinkers did not encompass the whole of society. Men speculated on the nature of the universe, but they saw no need for a steam engine. They tried to find man's place in the universe but gave little attention to social problems or to the organization of human society.

In the fifth century B.C., in Athens, philosophers and citizens had come together, and the average man had a brief sense of unity with all other members of society. His religion was service to the community; patriotism and religion were one and the same. This kind of involvement lasted for only a short time and only in a small portion of the world. During that time, a large number of artists, thinkers and statesmen lived in an active social and intellectual environment. In the third and second centuries B.C., however, a city such as Alexandria or Antioch could not have produced a Socrates. In the atmosphere of cities such as these, a Socrates would have retired to the Temple of the Muses to speculate on the universe and would not have engaged in dialogue with everyday citizens.

The Hellenistic man, citizen of the world but not citizen of the city in which he lived, found no meaningful group to belong to. The ideal of the polis, as described by Pericles and sought for by Plato and Aristotle, existed only as a dream. New forms of thought and of social organization had to be developed. The ideas of the Greeks had to expand in order to cope with the conditions brought about by the broadening of their world.

## Stoicism

Many different kinds of philosophies existed in the Hellenistic world. The most important of these philosophic schools was that of the *Stoics,* whose system of thought was called *Stoicism.* Stoicism provided the basic framework of thought and life for many people and lasted for many centuries. Many of the ideals of Stoicism are still alive, and men today might be Stoics without realizing it. The founder of Stoicism was a man by the name of Zeno (ZEE no), a Phoenician by birth, who lived from 336 to 264 B.C. He spent most of his time teaching on a long porch in Athens. The Greek word for such a structure was *stoa,* hence those who learned there were called Stoics. Stoicism represented a broadening of Greek thought and can be seen as the climax of Greek philosophy. The Stoics carried forward many Greek concepts, but they also added new ideas to cope with conditions existing in the Hellenistic age.

**The Gods and the Universe.** Years earlier, the great thinker Aristotle had attempted to understand and explain the laws which governed the natural world, laws which the Ionian philosophers had first discovered. The Stoics also believed in a universe governed by natural laws which human reason could understand. They accepted the many gods of Greece, but unlike Homer, they did not believe that all of these gods were real. The Stoics did not worship the individual gods; in their opinion, Zeus did not throw thunderbolts as some Greeks believed, but rather established the harmonious and rational universe. According to the Stoic philosophy, "the universe itself, as a perfect living creature, is rightly called God. The gods of popular religion represent different activities of the true god, and the foolish or immoral stories told about them are allegories intended to convey some moral truth." Zeus was identified with the entire universe, and so the Stoics were monotheists of a sort. What they lacked was a strong concept of an individual god. Zeus was more of an overall force than a distinct personality.

**A Philosophy of Self-sufficiency.** Just as Socrates had been concerned with the search for the good life, the Stoics were very

This second-century B.C. statue of an old market woman is a perfect example of the realism characteristic of the early Hellenistic age. The ideal of perfection has given way to the quest for realism.

The Metropolitan Museum of Art, Rogers Fund, 1909

interested in questions of personal ethics. In a world made large and uncertain by the breakdown of the polis, they provided a philosophy of life which offered man security and happiness. The Stoics developed the idea of self-sufficiency—*autarky* (aw TAR kee), they called it—and indicated the way it could be attained. Men were urged to reduce their desires and to have no strong commitments or loyalties. In so doing, they would be free of outside forces over which they had little or no control. The Stoics were convinced that blind chance, or fortune, ruled the world. The wise man should put his faith in nothing which could be taken from him; in so doing, he would never be disappointed. "[The] Stoics . . . addressed themselves to the task of redressing the imbalance between little man and huge world, of restoring the dignity to little man by arming him with *autarky* or self-sufficiency." The Roman philosopher *Seneca* (SEN ih kuh) expressed this basic Stoic idea in the following way.

> The wise man does not need to walk about timidly or cautiously, for he possesses such self-confidence that he does not hesitate to go to meet fortune nor will he yield his position to her. Nor has he any reason to fear her, because he considers not only slaves, property, and positions of honor, but also his body, his eyes, his hands—everything which can make life dearer, even his very self, as among things uncertain and lives as if he had borrowed them for his own use and was prepared to return them without sadness whenever claimed.

To push this kind of thinking to the extreme would be to live totally without possessions—or friends. Some Stoics did this, but for most men, Stoicism led to a temperate and modest life. This philosophy did not require the lack of possessions, honor or desires; rather, men were asked to regard such things as being not necessary for true happiness. A Stoic could be either rich or poor; what mattered the most was the way in which he regarded his condition. Epictetus (ehp ihk TEE tuhs), another Stoic, explained:

> In everything which pleases the soul, or supplies a want, or is loved, remember to add this: "What is its nature?" If you love an earthen vessel, say it is an earthen vessel which you love; when it has been broken, you will not be disturbed. If you are kissing your child or wife, say that it is a human being whom you are kissing; if the wife or child dies, you will not be disturbed.

Plato's philosophy (which taught that what man can see and touch is not true reality—only the world of ideas is) might well have served as a basis for these Stoic ideas about worldly possessions.

**Equality and Universalism.** Although the Stoics carried forward existing Greek ideas, they also developed original concepts. Socrates had been an Athenian patriot, tied to his native land; Aristotle believed that all non-Greeks were barbarians. The Stoics made no such distinctions. When Diogenes (die AHJ uh neez), an early Stoic, was asked to what state he belonged, he answered that he was a citizen of the world—*cosmopolite* (kahz MAHP uh lite). The Stoics made no distinction on the basis of race or nationality, regarding these as artificial and not natural distinctions. A man was a man throughout the entire universe, and the place of his birth or residence was unimportant. In the following excerpt from a poem honoring Zeno, we can see this universal spirit breaking through the old Greek idea of their own superiority.

> And if your country was Phoenicia,
> Why need we grieve; from that land Cadmus came,
> Who gave to Greece her written books of wisdom.

The ideal of the unity of mankind, created by the Stoics, is still an ideal of men today.

Along with their philosophy of universalism, the Stoics made no distinction between men on the basis of their wealth or position in society. The Stoics were, in theory, democrats. Socrates, on the other hand, had had little love for democracy and the common man, and Plato's ideal state was a rigid aristocracy. The Stoics, however, regarded social distinctions as being as artificial as national divisions. When Alexander the Great went to meet Diogenes, the king asked if he could do anything for him. Diogenes said that he could move away and stop blocking the sun. To Diogenes, Alexander was just another man. When a wealthy young man came to Zeno to seek instruction, Zeno first made him sit on a dirty bench and then sent him down among beggars so that he would rub against their rags. The young man soon went away.

**The Influence of Stoicism.** How widespread was Stoicism? In spite of its democratic tendencies, most of the men who embraced it were wealthy men of leisure who never considered developing democratic institutions as we know them. Stoicism was not a mass movement with support from the common people; its philosophy was too difficult and demanding for the average person to understand and put into practice. Most Stoics even accepted slavery as a natural condition for some men; Stoicism was not a revolutionary movement.

Nevertheless, the ideal of equality and the disdain for artificial distinctions were new ideas in the history of human thought. They led many Stoics to work for an improvement of human conditions and helped to make some rulers more generous, kind and open-minded than they otherwise might have been. One of the greatest Stoics was the Roman emperor Marcus Aurelius (aw REE lee uhs), who presided over a world empire with justice and wisdom.

Yet, Marcus Aurelius remained an emperor, an absolute ruler whose power was unlimited and whose career included some bloody wars. The fact that a Stoic could believe in the equality of man and still permit slavery to exist may strike us as contradictory and hypocritical. Yet, Thomas Jefferson, who wrote the words "all men are created equal," not only accepted the fact of human slavery but owned slaves himself. The gap between ideals and reality is often great, but this gap does not diminish the value of the ideals expressed. Ideas are often ahead of their times, and oftentimes, centuries pass until a moral ideal is so extended to change reality. This is why the wisdom of the Stoics, although created centuries ago, still has a message for men today. The following selections from Epictetus' writings can serve as examples.

> Men are disturbed not by the things which happen but by the opinions about the things: for example, death is nothing terrible, for if it were, it would have seemed so to Socrates. The opinion that death is terrible is the terrible thing. When then we are impeded or disturbed or grieved, let us never blame others, but ourselves, that is, our opinions. It is the act of an ill-instructed man to blame others for his own bad condition; it is the act of one who has begun to be instructed, to lay the blame on himself; and of one whose instruction is completed, neither to blame another nor himself.
>
> Whoever then wishes to be free, let him neither wish for anything nor avoid anything which depends on others. If he does not observe this rule, he must be a slave.
>
> Remember that it is not he who reviles or strikes you who insults you, but your opinion that these things are insulting. When then a man irritates you, you must know that it is your own opinion which has irritated you. Therefore try especially not to be carried away by the appearance. For if you once gain time and delay, you will more easily master yourself.

The wisdom contained in these sayings is profound, but we can sense in them a lack of involvement, a certain cold, distant quality, lacking in emotion. For example:

> We may learn the will of nature from the things in which we do not differ from one another; for instance, when your neighbor's slave has broken his cup or anything else, we are ready to say, "Such things happen." You must know then that when your cup is broken you ought to think as you did when your neighbor's cup was broken. Transfer this reflection to greater things also. Is another man's child or wife dead? There is no one who would not say, "Such is the life of man." But when a man's own child or wife is dead, forthwith he calls out, "Woe to me, how wretched I am." But we ought to remember how we feel when we hear that it has happened to others.

Stoicism was a philosophy for strong people, and the very goal of self-sufficiency required a detached and unemotional temperament. In the face of a friend's disaster, Epictetus advises, "So far as words, then, do not be unwilling to show him sympathy, and even to lament with him. But take care that you do not lament in your inner being also."

**The Development of Mystery Religions.** For many people, however, there was a need to "lament" in the inner being and to experience the deep involvement and personal commitment which Stoicism denied. Many men, perhaps all men, need to involve themselves with, or worship, a force greater than themselves and also to experience a sense of sacrifice and emotional release. Religion may well be a basic need of man. The official religion of the Greek cities and kingdoms was usually nothing more than a political ritual tied up with patriotism for either the polis or the king. In an age when local patriotism was not a strong force, such an official religion was usually no more than an empty and mechanical ritual. One historian has said of the Greeks, "Never did a people of advanced culture have a more infantile religion." In the Hellenistic age, when the polis no longer commanded the emotions of men, and when Stoicism appeared as a cold system of thought, various movements called *mystery religions* developed as if to fill the spiritual vacuum.

These mystery religions appealed to the senses and emotions of men. They were filled with dramatic, secret ceremonies during which the individual worshipper felt a kind of communion or identity with a particular god. Some of the religions led their worshippers to emotional frenzies and strange practices such as self-mutilation or denial of all worldly goods. For example, the cult of *Mithra* required all new members to be baptized in the blood of a bull. The person was placed in a pit covered by bars over which a bull was slaughtered.

THE HELLENISTIC WORLD 97

The gods of the mystery religions were usually old, Eastern nature gods or goddesses. The Egyptian goddess Isis (IE suhs) grew in importance during the Hellenistic period. Isis was the goddess of fertility originally associated with the Nile. The worshippers of Isis transformed the idea of the rebirth of nature into a notion of personal rebirth and immortality. Those who joined fully in the religion felt that they could gain immortal life through the powers of the goddess.

The mystery religions appealed to the mind as well as to the emotions. The priests of these religions were also scholars, claiming to possess secret knowledge of the universe and of divine forces. Therefore, knowledge and religious fervor were joined. This situation set the mystery religions apart from Stoicism, which placed its emphasis upon restraint and reason. The various religions of this sort can be seen as attempts to restore the unity of head and heart, mind and emotion, which had once existed in the polis.

Membership in a mystery cult was based on neither social standing nor nationality. Worshippers were drawn from all walks of life and found a common bond in their mutual commitment to the rules of the religion. In this, they were similar to the Stoics, but

Shown here is the "Seated Boxer," a life-sized bronze dating from the first century B.C. Unlike the earlier "Discus-Thrower" (page 44) who was more of an ideal than a reality, this late Hellenistic statue is that of a real human being, a real boxer, with broken nose and scarred, battered body.

*Alinari—Art Reference Bureau*

the emphasis upon emotionalism and secrecy made them appear as disruptive forces in society.

The mystery religions began in the East but in time spread throughout the entire Mediterranean world. They appealed to only a small number of people, but with their emphasis on emotion, the afterlife and the dark forces of nature, they represented a shift in the values established by the Hellenic mind. We shall see more of them as the history of the ancient world draws to a close.

## Judaism

In the Mediterranean world during the Hellenistic period, there was a group of people who were quite different from the overwhelming majority. They were the Jews, descendents of the Hebrews, who in earlier centuries had established a kingdom around the Syrian city of Jerusalem. About the year 1000 B.C., the kingdom of Israel had reached its peak of power. After that time, the Hebrews had been enslaved by the Babylonians, then ruled by the Persians; with the defeat of Persia, the ancient kingdom of Israel became a province in the Selucid kingdom. However, not all of the Jews lived in this ancient homeland. Like the Greeks, many of them migrated abroad, and during the Hellenistic period, Jews were living in most of the major cities. In spite of this migration, or dispersal, the Jews regarded Jerusalem as the Holy City.

The focal point of the Jewish religion (Judaism) was a collection of sacred writings containing the history, religious beliefs and ethical rules of the Jews. It was during the Hellenistic period that scholars and priests gathered together these writings into a unit which we now call the Old Testament, the first half of the Bible. Strict adherence to the teachings of this book made the Jews a close-knit group of people all sharing a common past and a common set of values, no matter where they might be living. Religion was the essential and pervading element of daily life. As there was no Hebrew state, the religious leaders became the most important people in the community.

**A Monotheistic Religion.** The Jews were monotheists. They believed that their God was the only true God. Unlike the Stoic conception of Zeus as the impersonal organizer of the universe, Judaism proclaimed a strongly personal God who not only had created the world, but who intervened in the history of the world, using the Jews as his instrument. Unlike all other people at that time, the Jews refused to accept the existence of other gods. Unlike the Greeks, for example, who saw in the Egyptian god Amon another form of Zeus, the Jews regarded gods other than their God as false and meaningless objects of worship. Their God was so majestic that it was forbidden to portray him in any form of art. Therefore, the Jews were cut off from the tradition of art and sculpture which was a major element of the culture of the entire Mediterranean world. In a polytheistic world, the Jews were unique. This uniqueness caused them to separate themselves from the rest of society.

**Ethics.** Judaism was a religion which emphasized ethics. The Bible contained not only particular rules and regulations but general ethical principles for men to follow. The Greeks, to be sure, were also concerned with discovering the proper standard for human behavior, but their gods did not provide such rules for them. The Jewish God, however, was above all an ethical god who established standards for men to follow. These standards were recorded in the Bible and did not have to be discovered by contemplation or reasoning; they were commands of God. Therefore, the God who created and controlled the forces of nature, the divine power who raised the storm and sent the thunder, also provided the rules by which man ordered his life. Worship and ethics were joined to a degree which would have astounded both Stoics and members of mystery religions.

**A Sense of History.** Perhaps the most unique element of Judaism was the concept of history. The Jews believed that God had made an agreement with them called a *covenant*. This covenant stated that if the Jews would worship only God and follow his commandments, he would give them a great nation. The Jews therefore directed their attention to the course of human events in order to seek the fulfillment of this promise. Thus, Judaism was a historical religion, deeply concerned with both past and future and filled with the concept of change.

The Greek view of the world is not historical in this deep sense. Both Plato and Aristotle sought the eternal and unchanging elements in the world. Thucydides, the greatest of the Greek historians, was primarily concerned with the history of his own time, not of ages past. There is no history of Greece written by an ancient Greek. The Old Testament, however, is primarily a *history* of the Jews from the time of their origins, showing how God chose them to play a major role in the history of the world.

In the past, when Israel had been a strong kingdom, the promise of the covenant had seemed to be fulfilled. But in later years, when the Jews were either ruled by others or scattered throughout the world, the promise was more of a hope than a reality. For example, consider the following passage from the Old Testament.

... For out of Zion shall go forth the law, and the word of the LORD from Jerusalem. He shall judge between the nations, and shall decide for many peoples; and they shall beat their swords into plowshares, and their spears into pruning hooks; nations shall not lift up sword against nation, neither shall they learn war any more.

ISAIAH 2:3-4

**Judaism in Perspective.** In spite of this gap between ideal and reality, the Jews were people whose thinking was focused on change, and a people whose thinking is focused on change are most likely to bring about change if given the opportunity. Progress only comes if change is acceptable. In fact, Judaism contained many qualities which seemed to be lacking in the prevailing ideal of the Hellenistic world. This religion fused a dynamic religious

The "Laocoön Group" illustrates the death of the legendary Laocoön and his two sons. This dramatic work is an example of the flamboyant quality of Hellenistic sculpture. The balanced energy of earlier art has been replaced by an unrestrained quality of artistic presentation.

*Alinari—Art Reference Bureau*

faith and a system of ethics into a unified view of life. The Stoics were strong on moral advice but weak on religious fervor; the mystery religions were powerful vehicles of religious ecstasy but were, for the most part, lacking in rules for human behavior. In Judaism, both elements of humanity were combined.

Judaism also produced a faith in a God who was demanding, transcendent and powerful yet at the same time was concerned with the daily affairs of men. This God was too majestic to be portrayed in even the best sculpture, yet a Hebrew writer could speak of walking with him.

> ... and what does the LORD require of you but to do justice, and to love kindness, and to walk humbly with your God?
> MICAH 6:8

Most important, the Jews had a sense of community, a social unit with cohesion and purpose, much like the Greek polis of the past.

## Cultural Discord

In spite of these attractions, most educated men of the Hellenistic age regarded the Jews as narrow-minded, superstitious and arrogant. To embrace Judaism would require the rejection of the gods of Homer, the poetry of Plato, the science of Aristotle, the pleasures of art and the tolerant attitude of the Stoics. The very strength of Judaism rested on those things which the Greeks found the most difficult to accept.

**Attempts at Hellenization.** Among those Jews who lived in the great Hellenistic cities, an attempt was made to bridge the gap between the Hebraic and Hellenic views of the world. During the third century B.C., the Old Testament was translated into Greek, the major language of the time. Along with the Greek language came Greek ideas, and out of this interaction of ideas, an attempt was made to blend the two cultures. A Jewish scholar, *Philo* (FIE low) *of Alexandria*, attempted to interpret the history and teachings of Judaism in the light of Greek philosophy. He tried to portray the Hebrew God more as a Platonic ideal and less as the God of a particular group of people. He tried to find and emphasize points of similarity in the ethical teachings of the Stoics and the Bible. Although there were some people who embraced this kind of Hellenized Judaism, the strict monotheism, the denial of art and the exclusive emphasis on Jewish history made it impossible to blend completely the two cultures.

**Opposition to Hellenization.** In fact, many Jews resisted any watering down of traditional values. When the Selucid king, Antiochus IV (an TIE uh kuhs), attempted to impose Greek culture on all of his subjects, he ran into stiff resistance from the Jews living in Jerusalem. Some Jews went along with the introduction of Greek theaters and schools, and one of the priests of the temple even changed his name from Joshua to Jason. However, in the year 168 B.C., a successful rebellion against this Hellenization broke out, led by a peasant named Judas Maccabaeus (mack uh BEE uhs). For a while, an independent Jewish state was created in the ancient homeland, but it was not a permanent establishment. Most Jews still lived far from the Holy City. The victory of the Maccabaeans is still celebrated in modern Judaism in the holiday of *Hanukkah* (HAH nuh kuh).

No doubt Judas Maccabaeus was attempting to fulfill the prophecy of a restored kingdom and to bring about the promises of God. However, for some Jews, the promised kingdom meant something other than an actual political state. The New Israel, unlike the old kingdom, might be a spiritual kingdom in which the God of the Jews would be recognized by all men as the true God. As long as the Hellenistic view of man and the world satisfied mankind, this kingdom could be only a dream. But if conditions changed, and if the accepted patterns of life and thought failed to satisfy men, the ideas of Judaism might provide an alternative way of life. Jerusalem might replace Athens as the center of civilization.

The history of man does not stand still. The power of man over his physical environment and in the realm of the mind and spirit continually grows. New political and social forms emerge, and new ideas seize the mind and spirit of man, propelling his creative forces onward, although not always upward. In the Hellenistic world, the forces of change came from two areas, both of which were least affected by the dominant Greek culture. From the Jews, there was, at least in potential form, a new culture based on faith in a dynamic God rather than on reason in a structured universe. But the Jews had no political power; their's was a power of spirit, an empire of ideas. Such an empire grows slowly, imperceptibly and, in the words of the Bible, "in the fullness of time."

**The Dawning of the Roman Civilization.** A second force was also growing; this force was in the form of a people to the west, on the Italian peninsula. The Romans, like the Jews, were unique in the Hellenistic world but for different reasons. The Romans were practical people who developed stable political institutions and who were animated by a military spirit. They were to become masters of the Mediterranean world. Their's was to be a political rather than a spiritual kingdom, an empire which was to provide a common government for ancient civilization. Their mission was different from that of the Jews, but they too had a sense of mission. According to the historian *Livy* (LIHV ee), the founder of Rome received this promise from the gods.

> At the break of dawn today, the Father of this city suddenly descended from heaven and appeared to me. Whilst thrilled with awe, I stood rapt before him in deepest reverence, praying that I might be pardoned for gazing upon him. "Go," he said, "tell the Romans that it is the will of heaven that my Rome should be the head of the world. Let them henceforth cultivate the arts of war, and let them know assuredly, and hand down with knowledge to posterity, that no human might can withstand the arms of Rome.

We will now turn to the Romans, the people who were to extend their rule throughout and beyond the Mediterranean and to bring about the climax of ancient civilization.

## *Define*

| | | |
|---|---|---|
| Hellenistic period | Zeno | mystery religions |
| Antioch | autarky | Philo of Alexandria |
| Carthage | Stoicism | Judas Maccabaeus |
| cosmopolitan | Diogenes | |

## *Review and Answer*

1. What were the basic elements of Hellenistic politics, society and thought, and how did they differ from those of fifth-century B.C. Athens?
2. Show how Stoicism supported a belief in individualism, universalism and equality. How did conditions in the Hellenistic world help to bring about this kind of philosophy?
3. What were the basic elements of the mystery religions, and what needs did they fulfill?
4. How did the basic beliefs of Judaism differ from the prevailing Hellenistic culture?
5. Can it be argued that Greek culture during the Hellenistic period had reached its limits and that the age represented a kind of vacuum needing new ideas and forces? Explain your answer.

# Reading III
# Greek Philosophy
## Plato and the Human Mind

The greatness of Greek civilization can be most clearly seen in the work of the Athenian philosophers, whose ideas long outlasted the empire of Pericles or the military exploits of Alcibiades. The philosophers turned their minds to timeless human questions and established principles of thought which have remained to this very day. Only one of these intellectual giants can be represented here—Plato of Athens, a man whose ideas should be investigated if the accomplishments of the Greeks are to be fully appreciated.

Plato, a pupil of Socrates, carried on his master's passionate search for truth. In his writings, Plato often used the form of the written dialogue and expressed his thoughts through the character of Socrates. Plato felt that it was a difficult but necessary task to determine what was right and what was wrong and to establish fixed standards for accurate judgment or wise decisions. Different people had different standards, and those living in different lands saw things in different ways. Even the Greek religion provided no firm basis for moral judgments; the gods were often inconsistent. Therefore, Greek thinkers had to use their own powers of reasoning to discover the absolute, unchanging standards by which to live.

For example, a group of people might agree that a certain action was either good or bad, or that a given picture was either beautiful or ugly. However, they would only be giving examples of goodness or beauty. Men could always give *examples*, but it was not easy to know what courage, beauty or goodness actually was. The world of the senses, from which examples are taken, often changes and nothing remains fixed. One action might be good when compared with another, but that same action might appear evil when compared with a third action. What is truth? This has been an eternal question. To the ancient Hebrews, wisdom was found in "the fear of the Lord," but the Greeks had no such faith in a single, stable God. To find order in diversity, and stability behind constant change, has been the quest of man from the time he existed. That quest took on a creative urgency in ancient Athens.

## *The Ideal Forms*

Plato believed that absolute standards and unchanging truth could be discovered by the proper use of reason, the concentrated application of the mind. He believed in the existence of a plane of reality, beyond what men could see and touch. In this plane of reality, the absolute existence, or forms, of things such as beauty, courage and goodness could be known through the use of human reason. In other words, what men see in the world is but a reflection of this higher reality. In fact, what we see—what our senses record—is not real at all, according to Plato, but rather shadows of the real, ideal forms which only our reason can comprehend. Once the ideal forms are understood, then and only then can man establish values for his life and place his experience in proper perspective.

Plato portrayed his vision of true reality in the following story, presented in the form of a dialogue. In this dialogue, the "shadows" represent the world of the senses—what man can see or hear or touch; the objects which cast the shadows represent the real forms that can only be known by man's reason.

And now, let me show in a figure how far our nature is enlightened or unenlightened:— Behold, human beings living in an underground den, which has a mouth open towards the light and reaching all along the den; here they have been from their childhood, and have their legs and necks chained so that they cannot move, and can only see before them, being prevented by the chains from turning round their heads. Above and behind them a fire is blazing at a distance, and between the fire and the prisoners there is a raised way; and you will see, if you look, a low wall built along the way, like the screen which marionette players have in front of them, over which they show the puppets. And do you see men passing along the wall carrying all sorts of vessels, and statues and figures of animals made of wood and stone and various materials, which appear over the wall?

You have shown me a strange image, and they are strange prisoners.

Like ourselves; and they see only their own shadows, or the shadows of one another, which the first throws on the opposite wall of the cave.

True, how could they see anything but the shadows if they were never allowed to move their heads? And of the objects which are being carried in like manner they would see only the shadows?

Yes.

And if they were able to converse with one another, would they not suppose that they were naming what was actually before them?

---

B. Jowett, trans., *The Dialogues of Plato* (New York: Macmillan, 1892), pp. 773-775.

Very true, the truth would be literally nothing but the shadows of the images. And now look again, and see what will naturally follow if the prisoners are released and disabused of their error. At first, when any of them is liberated and compelled suddenly to stand up and turn his neck round and walk and look towards the light, he will suffer sharp pains; the glare will distress him and he will be unable to see the realities of which in his former state he had seen the shadows. . . . And if he is compelled to look straight at the light, will he not have a pain in his eyes which will make him turn away to take refuge in the objects of vision which he can see, and which he will conceive to be in reality clearer than the things which are now being shown him?

True.

And suppose once more, that he is reluctantly dragged up a steep and rugged ascent, and held fast until he is forced into the presence of the sun himself, is he not likely to be pained and irritated? He will require to grow accustomed to the sight of the upper world. At first he will see the shadows best, next the reflections of men and other objects in the water, and then the objects themselves. The prison-house is the world of sight, the light of the fires is the sun, and you will not misapprehend me if you interpret the journey upwards to be the ascent of the soul into the intellectual world.

This dialogue tells us that, for Plato, true knowledge was found not in an examination of the world. Rather, true knowledge was found in a vision of the ideal forms, the real forms which exist far from the world of the senses, in what Plato called the "intellectual world." This kind of philosophy is called *idealism* because it claims that ideas (which are seen by the mind and known only to the reason) are real; the physical senses are deceptive.

As the dialogue shows, the path to the world of reality was difficult and painful; for Plato, intellectual insight was a kind of religious experience. It was through a ritual of questions and answers—a dialogue—that men moved from the level of opinion and appearances to the level of knowledge and reality.

### Definition Through Dialogue

The quotation which follows is but a fragment of one of Plato's Dialogues. In this Dialogue, Socrates is discussing the meaning of "piety" with Euthyphro (yoo THIH fro), a man who is bringing his own father to trial for murder. To Euthyphro, "piety" means pleasing the gods, and in his mind, the gods would not want murder to go unpunished. Plato, through the character of Socrates, begins the task of moving toward a full knowledge of this word "piety."

*Soc.* And what is piety, and what is impiety?

*Euth.* Piety is doing as I am doing; that is to say, prosecuting any one who is guilty of murder, sacrilege, or of any similar crime—whether he be your father or mother, or whoever he may be—that makes no difference; and not to prosecute them is impiety. And please to consider, Socrates, what a notable proof I will give you of the truth of my words, a proof which I have already given to others:—of the principle, I mean, that the impious, whoever he may be, ought not to go unpunished. For do not men regard Zeus as the best and most righteous of the gods?—and yet they admit that he bound his father [Cronos] because he wickedly devoured his sons, and that he too had punished his own father [Uranus] for a similar reason, in a nameless manner. And yet when I proceed against my father, they are angry with me. So inconsistent are they in their way of talking when the gods are concerned, and when I am concerned.

*Soc.* May not this be the reason, Euthyphro, why I am charged with impiety—that I cannot away with these stories about the gods? and therefore I suppose that people think me wrong. But, as you who are well informed about them approve of them, I cannot do better than assent to your superior wisdom. What else can I say, confessing as I do, that I know nothing about them? Tell me, for the love of Zeus, whether you really believe that they are true.

*Euth.* Yes, Socrates; and things more wonderful still, of which the world is in ignorance.

*Soc.* And do you really believe that the gods fought with one another, and had dire quarrels, battles, and the like, as the poets say, and as you may see represented in the works of great artists? The temples are full of them; and notably the robe of Athene, which is carried up to the Acropolis at the great Panathenaea, is embroidered with them. Are all these tales of the gods true, Euthyphro?

*Euth.* Yes, Socrates; and, as I was saying, I can tell you, if you would like to hear them, many other things about the gods which would quite amaze you.

*Soc.* I dare say; and you shall tell me them at some other time when I have leisure. But just at present I would rather hear from you a more precise answer, which you have not as yet given, my friend, to the question, What is "piety"? When asked, you only replied, Doing as you do, charging your father with murder.

*Euth.* And what I said was true, Socrates.

*Soc.* No doubt, Euthyphro; but you would admit that there are many other pious acts?

*Euth.* There are.

*Soc.* Remember that I did not ask you to give me two or three examples of piety, but to explain the general idea which makes all pious

---

B. Jowett, trans., *The Dialogues of Plato* (New York: Macmillan, 1892), pp. 386-389.

things to be pious. Do you not recollect that there was one idea which made the impious impious, and the pious pious?

*Euth.* I remember.

*Soc.* Tell me what is the nature of this idea, and then I shall have a standard to which I may look, and by which I may measure actions, whether yours or those of any one else, and then I shall be able to say that such and such an action is pious, such another impious.

*Euth.* I will tell you, if you like.

*Soc.* I should very much like.

*Euth.* Piety, then, is that which is dear to the gods, and impiety is that which is not dear to them.

*Soc.* Very good, Euthyphro; you have now given me the sort of answer which I wanted. But whether what you say is true or not I cannot as yet tell, although I make no doubt that you will prove the truth of your words.

*Euth.* Of course.

*Soc.* Come, then, and let us examine what we are saying. That thing or person which is dear to the gods is pious, and that thing or person which is hateful to the gods is impious, these two being the extreme opposites of one another. Was not that said?

*Euth.* It was

*Soc.* And well said?

*Euth.* Yes, Socrates, I thought so; it was certainly said.

*Soc.* And further, Euthyphro, the gods were admitted to have enmities and hatreds and differences?

*Euth.* Yes, that was also said.

*Soc.* And what sort of difference creates enmity and anger? Suppose for example that you and I, my good friend, differ about a number; do differences of this sort make us enemies and set us at variance with one another? Do we not go at once to arithmetic and put an end to them by a sum?

*Euth.* True.

*Soc.* Or suppose that we differ about magnitudes, do we not quickly end the differences by measuring?

*Euth.* Very true.

*Soc.* And we end a controversy about heavy and light by resorting to a weighing machine?

*Euth.* To be sure.

*Soc.* But what differences are there which cannot be thus decided, and which therefore make us angry and set us at enmity with one another? I dare say the answer does not occur to you at the moment, and therefore I will suggest that these enmities arise when the matters of difference are the just and unjust, good and evil, honourable and dishonourable. Are not these the points about which men differ, and about which when we are unable satisfactorily to decide our differences, you and I and all of us quarrel, when we do quarrel?

*Euth.* Yes, Socrates, the nature of the differences about which we quarrel is such as you describe.

*Soc.* And the quarrels of the gods, noble Euthyphro, when they occur, are of a like nature?

*Euth.* Certainly they are.

*Soc.* They have differences of opinion, as you say, about good and evil, just and unjust, honourable and dishonourable: there would have been no quarrels among them; if there had been no such differences—would there now?

*Euth.* You are quite right.

*Soc.* Does not every man love that which he deems noble and just and good, and hate the opposite of them?

*Euth.* Very true.

*Soc.* But, as you say, people regard the same things, some as just and others as unjust,—about these they dispute; and so there arise wars and fightings among them.

*Euth.* Very true.

*Soc.* Then the same things are hated by the gods and loved by the gods, and are both hateful and dear to them?

*Euth.* True.

*Soc.* And upon this view the same things, Euthyphro, will be pious and also impious?

*Euth.* So I should suppose.

*Soc.* Then, my friend, I remark with surprise that you have not answered the question which I asked. For I certainly did not ask you to tell me what action is both pious and impious: but now it would seem that what is loved by the gods is also hated by them. And therefore, Euthyphro, in thus chastising your father you may very likely be doing what is agreeable to Zeus but disagreeable to Cronos or Uranus, and what is acceptable to Hephaestus but unacceptable to Herè, and there may be other gods who have similar differences of opinion.

In this portion of the dialogue, we can see Plato, through the voice of Socrates, slowly wending his way beyond the usual definition of piety. The fact that Greek religion was polytheistic made it impossible to base morality on an imitation of the gods because the gods themselves would not agree on a proper mode of action. Plato had to pursue his dialogue in an attempt to grasp the essential meaning of piety, to see piety in its pure form, before he could judge any given action.

Euthyphro offered another definition when he stated that "piety . . . is what all the gods love, and that the opposite, what all the gods hate, is impiety." This attempt to make the gods act as one shows the value of monotheism as an ethical guide if the will of God can be known. Plato, however, in the person of Socrates, went beyond even a God-inspired morality when he asserted that to call piety "that which the gods love" was not an adequate definition.

*Soc.* I rather think, Euthyphro, that when I asked you what piety is you were unwilling to disclose its essence to me, and merely stated one of its attributes, saying that piety has the attribute of being loved by all the gods; but you have not told me what it is that has this attribute. So, if you have no objection, please don't conceal the truth from me, but make a fresh start and tell me what piety is; that it is loved by the gods or has any other attribute—we shan't quarrel about that.

Finding the gods of no help, Plato still pushed on to find the essence of true piety without divine help. This is a classic example of man using his reason to discover a true definition and standard for proper action. No stronger example of humanism—the worship of man and his power—can be found.

*True Knowledge*

Plato had faith that this true definition was possible to discover because the human soul, he believed, had once existed in the realm of true reality. The use of human reason caused the soul to remember the images of the true forms and then use those images to see the true reality of the world. The human mind, therefore, did not enter the world as a blank slate on which experience would be written. The images of reality existed in all men; the task of education was to recall those images to active memory. Hence, man was potentially perfect; proper thinking was the key to human perfection. Evil was merely the lack of true knowledge.

Armed with this kind of faith, Plato wished to see philosophers become kings or kings become philosophers. If such a change could occur, human society would be perfect, and all the humanistic dreams of the Greeks would come to pass. For this reason, Plato became the tutor of Dionysius, the ruler of Syracuse. Plato wanted the ruler to "take society and human character as his canvas and begin by scraping it clean." All would be rebuilt with the knowledge of true reality in mind. Actually, however, such a revolution could be accepted by few people, and Dionysius himself was not capable of following the intense quest for truth which Plato's system required. Discouraged, Plato left the world of politics and sought personal enlightenment rather than social reform. Describing the true philosopher, Plato said:

He contemplates a world of unchanging and harmonious order, where reason governs and nothing can do or suffer wrong; and like one who imitates an admired companion he cannot fail to fashion himself in its likeness. So the philosopher, in constant companionship with the divine order of the world, will reproduce that order in his soul and, so far as man may, become god-like.

Plato's concepts are difficult for the average person to grasp because they seem to fly in the face of man's experience with the world around him. Yet, the presentation of Plato's ideas was so compelling that his vision of reality has had a great influence—so great that our civilization has absorbed many of his ideas, and people today may be Platonists without realizing it. In fact, it has been said that the history of Western philosophy is no more than footnotes to Plato.

One area of Plato's influence can be seen in the belief that there is an unseen nonmaterial reality and that man is more than a bundle of material things, a collection of bone and tissue. Plato's belief that man is born with certain ideas and images in his mind has served to turn man's vision inward in an attempt to understand the geography of the human soul; modern psychology has a debt to Plato. Artists, poets and mathematicians have drawn inspiration from Plato; he, more than any ancient philosopher, has unlocked the powerful instrument which is the human intellect. Plato was more than a mere thinker. Through his dialogues, he explored the deep recesses of the human mind; in so doing, he presented to future generations avenues for growth which earlier men had not conceived possible. He taught Western culture how to think, and he continues to do so.

Hellenistic civilization was predominately Greek in its origin and expressions, but the leading ideas of the Hellenistic period spanned and united the different peoples of the Mediterranean basin. In spite of tremendous diversity, there was, as we have seen, a thin strata of common culture throughout the civilized portions of the lands around the great sea. Mediterranean civilization would have reached its final conclusion were it not for the Romans, who brought some fresh ideas and a good deal of energy to this geographical area. The Romans slowly but remorselessly spread their rule first throughout Italy, then through the Hellenistic world and finally beyond the Mediterranean lands themselves into the unknown territory called Europe. Civilization was both elaborated and spread by the Romans.

# UNIT IV
# The Roman Empire

# 7
# Italy and the Republic

Italy, like Greece, is a peninsula extending south from the mainland of Europe into the Mediterranean Sea. The Italian peninsula is, on the whole, less mountainous and more fertile than Greece. A single mountain range, the Apennines, runs down the eastern side of Italy, and the land sloping down to the west contains rich farmland and excellent harbors. Italy faces to the west, away from Greece and hence away from the ancient centers of civilization. This geographical fact might serve to explain why people living in Italy developed the arts of civilization later than those living in the eastern half of the Mediterranean area. At the time of Pericles and the flowering of Athenian culture, Rome was a small, insignificant farming village on the western coast of Italy.

## Early Italian Peoples

Most of the early Italians were Indo-European in background and had migrated to Italy around the start of the second millennium\* B.C. (2000 B.C.). The Mycenaeans in Greece and the Hittites in the Near East were also part of this general migration. In Italy, the various Indo-European tribes lived in separate groups, and there was little or no political unity. Some of the important Italian tribes were the *Sabines* (SAY bines), the *Samnites* and the *Latins;* the Romans were one of several Latin tribes. During the time of Homeric Greece, these inhabitants of Italy were not substantially different from people living in Spain or in the rest of Europe to the north. To Homer and the Greeks, they all would have been barbarians.

---

\* A *millennium* is a period of a thousand years.

114

**The Etruscans.** Such a description could not have applied to two early inhabitants of Italy, the *Greeks* and the *Etruscans*. The Etruscans lived in a land they called Etruria, which was located roughly around the modern Italian city of Florence in central Italy. The origins of the Etruscans are still uncertain, but most historians believe that either they or their ideas originated in Asia Minor. Their language is only now in the process of being translated, and indications are that they were not of Indo-European background.

The Etruscans lived in cities, practiced trade and manufacturing, developed an elaborate monarchy and were deeply religious. It was they who introduced the practice of *divination* to Italy, a ritual in which the priests examined the entrails of animals in order to predict the future. The Etruscan priests also had a system for interpreting the flight patterns of birds, the study of which was thought to lead to an understanding of the will of the gods. Religious practices such as these, as well as the institution of a priesthood, were taken over by the Romans.

The Etruscans had trade contacts with both the Carthaginians in northern Africa and the Greeks who had migrated to southern Italy. They were skilled builders, and in fact, they may have been the first to use the arch as a basic element of their buildings. Their craftsmanship was the equal of the Greeks' and far superior to the rest of the Italians'. Whether or not any great Etruscan literature will be discovered remains to be seen, but it is clear that these people had a significant influence on the Romans. Many practices and ideas which were once thought to be Roman are, in reality, Etruscan borrowings. Gladiatorial contests,* which were later popular in Rome, were also of Etruscan origin.

**The Greeks.** The southern half of Italy and the island of Sicily gradually filled up with Greek cities inhabited by immigrants from Greece. In time, these cities, of which Syracuse was the most important, became as wealthy and civilized as the cities in Greece itself. During the Hellenistic period, Syracuse was a major intellectual center, home of the famous scientist Archimedes. Although the Greeks had to share the central and western Mediterranean with the Carthaginians, their presence in Italy was powerful and secure. They served as a link between Italy and the civilized world to the east.

---

* Gladiatorial contests involved a duel to the death between a person (often a slave or captive) and another person or a wild animal; they were held in public arenas for the entertainment of the spectators.

This bronze Etruscan statuette of a female dancer dates from an early period in the history of Italy. Its style is stiff and formal, much like early Greek art and Egyptian sculpture.

*Courtesy, Museum of Fine Arts, Boston*

The Greek city of Cumae (KYOO mee) was close to Rome, and it was here that contact between Greeks and Romans was made. The Romans, in fact, devised the word *Graecus* to describe these Hellenic peoples, a word from which the English word Greek originates. The most important Greek city on Italy itself was called *Neopolis* (meaning new city). This is the modern city of Naples, called Napoli in Italian. The Greek origins of this city can be seen clearly in its very name.

**The Latins.** The Latin tribes to which the Romans belonged lived in the valley of the Tiber River between the Etruscans and the Greeks. The city of Rome was founded on one of seven hills located near the Tiber; in time, the Romans incorporated all of the hills into their city. It was not a large city, but it was an independent state similar to the Greek city-state, or polis, which had once flourished in Greece and was now the basic political unit of the Mediterranean area. The location had many advantages. The Romans controlled the river which ran to the sea as well as the trade routes which ran north and south along the peninsula. It was this city and these people who would one day rule the entire Mediterranean area. Rome eventually became not only the most important city in the Mediterranean world but also the most influential city in the history of western European civilization. What the Romans did is therefore of importance to us.

## Early Roman Society

**The Farmer-soldier.** The early Romans were farmers; they manufactured no more than they needed and traded very little. They were men of the soil, not of the marketplace. Each Roman family owned a plot of land from which a livelihood was drawn. Because of the valuable location of the city, the Romans were under pressure from other peoples, and war was a frequent occurrence. Unlike the Egyptians, who were protected by miles of desert, the Romans were forced to draw together and to cultivate the art of war. Therefore, the average Roman was a "farmer-soldier" who divided his life between these two occupations.

This quality of Roman society can be illustrated in the career of *Cincinnatus*, an early Roman who, when summoned to battle, left his plow in the middle of the field, took up his weapons and joined with other farmers to defend the tribe from attack. After the battle, Cincinnatus did not pursue the path of military glory in the manner of the Greek hero Alcibiades. Rather, he returned to his field and resumed the quiet life of the farmer. In the actions of Cincinnatus, we can glimpse an essential difference between the Greek and the Roman temperament. Even the Roman god of war, *Mars*, was also the god of the fields. It is interesting to note that George Washington, after his career as a general in the Revolutionary War, returned to his farm in Mount Vernon and formed an organization of former officers called the Order of Cincinnati.

**Respect for Authority.** The quiet and stable sense of duty which the early Romans had was reinforced by their traditional family structure. The father was the head of the household, and all members of the family respected and bowed to his will. His power and authority did not rest on his own personal skill or strength but in the fact that he embodied the spirit of the family, a spirit which was passed on from father to son. In Roman homes, statues of former fathers were on constant display; this was a way of making visible the continuing spirit (described by the Romans as *genius*) of the family. This quality of respect, and stability, represented a conservative attitude which maintained old ideals and gave the Roman family great strength. Household gods were important divine forces in Roman life and are witnesses to the importance of the family as the essential component in Roman society.

The respect for proper authority and loyalty to the group which was nurtured in the Roman family was gradually transferred to the Roman state as it grew. The commands of rulers were obeyed as if they were commands of a father, and the common good was more important than individual pleasures or desires. This respect for authority and for the traditions of the past can be seen in the following incident in which a Roman official (the consul) was obligated by law to punish his own sons for treason. In the words of a Roman historian:

> Their punishment created a great sensation owing to the fact that in this case the office of Consul imposed upon a father the duty of inflicting punishment on his own children; he who ought not to have witnessed it, was destined to be the one to see it duly carried out. Youths belonging to the noblest families were standing tied to the post, but all eyes were turned to the Consul's children, the others were unnoticed. The Consuls took their seats, the lictors were told to inflict the penalty; they scourged their bare backs with rods and then beheaded them.

This kind of patriotism and acceptance of rules, even in the face of the strongest of human emotions, gave the Romans a cohesiveness and solidarity which enabled them to survive as a group and to become the strongest people in Italy. They were, on the whole, serious and unsentimental people whose temperament could be summed up in the Roman word *gravitas*, a word meaning heaviness or seriousness. This quality can be seen in many aspects of Roman culture.

**Religion.** In the Roman religion, there were gods of nature, gods of the city and gods of the household. The Romans did not portray their gods as colorful personalities, and so there was no Roman mythology in the early days. Religion was highly ritualistic and was usually concerned with practical matters such as the fertility of the soil, the hoped-for birth of a male child and the safety of the household and state. In the family, the father acted as priest, performing the necessary ceremonies to secure the safety and prosperity of the household and family. In the city, the priests were public officials who used religious ceremonies to secure the favor of the gods. Such favor was usually gained through the proper performance of rituals—rituals which served to bind the people together through a common focus of worship.

## ITALY AND THE REPUBLIC

One of the possible meanings of the Latin word *religio*, from which comes the English word religion, is "to bind." Roman religion was in many ways a binding operation. The gods were bound to support the Roman state as a result of proper worship, and the people were bound together through worship of the same gods. Roman religion had little spiritual or intellectual content and was primarily a patriotic operation. The high priest, called the *Pontifex Maximus*, held one of the most important offices in the Roman government. There was no Roman religious literature as was the case with the Hebrews. Nor, in the early days, was there a Roman Homer who could use religion as a means of exploring the soul and spirit of man. For the Romans, *pietas*—what we would call "piety" —meant loyalty to home, city and established ways rather than an intense personal religious feeling. Order and practicality were some of the legacies of Roman religion.

### The Roman Republic

During the early years of Rome's existence, the city was under the domination of the Etruscans. Several of the early kings of Rome were themselves Etruscans. However, as the Romans devel-

This sculpted head of a Roman conveys much of the personal qualities of the early Romans. It is a somber face, expressing the qualities of gravitas and secure fortitude.

*Courtesy, Museum of Fine Arts, Boston*

oped their own cultural forms and a sense of their own identity, resistance to Etruscan rule grew. In the year 509 B.C., a leading Roman by the name of *Lucius Junius Brutus* led a successful rebellion against the Etruscan king, *Tarquin the Proud.* The revolt led to the establishment of Rome as a separate political entity. Rather than constructing a Roman monarchy, the leaders of the new state established a form of government which they called a *republic.* From that time on, the word king (*rex*) was a hated word among the Romans.

The Roman republic was a fairly common kind of government on the surface, not very different from others at that time. The state was ruled by members of the leading families, at first by descendants of the original men who had expelled the Etruscan kings and established the republic. It was a rule of the few, an aristocracy of birth. However, the spirit of the Roman republic was different from that which existed in other governments. The word republic itself suggests that something more than aristocracy was involved; it was derived from two Roman words—*res,* meaning things, and *publicae,* meaning of the people. The closest English synonym is the word commonwealth, a word which also implies a sense of the common good and of the involvement of the people in the government. Roman government, like Roman religion, was to have a distinctive quality.

**Political Structure.** The leaders of the state were called *patricians* (from the Roman word *pater,* meaning father), implying that they were the fathers of the state. They met together in a body called the *senate,* which was a permanent and powerful political group. Each year, the citizens chose two men who were jointly responsible for the actual running of the state. These two men, called *consuls,* acted as king but ruled for only one year. The consuls had equal power so that they could check one another. In such a way, the Romans hoped to prevent a relapse to the rule of one man—a monarchy. After serving as consul, a man could join the senate. In times of great emergency, a single ruler, called a *dictator,* could be chosen to rule for a short period of time. Dictatorship was resorted to only under unusual circumstances, and the term of the dictator was severely limited.

The great majority of Romans were not related to the leading families; they were called *plebians.* Plebian status was determined by birth, and therefore a plebian might be either rich or poor; some plebians were actually wealthier than some patricians. Although there was an assembly of the plebians possessing some power, final authority was clearly in the hands of the patricians. Plebians were forbidden by law to hold the office of consul, and marriage between the classes was forbidden. As in the case of Greece, noble blood carried with it the right to rule. In Roman society, the great importance accorded to the family and its continuing spirit reinforced a government by birth.

**The Plebian Revolt.** As the city of Rome grew in power and wealth, the plebians became restive. They argued that the republic was being untrue to its name; it was not, they said, a "thing of the people." Class friction grew, and eventually, open war broke out between patricians and plebians, just as it had in the earlier city-states of Greece. The Roman and the Greek polis faced political and social problems which were remarkably similar.

In order to dramatize their argument, the plebians as a group left the city. This secession threatened to bring about the disintegration of the Roman republic and its destruction by more unified peoples. In the words of Roman historians:

> From the very beginning of the republic the strong were encroaching on the weak, and for this reason the people were alienated from the senate. After the expulsion of the kings, the ruling classes exercised justice and moderation only till the dread of Tarquin and the fierce war with Etruria had subsided. From that time the patricians began to tyrannize over the plebians as over slaves, to scourge and pirate their lands, exclude them from government and monopolize it for themselves. Greatly oppressed by these severities and still more by the illegal interest on debts, the people had also to contribute taxes and personal service for incessant wars.

> In the city there was great panic; everything was at a standstill because of mutual apprehensions. The plebians left behind feared violence from the senators, who in turn feared the plebians remaining in the city, uncertain whether they should prefer them to stay or leave. "How long," they asked, "will the crowd of seceders remain quiet? What will happen if foreign war should break out in the meanwhile? Certainly the only remaining hope is harmony in the citizen body, and harmony must be achieved by fair means or foul." They decided to make their advocate Menenius Agrippa, an eloquent man, and a favorite of the plebians because he was himself a plebian born. When he was admitted into the [plebian] camp he is said merely to have told this tale, in the unpolished old-fashioned style:

> Once when a man's parts did not, as now, agree together but each had its own program and style, the other parts were indig-

nant that their worry and trouble and diligence procured everything for the belly, which remained idle in the middle of the body and only enjoyed what the others provided. Accordingly they conspired that the hands should not carry food to the mouth, nor the mouth accept it nor the teeth chew it. But while they angrily tried to subdue the belly by starvation, the members themselves and the whole body became dangerously emaciated. Hence it became evident that the belly's service was [necessary], that it nourished the rest as well as itself, supplying the whole body with the source of life and energy by turning food into blood and distributing it through the veins.

By thus showing that the plebians' anger against the senators was the internal sedition in a body, he swayed the men's minds. Negotiations for concord were then undertaken. The terms included a provision that the plebians should have their own magistrates who would be sacrosanct and possess power to aid the common people against the consuls; it would not be lawful, moreover, for a patrician to hold this magistracy. In this way the tribunes of the people were created.

The concept of the state as an interconnected organism patterned after the human body was a powerful political idea, an idea invented by the Romans.

**Reform.** When the plebians returned to Rome, they were given the right to choose a magistrate of their own called a *tribune*. The man holding this office was a spokesman for plebians who looked out for their interests. Tribunes were given power to halt any law being passed by the senate merely by saying *veto*—"I forbid." This is the origin of the veto power held in the United States government by the President; the President is a kind of tribune of the people who can check the actions of the Congress. It is interesting to note that the word tribune appears in the titles of many modern newspapers.

The plebians made other gains. Around the year 450 B.C., the basic laws of the state were written down, supposedly on the *Twelve Tables,* so that all men might know of their rights and obligations. In time, laws were passed which granted to the assembly of the plebians the right to pass final judgment on laws. Plebians could be elected to the office of consul, and hence they gained the right to be admitted to the senate. Marriage between patrician and plebian was made legal. By laws such as these, the division between the classes was lessened, and cooperation grew. Members of the same body, in this case, a "body politic," would have to work together if the social organism were to be healthy and strong.

An aqueduct is a massive trough or channel which conveys water over great distances. The Claudian Aqueduct shown here was one of many which delivered fresh mountain water to ancient Rome. It is an impressive example of Roman practical genius and engineering skill.

**The Aristocracy.** Although the plebians gained rights which gave them a political power equal, in theory, to that of the patricians, the Roman republic was still, in fact, a government of the few. The senate was no longer restricted to descendants of the original noble families. However, the prestige of being a member of an old family gave a man automatic political power. Plebians who joined the senate by way of consulship merely became members of the aristocracy and thereafter supported the rule of the few, of which they had become a part.

Consuls and other officers were chosen by vote of the people, but even in elections, the aristocracy had ultimate power. Such modern things as insurance, Social Security and trade unions did not exist, and so the Romans who were poor became dependent on wealthy Romans for protection and security. Such dependents were called *clients,* and clients, although they were free men, were followers of individual, powerful Romans—their *patrons.* At election time, the clients usually showed their gratitude by voting as their patrons wished. We might call such an arrangement corrupt, but it was a gentle way of binding men together, and it served to guarantee an effective rule of the few within a democratic system.

Above all, the senate usually managed to rule with the interests of the entire population in mind, and so the majority of the people were content and did not want to revolt. Rome was a democracy in theory but an aristocracy in practice. Its government fit into no set or logical mold. It was a government for the people and, to an extent, of the people, but it was not a government by the people. The initials S.P.Q.R. which adorned Roman shields and standards spelled out the reality of the situation—*Senatus Populusque Romanus* (the Senate and People of Rome).

**Stability.** The crisis of the Roman republic, the struggle between the patricians and plebians, was quite similar to the conflict between the rich and the poor, the nobles and the peasants, in seventh- and sixth-century B.C. Greece. However, the solution to this political problem in Rome was not brought about by a single lawgiver; there was no Roman equivalent of Solon. It seems as if the political genius of the Roman people themselves had brought about a stable and balanced political structure. For this reason, the Roman constitution* was more sound than that of the Greek states, whose governments often fluctuated between democracy and tyranny. The reason for this difference might well be found in the temperament of the Roman people themselves. As a prominent Roman once said, "On ancient men and morals the Roman state stands."

But it was not only "ancient men and morals" which enabled the Romans to build lasting political institutions. The availability of fertile land in Italy enabled them to expand and to provide land for a growing population. Faced with a similar problem, the Greeks had had to migrate to distant places, thereby making the Greek world less unified than the Roman. In the process of expansion, the Romans incorporated the peoples of conquered lands in Italy into their own system of government. Full citizenship rights were given to some Italians, and partial rights were given to others. Cities which were troubled by uncivilized tribesmen from the mountains often invited the Romans to join with them in their wars. Alliances were thus formed, and Rome gradually became the policeman of Italy. Alliance with Rome was often a wise policy for a city to follow, as the Romans required little of their allies. The Romans were a relatively simple people, not driven by the desire for glory and conquest which infected the Greek spirit.

---

* The term "Roman constitution" describes the way in which the Roman state, or body politic, was constituted. A constitution existed in the sense that the British constitution exists today—it was an accumulated body of laws and traditions rather than a single document.

## Contact with Greece

In the south of Italy during the fourth century B.C., the Roman and Greek worlds joined together. The Greek cities of Italy were centers of wealth, learning and the restless spirit of Hellenic culture. As we might expect, these cities were frequently at war with each other, and Roman military skill was often called upon. Gradually, the Romans became involved in the politics and wars of the Greek world. The senate soon found that the stability of the Roman order required the incorporation of all of Italy into the Roman system.

In the year 281 B.C., one of the Greek cities in the south of Italy employed the services of a Greek general by the name of *Pyrrhus* (PIHR uhs) to fight against the Romans. This military man was practiced in the Macedonian art of war and represented the best of military skill in the Hellenistic world. Although Pyrrhus defeated the Roman army, he sustained such losses that it was clear that no Greek general could restrain the power of Rome forever. Roman soldiers were more than professional fighting men; they were products of a long tradition of iron discipline and deep-rooted patriotism. They represented a new force in the Mediterranean world, a force which not only won wars but produced stable and effective government over large areas.

By the mid-third century B.C., Romans were scattered throughout Italy south of the River Po, and Rome was the dominant city on the peninsula. Some land was annexed to Rome, but most of Italy was not ruled directly by Romans. Cities merely allied themselves with Rome, and the senate let them run their own internal affairs as they saw fit. Also, none of the non-Roman states could ever join together long enough to challenge the power of Rome. The acquiring of new lands, the expanding of trade routes and the extending of an effective government made Rome a major power in the western Mediterranean. The farmer-soldiers of Rome now gazed upon the rich and exciting civilization which lay to the east.

## *Define*

Etruscans
divination
Cincinnatus

*genius*
*gravitas*
Pontifex Maximus

*pietas*
Lucius Junius Brutus
Roman republic

patricians        dictator        clients
senate            plebians        patrons
consuls           tribune         Pyrrhus

*Review and Answer*

1. In what ways was the geography of Italy significantly different from that of Greece?
2. What were the important qualities which gave Roman society and values a distinctive mark?
3. Explain Menenius Agrippa's comparison of society with the human body (pages 121-122). What does this tell us of the Roman view of the state?
4. What was so significant about the initials S.P.Q.R.?
5. In what ways did the Roman republic remain an aristocracy in spite of political reforms in the direction of democracy?

# 8
# The Mediterranean and the Empire

As the Romans moved about the southern tip of Italy, they came face to face with a hard decision. Across the sea was the wealthy and powerful city of Carthage, with colonies on the island of Sicily and in control of the entire western portion of the Mediterranean. Roman leaders had to decide whether to avoid a conflict with these people and so remain an Italian power or whether to come to blows with Carthage and so move out into the wider world. The decision to expand produced a titanic struggle with Carthage which put Roman institutions to a severe test and led the Romans on a clear path to gaining a world empire.

## The Punic Wars

Carthage itself was in North Africa, but it had established colonies in Spain and Sicily. In Spain, the Carthaginians had encountered uncivilized tribesmen, but in Sicily, they collided with highly developed Greek cities. Friction grew, and when the Greek city of Messina (muh SEE nuh) in Sicily was threatened by Carthage, the leaders appealed to Rome for assistance. In the senate, debates took place as to whether it was in the interest of Rome to assist this Greek city and so to run the risk of a major conflict with the Carthaginian empire. Some argued that if Sicily fell under the domination of Carthage, Rome would ultimately be threatened. The decision was made to assist Messina. Thus began the first of several wars with Carthage, wars which were to determine who would control the western Mediterranean.

The Carthaginians were of Phoenician origin, Carthage having once been a Phoenician colony founded centuries earlier. This is why the Romans used the word *poenicus* (POY nih kuhs), later *punicus* (POO nih kuhs), to describe the Carthaginians; this is also why the wars with Carthage are usually called the *Punic* (PYOO nihk) *Wars*. Although Carthage controlled extensive lands along the coast of Africa, it was primarily a sea power. The empire was ruled by a merchant oligarchy whose wealth was based on a mixture of agriculture and trade. The western Mediterranean was a Carthaginian lake, and the *First Punic War* (264-241 B.C.) was fought on the island of Sicily and the surrounding waters.

**The First Punic War.** This war was like a struggle between an elephant and a whale; the Romans were superior on land, and the Carthaginians were in control of the sea. Faced with this situation, the Romans had to learn the technique of naval warfare. They captured a Punic ship, copied its plan of construction and began the slow process of training naval officers.

In the days before long-range cannons, sea-fighting was not very different from land-fighting. Men tended to look upon ships as extensions of the land, and so ships were made with large gangplanks and ample space for soldiers. In an actual battle, the attacking ship would draw close to the enemy, lower the gangplank and so permit the army to rush over and do battle with the soldiers on the enemy ship.

When the first Roman fleet put out to sea, mistakes were made and the Romans suffered many setbacks. Nonetheless, in spite of their awkwardness on the sea, the Romans eventually defeated the Carthaginians and soon found themselves in control of the islands of both Sicily and Sardinia.

**New Provinces—New Problems.** The acquisition of land outside of Italy posed problems. The Romans had not developed political institutions to deal with distant possessions, lands which the Romans called *provinces*. In addition to this political problem, the opening of new lands made it possible for adventurous Romans to become wealthy through trade, farming or tax collecting. Wealth began to move into Rome, and the control of that wealth became a social and political problem. The old ruling class was primarily agricultural, and many senators regarded trading and tax collecting as beneath the dignity of a patrician. Therefore, a new class of Romans, mostly of plebian background, began to emerge.

This "middle class"—those above the impoverished peasants but below the rich nobility—took on the job of running the provinces and providing the services a growing government required.

New offices had to be created to govern the provinces, and the Romans dealt with this problem merely by extending existing offices. Consuls, after their terms of office were over, were sent to the provinces to rule there as consuls. These *pro-consuls*, as they were called, were provincial governors, and the holding of such an office soon became one of the routes to wealth and power.

**The Second Punic War.** The defeat of Carthage did not go unavenged. One of the leading Carthaginian families, the Barca family, had a son by the name of Hannibal, who, as a child, was forced by his father to swear an oath of eternal hatred toward Rome. When this child grew to manhood, he gathered together an army of Africans, Spaniards and Carthaginians and launched a massive invasion of Italy. Most of his soldiers were mercenaries (soldiers who fought for pay), but the brilliant generalship and powerful personal qualities of Hannibal fused them into an effective fighting force. The army of Hannibal did not have the built-in unity and commitment that a Roman army had. Unity was created and imposed by a single man without whom Rome would have been far less threatened. Therefore, it is unfortunate that so little is known of Hannibal himself, and most of it from Roman sources.

Hannibal launched his attack from what is now Spain, moved along the southern coast of present-day France and entered Italy after crossing the Alps. This march, involving foot soldiers, mounted warriors and elephants, is one of the most exciting tales in military history. When Hannibal descended into the Po Valley and turned his army toward Rome, the very existence of Roman civilization was at stake. Hannibal's invasion of Italy and the battles he fought there constituted the *Second Punic War* (218-201 B.C.).

**The Genius of Hannibal.** In battle after battle, the Romans were defeated. Hannibal displayed a kind of military genius which no Roman consul could equal. In one instance, he attacked from the rear after luring the Romans into the battlefield. In the battle of Lake Trasimene, he attacked from the side as the Roman army was moving through a fog. In another encounter, he escaped by night from a Roman trap by tying lamps to the horns of cattle, thereby drawing the Romans away from his army which escaped by another route. Hannibal came armed with political weapons as well. He offered Italian cities and tribes freedom from Roman rule if they would support him. Hannibal remained in Italy a total of fourteen years, living off the land and destroying the Roman order.

## 130 THE ROMAN EMPIRE

In the war with Hannibal, the Romans were both helped and hindered by their political system. The practice of having two consuls, chosen for only one year, led to confusion, especially when each consul took command on alternate days. During the extended crisis of Hannibal's invasion, real power rested in the senate. Occasionally, dictators were chosen for brief periods, but the fact that there was no king, no single ruler around whom the nation could rally, left the senate as the only effective body. The war was the supreme test of the Roman system of government, and it was the finest hour for the Roman senate, acting on behalf of the Roman people. Hannibal's flashing horsemen were met by Romans bearing standards which read S.P.Q.R.

The dramatic events of the Second Punic War, often called the Hannibalic War, cannot be covered in detail. Rather, an essential question needs to be posed. Why was it that Rome could withstand the onslaught of a superior military force for so long a time? The answer to this question lies in the strength of Roman political culture.

This tombstone sculpture of a Roman husband and wife (Cato and Portia) shows not only the strength of Roman character but emphasizes the continuing power and influence of the family in Roman culture. Stability and security are important ingredients of this work of art.

Anderson

**Roman Military Leaders.** After the early battles, in which the Romans attacked Hannibal's forces with speed and daring, only to be defeated, a new kind of strategy was developed. It was associated with a Roman consul by the name of *Fabius* (FAY bee uhs) and consisted of a policy of not joining the enemy in open battle but of following him and sniping at his flanks, hoping eventually that his provisions would run out and his morale would be destroyed. This policy has led to the coining of the word *Fabian*, which means the use of delaying tactics. By using this strategy, however, farmlands belonging to wealthy Romans were left to be plundered and ruined by Hannibal's army. Protests grew against Fabius and his policy, especially when it became known that Hannibal had deliberately avoided harming lands owned by Fabius himself. Yet Fabius was never driven from office; he remained in command until his term of office was over.

Eventually, the strategy was changed, and a consul by the name of *Varro* (VAIR oh) decided on open attack near the village of Cannae (CAN ee). To meet this attack, Hannibal ordered his army to give way at the center, thereby drawing the Roman army deep into the Carthaginian ranks. Encouraged by this early victory, Varro pressed on—only to have his army crushed from both sides as if between a pincer. The battle at Cannae established a classic style of warfare which has been used again and again by military strategists. The German army used a modified version of the Cannae strategy in the attack on France in the First World War.

After the disaster of Cannae, the Roman army was demolished, and the city of Rome itself was exposed to attack. However, at this point, a curious and significant thing happened. Varro departed from the sensible policy of Fabius and brought about a calamity. One might expect the Romans, especially Fabius, to take out their frustration on the unwise consul. This, however, was not the case, as the following account, describing what happened after Cannae, shows.

> Above all, let us admire the high spirit and equanimity of this Roman commonwealth; that when the consul Varro came beaten and flying home, full of shame and humiliation, after he had so disgracefully and calamitously managed their affairs, yet the whole senate and people went forth to meet him at the gates of the city, and received him with honor and respect. And, silence being commanded, the magistrates and chief of the senate, Fabius

amongst them, commended him before the people, because he did not despair of the safety of the commonwealth, after so great a loss, but was come to take the government into his hand, to execute the laws, and aid his fellow-citizens in the prospect of future deliverance.

Varro had failed, but he was still a consul and as such was accorded honor. The deep respect which the Romans gave to their government saved the city from panic and disintegration. To the Romans, it was the office, and not the man, which counted.

**Hannibal's Defeat.** Hannibal never attacked the city of Rome, and in time, the Romans launched a counterattack on Carthage itself, forcing the great general to return to Africa. If Rome had been defeated, the future development of Italy and of later civilizations would have been different from what it was. We ourselves might have been different people.

Why Hannibal failed to deal the final blow to Rome is difficult to say. He had no siege equipment, and so the taking of a fortified town would have been extremely difficult. Also, some of the Italian cities had been well treated by Rome, and in the face of Carthaginian domination in Italy, they began to have second thoughts about allying with Hannibal. The Carthaginians fought well; whether they governed well was questionable. Therefore, Hannibal did not have the full support of the Italian population. Also, Hannibal himself found it difficult to consolidate his gains; he was more effective in attack. A fellow officer once said to him, "You know, Hannibal, how to gain a victory, but not how to use it." The same can be said for many military geniuses, even today.

Roman legend states that when Hannibal appeared about to attack Rome, the army and people left the city on their way to Spain, in high spirits and with banners flying. While this exodus was taking place, the land in and around Rome was still selling at a high price, indicating that no one doubted that Hannibal would be defeated and the Romans would return. Whether or not these courageous gestures actually occurred or whether they had any effect on Hannibal, we will never know. However, it is true that Roman character, as shown in the respect they gave to their institutions and laws, served as the greatest defense of their state.

**The "New" Senate.** There was no single Roman hero of the war. Rather, the Roman senate as a whole guided the state through its trials. It emerged after the war as the strongest ruling body in the western Mediterranean. To wield this kind of power, the senate had to have the respect and automatic support of the citizens. It had to be a small, select body in order to have any kind of prestige. But, at the same time, it could not be a thoroughly closed group, a narrow oligarchy.

During the second century B.C., the senate no longer consisted only of members of old patrician families; it also contained men who had held the office of consul. This procedure not only kept the senate full of experienced statesmen, but it permitted plebians to enter the ranks of the ruling class. The old aristocracy of birth became an aristocracy of officeholders, which came close to being an aristocracy of talent. A visitor to Rome once remarked that dealing with the senate was like meeting with an assembly of kings.

## The Expanding Empire

The victory over Hannibal did more than enhance the prestige of Rome. It made the Romans responsible for lands formerly held by Carthage. Also, the power of Rome did not go unnoticed in the courts of the great Hellenistic kings in the East. These Eastern states were often at war with each other, each attempting to rule the area which had once been unified by Alexander the Great. Rome, the power in the West, could serve as an ally in this struggle. Also, during the Second Punic War, Hannibal had attempted to enlist the aid of Macedonia. Therefore, after the war, the Roman government could no longer remain indifferent to the actions of this Greek kingdom.

**Macedonia.** Some of the smaller Greek city-states saw in Rome a possible ally against the Macedonians and sent appeals to the senate. Since many Romans had acquired an admiration for Greek culture, they were moved by appeals from the cities which were the birthplaces of Hellenic civilization. Also, on strictly military grounds, it was wise to keep Macedonia from becoming too strong. A Macedonian attack on Rome in alliance with the twice-defeated Carthage was always a possibility. Therefore, in the same haphazard way in which Rome had become dominant in the West, Roman involvement in the East began. In the year 215 B.C., the first of four Macedonian Wars began, and by the middle of the second century B.C., what is known as the Roman Empire was coming into being.

**Roman Reasons for Expansion.** It has been argued that Rome built its empire as a result of defensive and generous motives, and this argument is not without merit. The need for protection against a hostile alliance between Macedonia and Carthage was clear. Also, the Roman admiration of Greek culture was genuine. Many wealthy Romans had become aware of the Homeric poems, Greek mythology and Athenian drama and philosophy. Roman minds, trained in the sober, practical virtues of home and state, were excited by the brilliance and beauty of Greek ideas and values. The heroic humanism of Homer, the keen intelligence of Socrates and the radiant beauty of Greek sculpture cut through the tough fiber of the traditional Roman *gravitas*. This cultural invasion of Rome produced a division between traditional Romans and those who could be called Hellenized Romans. The beauty and brilliance of Hellenic civilization could not be denied, and many Romans were increasingly drawn to the East, toward the original home of civilization.

Along with these rather noble motives for building an empire, there existed less generous ones. New provinces meant more wealth for more people; economic forces pulling Rome to the East were as strong as the cultural ones. Large estates could be built if slaves could be procured to provide the labor for field and pasture. Captives taken in war were usually sold into slavery, and the slave trade itself was a profitable business. Money and movable items, particularly art works, were stolen outright as the prizes of victory. The expansion of trade and of economic activity in general led to the continued growth of a wealthy merchant class. Also, the obvious military success of the state produced a feeling of pride and a desire for increasing success in battle. The motives for acquiring power are always mixed.

**Military Exploits in the East.** In the year 197 B.C., the Roman army dealt a substantial blow to the Macedonians, thereby proving that Roman military organization was superior to the system of fighting which had been devised by Alexander. A Roman army had broken the Macedonian phalanx! The cities of Greece were liberated and placed under Roman protection. However, when it became clear that the Greek cities wanted complete freedom to pursue their own policies, sometimes in opposition to Rome, even they had to be subdued. Now that Romans were living in Greece, studying philosophy and art in Athens and earning their living abroad, Rome could not let events take their own course. In the year 146 B.C., the Roman army destroyed the city of Corinth, and all of Greece was made an outright Roman province. In the same

notebook ↓

## Rome and the Western Mediterranean
(c. 3RD Century B.C.)

▨ LANDS CONTROLLED BY CARTHAGE
— ROUTE OF HANNIBAL   Cumae GREEK CITIES

Through the Pyrenees and across the frozen Alps, the brilliant, ruthless Hannibal led his troops toward Rome. Out of the approximately 60,000 men who began the march, only 26,000 survived to descend to the Po Valley and begin the bloody trek to Rome.

year, Carthage, having raised a third war against Rome (the *Third Punic War*, 149-146 B.C.), was totally destroyed. Roman governors were installed along the coast of North Africa.

Rome could not stop with Greece; the logic of empire was inevitable. The states of Asia Minor, in particular, the kingdom of Pontus ruled by the ambitious King *Mithridates* (mith rih DAY teez), posed a threat to Greece—and Greece was now the eastern border of the Roman Empire. Therefore, the Romans were compelled to become involved in the affairs of Asia Minor. They built up alliances and dispatched armies. In the year 88 B.C., the first of three Mithridatic Wars began. During the first century B.C., Asia Minor became a major area of Roman activity, just as the island of Sicily had been almost two hundred years earlier. Tax collectors, governors, generals and merchants increased the scope of their activity; wealth, glory and Greek ideas flowed into the city of Rome. Like the Greeks of an earlier age, the Romans seemed to be everywhere; unlike the Greeks, they came not as individual colonists or conquerors but as members of a coherent military and political organization.

**Problems in the West.** In the West, Spain had been a Roman province since the defeat of Hannibal. In order to secure the land route to Spain, the Romans had to subdue the tribes living north of the Po River and in the southern portion of Gaul.* The land between the Po and the Alps was called *Cisalpine Gaul* (Gaul this side of the Alps). The large area to the north stretching to the English Channel was called *Transalpine Gaul* (Gaul across the Alps). The barbarians living in these lands were an occasional threat to Rome. They had attacked the city as far back as 390 B.C. and as recently as 133 B.C. Therefore, although Rome was fast becoming the capital city of an empire, it was situated near the edge of the civilized world.

The wars with Carthage, especially the victory over Hannibal, made it necessary for Rome to establish its rule in backward lands. The victory over Carthage also involved Rome in the affairs of the peoples and kingdoms of the East. This gradual development of an empire by a people whose basic patterns of life and system of government were designed for a city-state could not help but have an effect on the Romans and their society. Rome as an Italian power and Rome as a world power were two different things.

---

* Gaul was the territory consisting of what is now northern Italy, France, Belgium and the southern part of the Netherlands.

### Define

| provinces | Fabian | Cisalpine Gaul |
| pro-consul | Varro | Transalpine Gaul |
| Hannibal | battle of Cannae | |
| Fabius | Pontus | |

### Review and Answer

1. How can it be argued that the Roman Empire was built by accident and with no set plan?
2. How did the struggle between Rome and Carthage bring out certain basic traits of Roman character and traditions?
3. How did the gaining of new lands affect Roman government and values?

# 9

# The Empire and the Roman Constitution

Just how Rome was forced to change by becoming an empire is an interesting story. A series of wars coupled with territorial expansion had as much of an impact on Rome itself as it did on those people whom Rome now ruled. The social and political changes which occurred within the Roman republic called forth an incredible number of great personalities. The significance of Roman history during this period is not without interest for modern Americans, who live in a nation recently risen to the rank of the most powerful nation in the world.

## A Changing Social Structure

The foundation stone of Roman society and the essential element of its political structure was the "farmer-soldier," a type of man personified by Cincinnatus. As long as Roman military activity was restricted to Italy, the army could be staffed by such men. The crown of the Roman government was the senate, that "assembly of kings" which had guided the country through the Punic Wars. As long as the senate was responsible for Italian affairs and no more, it provided an efficient and elegant government. However, Roman involvement throughout the Mediterranean world profoundly altered these two essential elements of Roman society and politics.

**The "New" Soldier.** An army different from the kind Cincinnatus had known was needed to wage war in Asia Minor and to pacify barbarian tribes north of the Alps. In this new army, soldiers often spent years away from home, during which time their farms were likely to fall into disrepair. The Roman soldier of the second century B.C. was more soldier than farmer. At the same time, the very empire these soldiers were creating brought about a new wealthy class in Rome, whose members frequently bought up farms belonging to the distant soldiers. These farms were frequently worked by slaves who had been acquired in foreign wars; sometimes, landlords with large holdings turned farmland into pastureland for the raising of livestock. The use of slaves for both farming and herding tended to force less wealthy farmers off their land and hence out of work.

The need for long-term soldiers and the decline of small farms made soldiers dependent on their generals for war treasures or for the reward of land when they returned to Rome. A general who had conquered an Asian province was a powerful figure since he was supported by a large number of landless men who were willing to follow their leader in return for wealth and security. Men without land migrated to the cities, especially Rome, in search of employment. These people had no property or wealth; all that they

Shown here is all that remains of the Roman Forum today. The Forum was to Rome what the Acropolis was to Athens—the political, religious and economic heart of the city. It was these ruins which aroused thinkers to reconstruct the history of Roman civilization.

could offer the state were their offspring (*proles*) as soldiers. Such a class of people was called the *proletariat*. The Roman proletariat grew as the Roman Empire grew; it might even be said that one caused the other.

**The Senate.** The growth of an empire led to changed political conditions as well. Provinces were added without the development of a body of officials adequate to administer them. The senate in Rome found it increasingly difficult to control the actions of proconsuls and others in the distant provinces. Provincial Romans (those in the provinces) and their friends at home often grew rich from exploiting the new subjects. Since it was only Romans and some Italians who had Roman citizenship, the provincial people did not have the legal and political power to prevent abuses against them. Tax collecting, for example, was not handled by the government. Rather, the right to collect taxes was sold to individual businessmen, who agreed to turn over a certain amount of money to the government each year. Any additional money which could be collected was kept by them. Arrangements such as these produced discontent in the provinces and created millionaires in Rome.

Therefore, the close union of the Roman body politic was weakened; a gap grew between the rich and poor, and the senate, capable of ruling a city-state, was unable to cope fully with the ruling of an empire. The very strength of the Roman temperament was its conservative quality, the tendency to continue the old traditional practices. However, in the face of changed conditions, this quality became a source of weakness. The Empire required new political forms and a new social policy, but the senate assumed that the old ways were the best—they always had been. With a growing proletariat and inadequate public control, it was now possible for an ambitious general or politician, bribing men with ill-gotten wealth, to usurp power from the senate and perhaps become a tyrant. The Greek general Peisistratus had done just that in Athens four hundred years earlier.

## Internal Crises

**Tiberius Gracchus.** In the year 133 B.C., a major political crisis occurred, and the Romans needed the wisdom of a Solon. The tribune for that year was *Tiberius Gracchus* (GRAHK uhs), a man who was deeply concerned about social conditions. As he commented:

> The savage beasts in Italy have their particular dens, they have their places of repose and refuge; but the men who bear arms, and expose their lives for the safety of their country, enjoy in the meantime nothing more in it but the air and light; and having no houses or settlement of their own, are constrained to wander from place to place with their wives and children.

The men who were called the masters of the world had not one foot of ground which they could call their own. Class war, which had plagued the Greek city-states, was about to trouble the Roman state.

Tiberius Gracchus attempted to pass laws which would limit the size of estates and make more land available to the poor. He also wanted to extend Roman citizenship to more Italians. The senate, consisting mainly of wealthy landowners, refused to pass measures for land reform and was unwilling to extend Roman citizenship and the privileges which went with it. Faced with this rebuff, Tiberius Gracchus broke a longstanding custom and refused to step down from his office when his term was finished. He rallied his followers and used force in an attempt to solve what he regarded as serious social problems. In the ensuing struggle, he was assassinated, as was his brother *Gaius* (GAY uhs) *Gracchus* who proposed similar reforms a short time later. The revolt of the Gracchi (GRAHK eye) showed that the existing political system was unable to solve, in a legal way, the serious problems that had arisen.

**Gaius Marius.** About thirty years later, foreign problems touched off a more serious internal crisis which led to open civil war. In 111 B.C., a powerful African king by the name of *Jugurtha* revolted against Roman rule. As general after general was sent by the senate to put down the revolt, Jugurtha grew stronger. Word spread that the senators were being bribed not to win the war, and it was rumored that every senator had his price. The "assembly of kings" had become a den of corruption! Finally, *Gaius Marius*, a general of plebian origins who had waged a successful war against the barbarians in Gaul, was given command. He and his loyal troops went to Africa and in a relatively short time defeated Jugurtha. Upon his return to Rome, Marius was elected consul and, in direct violation of the law, was reelected seven times. Marius came close to becoming a tyrant.

## THE EMPIRE AND THE ROMAN CONSTITUTION

Marius' political success stemmed from the fact that his army consisted not of farmer-soldiers but of land-hungry men who looked to him for their needs. It was they who helped elect him seven times. Against this kind of political power, the senate had little influence. The prestige of the senate was declining, and the political system which had served so well for centuries seemed incapable of providing an effective government for an imperial state. Marius was a new breed of man, a soldier-politician, whose career ushered in the turbulent, tempestuous collapse of the Roman republic.

There had been brilliant and popular generals before. A century earlier, *Scipio,* called "Africanus" for his spectacular defeat of Hannibal, had returned home in triumph at the head of a jubilant army. Scipio admired the Greek style of life and politics and was familiar with the tales of Greek military heroes. Perhaps he could see himself as the Alexander of Rome, but the social ingredients were lacking for such a career. His army was disbanded, and his men returned to their farms, following the pattern of Cincinnatus. In the case of Marius, however, there were few farms to receive the soldiers, and so they supported their ambitious general. Marius' career was an example of how a man could gain power in the provinces and then return to Rome, stronger than the senate itself.

**In this artist's reconstruction of the Roman Forum, the temples and other public buildings show a marked resemblance to Hellenic styles of architecture, indicating the Roman dependence on Greek forms. However, the arch, a Roman invention, can be seen in some buildings.**

*Fototeca Unione*

**Cornelius Sulla.** Following the death of Marius, a civil war broke out in Italy. The supporters of the senate took to the field, led by the patrician Cornelius Sulla, who eventually established order and restored power to the senate. At the same time, a number of Italian cities revolted against Roman rule and were pacified only by the granting of Roman citizenship rights. In the course of this civil war, many Romans were executed, and their property taken by those on the winning side. Bitter feelings were to linger on, and the political climate was poisoned by personal hatreds often passed on from father to son. Some land was made available in Cisalpine Gaul, and the Roman proletariat was provided with free rations of grain. Sustenance in the form of free grain, and amusement in the form of gladiatorial contests and chariot races, provided a means for keeping the poor quiet. Such a policy, however, could be no more than a temporary measure.

## The Empire Within

**Political and Social Problems.** The senators, jealously protecting their privileges, were unwilling to expand the government so as to control the Empire in an efficient manner. Therefore, individual senators, tax collectors, governors and generals had a great deal of personal wealth and power. Commanders in the field had unlimited power, and wealthy public officials paid for public games and banquets out of their own pockets. Individuals were often stronger than the government, and loyalty to a powerful man was often more compelling than loyalty to Rome. The growing knowledge of Hellenic culture also served to weaken the old Roman virtues. The Greek notion of *arete* emphasized the full development of individual powers. The heroes of the *Iliad* and the careers of Greek generals, Alexander above all, served as enticing examples for powerful Romans to follow.

The Rome of the first century B.C. was exceedingly different from the Rome which, two hundred years earlier, had struggled against Hannibal. The city itself, although close to the barbarian frontier, was the leading city in the Mediterranean basin. Decisions made there affected the rest of the known world, and it was from Rome that the rulers of the Empire fanned out to seek their fortunes. It was a wealthy city, but its prosperity was the result of wealth gained from imperial conquests. Well-to-do people maintained large villas in the countryside and had elaborate homes in Rome. Close to these mansions of the rich were decaying slums, which were inhabited by the landless proletariat kept alive by the doles of grain and amused by public spectacles. Rome was an active city which rivaled and surpassed older cities such as Alexandria and Antioch, mainly because it was the center of military and political power.

**The Roman Army.** The fact that the Romans were often divided against each other should not lead to the impression that the Empire was weak. Roman officers and soldiers were courageous and disciplined, filled with a confident belief in the power of Rome to unify and civilize the world. The traits which had made them masters of Italy were turned to the cause of building a world empire. The monarchs of the East, the Selucids and Ptolemies, could not command the kind of unity nor produce the kind of morale among their subjects that a Roman general could arouse in his soldiers. A mixture of confidence and success is both irresistible and contagious. The story is told of a Roman general who asked a prince to decide whether or not he wished to surrender. When the prince hesitated, the Roman drew a circle around him in the sand, saying that he must make his decision before he moved out of the circle. Faced with this kind of resolution, the prince surrendered.

**The Rise of New Leaders.** Such spirit and such an empire produced great men, jealous of each other and driven to constant competition for power. This rivalry was given free reign by the lack of any strong and effective central government. One such powerful individual was Gnaeus Pompeius, usually called *Pompey* (PAHM pee). Pompey built his military reputation by suppressing a slave revolt, clearing the eastern Mediterranean of pirates and extending Roman rule throughout Asia Minor into Syria and as far as the borders of Egypt. It was Pompey who dismembered the Selucid empire and established Roman provinces and allied states in the Near East. In 64 B.C., Pompey entered the city of Jerusalem. Although Pompey once held the post of consul, his power did not result from this office; rather, it rested upon his army and his military exploits throughout the empire.

Another striking personality was *Crassus*, whose strength came not from military skill but from great personal wealth. Crassus owned extensive property and was in charge of several provinces. He was in a position to buy votes in Rome and to build what we today would call a political machine. He offered lavish banquets and public spectacles for the poor and often loaned money to ambitious generals or politicians. Pompey the general and Crassus the millionaire could work together and so be in a position to control the government of Rome and the empire which went with it. The senate, supported by ancient customs and values, was unable to withstand this kind of pressure. Years earlier, it had been said, "The Carthaginians obtain office by bribery, but among the Romans the penalty for it is death." Such was not now the case, and bribery could take many forms.

**Julius Caesar.** A third and most important individual was Julius Caesar, a nephew of the famous Marius. Caesar worked his way up through the minor public offices to the post of consul. He was neither as glamorous as Pompey nor as wealthy as Crassus. He developed slowly, and his early career was unexceptional. He traveled throughout the Roman world, studied in Athens and held government posts in Spain. He, like others, was ambitious, and once, while gazing at a statue of Alexander the Great, he wept, realizing how much Alexander had accomplished as a very young man.

While Pompey was establishing his military reputation and political power in the East, Caesar assumed the command of the Roman armies in the backward province of Gaul. During his ten-year stay, through leadership, diplomacy and intelligence, he reduced the Gallic* tribes to Roman rule and extended the influence of Rome into an area which includes most of modern-day France. Caesar's work in Gaul was the basis of his future success. He fought hard and ruled well, encouraging the leaders of the Gauls to accept Roman rule and Roman ways. In so doing, he brought Graeco-Roman civilization to Gaul. The remains of this influence can be seen in everything from the Roman aqueducts and theaters of southern France to the French language itself. He brought to the Gallic tribes the intellectual and practical knowledge of Rome, thereby pulling a large portion of Europe out of barbarism. He recorded his accomplishments in his *Commentaries on the Gallic Wars*, a work of literature which is still studied for its vigorous and effective Latin style.

However, Caesar's motive was not to bring civilization to the barbarians or to create the basis for the modern French nation. His major goal at this time was the capture of supreme power in

---

* *Gallic* means of or relating to Gaul or the Gauls.

This portrait bust of Julius Caesar, the great Roman dictator and soldier, shows signs of the strenuous life he led. He appears in this sculpture as the vigorous man of action.

*Anderson—Art Reference Bureau*

Rome, a goal made possible by the confusion which existed in the capital city. In the year 60 B.C., Pompey, Crassus and Caesar joined together in an informal and secret alliance called a *Triumvirate*, pledging to work together toward the gaining of power. It is significant that this powerful alliance of men had little to do with the proper government offices which any of them might hold. Clearly, the Roman government had not kept pace with the march of events. Effective power was no longer in the hands of the Roman senate.

**Caesar vs. Pompey.** Crassus was killed in 53 B.C. while leading an army against the Parthians, a people living in the land once inhabited by the Persians. His death left Pompey and Caesar as the strongest men in Rome. Pompey was a popular and effective general whose main support was in the East and among many of the senators. In 52 B.C., by special concession, he was made the only consul—a testament to his power.

Caesar, an efficient and broad-minded governor of Gaul, had behind him a splendid military and political achievement as well as a seasoned army of loyal men. His command in Gaul had been extended beyond the usual limit, and when in 49 B.C., he wished to run for the office of consul, the senate ordered him to disband his army before entering Rome. Fearing that to do this would place him at the mercy of Pompey, Caesar defied the senate and led his army across the River Rubicon into Italy. The breakdown of civilian control over the military, a tendency which began with Marius, reached its peak on the banks of the Rubicon, when the soldiers shouted defiantly, "We are not civilians; we are Caesar's soldiers."

The crossing of the Rubicon brought the long-expected confrontation with Pompey to a head. As Caesar approached Rome, senators and statesmen fled either to his or to Pompey's camp; Pompey withdrew to Greece, to the East, the source of his strength. The entire Empire was now plagued with civil war; it had become a giant arena for gladiators. To this struggle, Caesar brought with him not only military skill but wise and enlightened leadership. He was not tied to the old ways, and he had new ideas about how a large empire needed to be run. In Greece, Pompey's army was defeated, and Caesar accepted the support of Pompey's followers. Pompey fled to Egypt and there was assassinated. Caesar was now the sole master of the Roman Empire; there was no individual who could equal him.

**Cicero.** Before looking at Caesar's dictatorship and his plans for reforming the Roman government, it would be well to mention one other important individual, *Marcus Tullius Cicero* (SIS uh roe), who lived from 106 to 43 B.C. Cicero's fame does not rest on his military exploits but rather on his literary creations and political ideals. Cicero, a lawyer by profession, admired the old traditions of Rome and wished to see both the balanced constitution and the rule of law maintained. He was not a member of an old patrician family and had not even been born in the city of Rome. Cicero was by temperament a scholar-politician, and he was deeply influenced by Greek ideas, especially Stoicism. He saw the great strengths of old Roman customs and institutions, but he also tried to instill in his followers some of the intellectual and spiritual ideas of Greek philosophy. He was a Roman who wanted to integrate Roman practicality and the Greek intellect; he saw in the growing Roman Empire the possibility of bringing into reality the union of mankind of which the Stoics had dreamed.

Cicero's writings on political, ethical and religious questions are a summation of the Graeco-Roman heritage, and their influence upon later ages has been profound. His writing style itself has served as the basis for the study of the Latin language and has had a great influence on writing and public speaking in the English language.

Cicero had a philosophy of government which attempted to bring together freedom and order and to retain the closeness of a small republic in the midst of a great empire. He is an example of a liberal statesman, a man who wished to sustain justice under the rule of law and to preserve individual freedom. The ideals and actions of Cicero can serve as a model for statesmen and politicians even today. The fact that he failed to translate his ideals into reality shows how difficult it is to have both freedom and order. As Cicero said, "We are servants of the law in order that we may be free."

Cicero established his early reputation in the year 70 B.C. by prosecuting a corrupt provincial official by the name of *Verres*, a man who had enriched himself at the expense of the inhabitants of Sicily. One of Cicero's greatest moments came seven years later when a band of revolutionaries under the leadership of a bankrupt and power-hungry nobleman named *Catiline* plotted to take over the Roman government by force. Cicero exposed the conspiracy and asserted the power of the senate and laws of Rome against Catiline. Cicero's speeches against Catiline stand to this day as

Cicero was a statesman and scholar who became entangled in the struggles for power during the first century B.C. He was more a man of thought than a man of action, a quality which perhaps can be glimpsed in this portrait bust of him.

*Alinari—Art Reference Bureau*

eloquent statements of the value of respect for established laws and procedures. The *Catiline Orations* are much like the *Philippics* of Demosthenes; Cicero was in many ways the Demosthenes of Rome.

## The End of the Republic

Like Demosthenes, who resisted the tyranny of Philip and Alexander of Macedonia, Cicero was suspicious of Caesar's rise to absolute power. Yet, Caesar brought with him many new ideas, and he had a clear vision of the reforms which would have to take place if Rome were to rule a world empire effectively. Caesar, because of his dictatorship, was in a position to give Rome a leadership and government suited to its responsibilities. In the process, many of the traditional elements of Roman government would have to be abandoned and individual liberties diminished. It seemed that a republic and an empire could not exist at the same time; political freedom and the rule of a large area were apparently incompatible. For Caesar, such a situation posed no problem; he had the instincts of a leader. For Cicero, however, Caesar's rule seemed a high price to pay for effective government, and the acceptance of dictatorship was an admission of the failure of the Roman republic.

**Caesar's Struggle for Reform.** Caesar was prepared to rule as a dictator for life, yet he did not use absolute power for his own pleasure. He extended Roman citizenship to the inhabitants of Cisalpine Gaul and thereby set the pattern for extending citizenship to all people under Roman rule. He centralized the administration of the government and attempted to cut down some of the powers of provincial governors and tax collectors. He established a new calendar which would be accurate and perpetual—one of the twelve months (July) is even named after him—and he began plans for draining the disease-ridden marshes which lay close to Rome. What his full record of accomplishments would have been is impossible to say, for he was killed just seven months after he assumed full power.

Caesar was killed by a group of Romans who saw in him a threat to the old traditions of the republic. Although he had refused the title of king, he was acting like one, even to the extent of having his likeness engraved on coins, a practice common with

*Fototeca Unione*

This impressive Roman arena, or amphitheater, is not in Rome but in Nimes in southern France. It is a monumental record of the implantation of Roman civilization beyond the confines of Italy.

other divine rulers. The leader of the opposition to Caesar was Marcus Brutus, a descendant of Junius Brutus who, centuries earlier, had driven the hated Etruscan king Tarquin from Rome and who had helped establish the republic. History weighed heavily on the young Brutus as he watched the accession of Caesar to royal power—and as he plunged one of the daggers into Caesar on March 15, 44 B.C. The assassination of Caesar was performed in the name of freedom and the ancient traditions of Roman government. Men like Cicero favored the action but regretted the means employed. What they perhaps regretted most was the fact that no other means was available against what they saw as tyranny. The problem they faced is with us today.

**Marc Antony.** The death of Caesar left a huge vacuum in the government, and soon there was a struggle to fill it. The senate had lost so much prestige and influence that it could not prevent a struggle of new giants from breaking out. Caesar's closest follower, Marc Antony, spoke eloquently of the genius of the dead ruler and convinced many Romans that the killing of the dictator had been a serious mistake. Cicero, one of Caesar's opponents who now resisted Marc Antony's bid for power, lost his life in the civil war which followed Caesar's death. Cicero, like Demosthenes before him, had attempted to resist a new form of government because he saw it as being hostile to freedom. Most men of good will are like Cicero; they are open-minded, ready to change, but are unwilling or unable to face the often brutal reality which change produces. The basic weaknesses of the Roman republic could no longer just be discussed, and when moderate men failed to bring about changes, ruthless men appeared and swept all before them. Caesar had become the Alexander of Rome, and his death could not change the circumstances which had produced him.

Brutus, the leader of the anti-Caesar forces, fled to Greece and there was defeated by the forces of Marc Antony. Antony then moved eastward and began the process of incorporating Egypt, the last great independent state, into the Empire. Rather than take Egypt by force, he formed an alliance with the queen, Cleopatra, a descendant of the Macedonian rulers of the Nile.

Antony was the logical successor to Caesar, but he lacked the discipline and commitment which Caesar had displayed. He found Egypt to his liking, and his alliance with Cleopatra kept him there and made it possible for a rival to appear in Rome. Antony was in effective command of the East; the young *Octavian*, a grandnephew of Caesar and potential rival, shared power with Antony by controlling Italy and the West.

**Octavian vs. Antony.** Caesar had destroyed what was left of the Roman republic and had paved the way for dictatorship. Therefore, a struggle between Antony and Octavian would be, in reality, a struggle for control of the entire Mediterranean world—and such a struggle seemed almost inevitable. If neither one succeeded in gaining full power, it was probable that the unity which had been brought about by centuries of labor would be broken. The Empire which as yet lacked strong and centralized institutions could well break down into separate parts. It was rumored that Antony even wanted to shift the capital from Rome to Alexandria in Egypt.

Antony appeared to be in a strong position. He was situated in the East, which was wealthier and more populated than the West, and he had the resources of the Egyptian monarchy behind him. Octavian, although no more willing to let the senate rule than his granduncle had been, did have powerful friends in the senate who supported him against Antony and his Eastern allies. The struggle between these two men was imminent, and the fate of the civilized world rested in this combat. The passions and personalities of these last days of the Roman republic have fascinated later generations. Two of Shakespeare's great plays, *Julius Caesar* and *Antony and Cleopatra*, are powerful recreations of this era in man's history.

**Emperor Caesar Augustus.** In the sea off the Greek city of Actium, in the year 31 B.C., these two political gladiators met in battle. Octavian was triumphant; Antony returned to Egypt and there committed suicide, to be followed by Cleopatra a short time later. The oldest of monarchies, the kingdom of the Nile, at last became a Roman province. With a power stretching from the English Channel to the Euphrates River, Octavian was now in a position to bring to completion the work begun by Caesar. There was little opposition to Octavian, for reasons which will be discussed in the next unit. Octavian took the title of *Caesar*, which soon came to be the word for "ruler." He also adopted the titles of *Emperor* (from *imperator*—leader of the army), and *Augustus*, meaning august or full of awe. In the East, he was spoken of as a "savior," as a divine personage who would bring peace and unity to the Roman world.

By the end of the first century B.C., the Roman world had become coequal with the known world. The little city on the banks of the Tiber was now the capital of the world. The history of Rome merged with the history of ancient civilization, a civilization stretching back for three thousand years. The mission of Rome to become "the head of the world" had been accomplished. In the process of becoming an empire, Rome had changed, and the civilization of the ancient world, the civilization of the Mediterranean, was reaching its climax. It was true, as the prophets had said, that "no human might can withstand the arms of Rome"; but in the climax of ancient civilization, forces would be unleashed which some thought were not of human origin, for during the reign of Caesar Augustus, a different kind of savior was born. That drama is the subject of the next unit.

## Define

| | | |
|---|---|---|
| proletariat | Crassus | Marc Antony |
| Tiberius Gracchus | Julius Caesar | Octavian |
| Gaius Marius | Triumvirate | *imperator* |
| Cornelius Sulla | Cicero | *augustus* |
| Pompey | Marcus Brutus | |

## Review and Answer

1. What were the specific economic, political and social consequences of the extensive expansion of Roman rule?
2. Show how the careers of the Gracchi and Gaius Marius were a result of the new political and economic forces at work within the Empire.
3. Why was the government of the republic unable to withstand the blows of such military leaders as Caesar and Pompey?
4. What basic and continuing political and ethical issues were raised by Cicero's position during the last years of the Roman republic?
5. What issues could be raised in a debate about the wisdom of assassinating Caesar?

# Reading IV
# The Merging of Greece and Rome
## Polybius and the Roman Constitution

Roman genius did not lie in the direction of abstract or theoretical thought. As we have seen, the Romans had a keen practical instinct for government. Perhaps their greatest accomplishment was the creation of an open yet stable political order, an accomplishment which had eluded the Greeks. The Greeks, however, could analyze political structures and present the logic of a government with perfect clarity. The Romans, builders of an empire, found it difficult to describe in any logical way their own government or to explain why it worked as well as it did. It took a Roman to govern well, but it took a Greek to explain how a government worked. In this sense, the fusion of Greek and Roman culture was a happy mixture, a mixture which can be seen in the following document.

Polybius (poe LIHB ee uhs) was a Greek who was captured by the Romans in one of the Macedonian Wars of the second and first centuries B.C. Sent to Rome, Polybius became acquainted with both military and political leaders who admired his mind and appreciated his interest in things Roman. Whereas the Roman historian Livy wrote a patriotic history of Rome, Polybius attempted to analyze, as an outsider, the growth of the Roman republic and the development of the Roman Empire. In his history, Polybius described and analyzed the Roman constitution, the basic structure of the republic. His analysis not only described with clarity the delicate balance attained by the Roman state but raised many general questions about the nature of politics itself.

As for the Roman constitution, it had three elements, each of them possessing sovereign powers: and their respective share of power in the whole state had been regulated with such a scrupulous regard to equality and equilibrium, that no one could say for certain, not even a native, whether the constitution as a whole were an aristocracy or democracy or despotism. And no wonder: for if we confine our observation to the power of the Consuls we should be inclined to regard it as despotic; if on that of the Senate, as aristocratic; and if finally one looks at the power possessed by the people it would seem a clear case of a democracy. What the exact powers of these several parts were, and still, with slight modifications, are, I will now state.

---

Evelyn S. Shuckburgh, trans., *The Histories of Polybius* (London: Macmillan, 1889), pp. 468–474.

The Consuls, before leading out the legions, remain in Rome and are supreme masters of the administration. All other magistrates, except the Tribunes, are under them and take their orders. They introduce foreign ambassadors to the Senate; bring matters requiring deliberation before it; and see to the execution of its decrees. If, again, there are any matters of state which require the authorisation of the people, it is their business to see to them, to summon the popular meetings, to bring the proposals before them, and to carry out the decrees of the majority. In the preparations for war also, and in a word in the entire administration of a campaign, they have all but absolute power. It is competent to them to impose on the allies such levies as they think good, to appoint the Military Tribunes, to make up the roll for soldiers and select those that are suitable. Besides they have absolute power of inflicting punishment on all who are under their command while on active service: and they have authority to expend as much of the public money as they choose, being accompanied by a Quaestor who is entirely at their orders. A survey of these powers would in fact justify our describing the constitution as despotic,—a clear case of royal government. Nor will it affect the truth of my description, if any of the institutions I have described are changed in our time, or in that of our posterity: and the same remarks apply to what follows.

The Senate has first of all the control of the treasury, and regulates the receipts and disbursements alike. For the Quaestors cannot issue any public money for the various departments of the state without a decree of the Senate, except for the service of the Consuls. The Senate controls also what is by far the largest and most important expenditure, that, namely, which is made by the Censors every *lustrum* for the repair or construction of public buildings; this money cannot be obtained by the Censors except by the grant of the Senate. Similarly all crimes committed in Italy requiring a public investigation, such as treason, conspiracy, poisoning, or wilful murder, are in the hands of the Senate. Besides, if any individual or state among the Italian allies requires a controversy to be settled, a penalty to be assessed, help or protection to be afforded,—all this is the province of the Senate. Or again, outside Italy, if it is necessary to send an embassy to reconcile warring communities, or to remind them of their duty, or sometimes to impose requisitions upon them, or to receive their submission, or finally to proclaim war against them,—this too is the business of the Senate. In like manner the reception to be given to foreign ambassadors in Rome, and the answers to be returned to them, are decided by the Senate. With such business the people have nothing to do. Consequently, if one were staying at Rome when the Consuls were not in town, one would imagine the constitution to be a complete aristocracy: and this has been the idea entertained by many Greeks, and by many kings as well, from the fact that nearly all the business they had with Rome was settled by the Senate.

After this one would naturally be inclined to ask what part is left for the people in the constitution, when the Senate has these various functions, especially the control of the receipts and expenditure of the exchequer; and when the Consuls, again, have absolute power over the details of military preparation, and an absolute authority in the field? There is, however, a part left the people, and it is a' most important one. For the people are the sole fountain of honour and of punishment; and it is by these two things and these alone that dynasties and constitutions and, in a word, human society are held together: for where the distinction between them is not sharply drawn both in theory and practice, there no undertaking can be properly administered,—as indeed we might expect when good and bad are held in exactly the same honour. The people then are the only court to decide matters of life and death; and even in cases where the penalty is money, if the sum to be assessed is sufficiently serious, and especially when the accused have held the higher magistracies. And in regard to this arrangement there is one point deserving especial commendation and record. Men who are on trial for their lives at Rome, while sentence is in process of being voted,—if even only one of the tribes whose votes are needed to ratify the sentence has not voted,—have the privilege at Rome of openly departing and condemning themselves to a voluntary exile. Such men are safe at Naples or Praeneste or at Tibur, and at other towns with which this arrangement has been duly ratified on oath.

Again, it is the people who bestow offices on the deserving, which are the most honourable rewards of virtue. It has also the absolute power of passing or repealing laws; and, most important of all, it is the people who deliberate on the question of peace or war. And when provisional terms are made for alliance, suspension of hostilities, or treaties, it is the people who ratify them, or the reverse.

These considerations again would lead one to say that the chief power in the state was the people's, and that the constitution was a democracy.

Such, then, is the distribution of power between the several parts of the state. I must now show how each of these several parts can, when they choose, oppose or support each other.

The Consul, then, when he has started on an expedition with the powers I have described, is to all appearance absolute in the administration of the business in hand; still he has need of the support both of people and Senate, and, without them, is quite unable to bring the matter to a successful conclusion. For it is plain that he must have supplies sent to his legions from time to time; but without a decree of the Senate they can be supplied neither with corn, nor clothes, nor pay, so that all the plans of a commander must be futile, if the Senate is resolved either to shrink from danger or hamper his plans. And again, whether a Consul shall bring any undertaking to a conclusion or no depends entirely upon the Senate: for it has absolute authority at the end of a year to send another Consul to supersede him, or to continue the existing one in his command. Again, even to the successes of the generals the Senate has the power to add distinction and glory, and on the other hand to obscure their merits and lower their credit. For these high achievements are brought in tangible form before the eyes of the citizens by what are called "triumphs." But these triumphs the commanders cannot celebrate with proper pomp, or in some cases celebrate at all, unless the Senate concurs and grants the necessary money. As for the people, the Consuls are pre-eminently obliged to court their favour, however distant from home may be the field of their operations; for it is the people, as I have said before, that ratify, or refuse to ratify, terms of peace and treaties; but most of all because when laying down their office they have to give an account of their administration before it. Therefore in no case is it safe for the Consuls to neglect either the Senate or the good-will of the people.

As for the Senate, which possesses the immense power I have described, in the first place it is obliged in public affairs to take the multitude into account, and respect the wishes of the people; and it cannot put into execution the penalty for offences against the republic, which are punishable with death, unless the people first ratify its decrees. Similarly even in matters which directly affect the senators,—for instance, in the case of a law diminishing the Senate's traditional authority, or depriving senators of certain dignities and offices, or even actually cutting down their property,—even in such cases the people have the sole power of passing or rejecting the law. But most important of all is the fact that, if the Tribunes interpose their veto, the Senate not only is unable to pass a decree, but cannot even hold a meeting at all, whether formal or informal. Now, the Tribunes are always bound to carry out the decree of the people, and above all things to have regard to their wishes: therefore, for all these reasons the Senate stands in awe of the multitude, and cannot neglect the feelings of the people.

In like manner the people on their part are far from being independent of the Senate, and are bound to take its wishes into account both collectively and individually. For contracts, too numerous to count, are given out by the Censors in all parts of Italy for the repairs or construction of public buildings; there is also the collection of revenue from many rivers, harbours, gardens, mines, and land—everything, in a word, that comes under the control of the Roman government: and in all these the people at large are engaged; so that there is scarcely a man, so to speak, who is not interested either as a contractor or as being employed in the works. For some purchase the contracts from the Censors for themselves; and others go partners with them; while others again go security for these contractors, or actually pledge their property to the treasury for them. Now over all these transactions the Senate has absolute control. It can grant an extension of time; and in case of unforeseen accident can relieve the contractors from a portion of their obligation, or release them from it altogether, if they are absolutely unable to fulfil it. And there are many details in which the Senate can inflict great hardships, or, on the other hand, grant great indulgences to the contractors: for in every case the appeal is to it. But the most important point of all is that the judges are taken from its members in the majority of trials, whether public or private, in which the charges are heavy. Consequently, all citizens are much at its mercy; and being alarmed at the uncertainty as to when they may need its aid, are cautious about resisting or actively opposing its will. And for a similar reason men do not rashly resist the wishes of the Consuls, because one and all may become subject to their absolute authority on a campaign.

The result of this power of the several estates for mutual help or harm is a union sufficiently firm for all emergencies, and a constitution than which it is impossible to find a better. For whenever any danger from without compels them to unite and work together, the strength which is developed by the State is so extraordinary, that everything required is unfailingly carried out by the eager rivalry shown by all classes to devote their whole minds to the need of the hour, and to secure that any determination come to should not fail for want of promptitude; while each individual works, privately and publicly alike, for the accomplishment of the business in hand. Accordingly, the peculiar constitution of the State makes it irresistible, and certain of obtaining whatever it determines to attempt. Nay, even when these external alarms are past, and the people are enjoying their good fortune and the fruits of their victories, and, as usually happens, growing corrupted by flattery and idleness, show a tendency to violence and arrogance,—it is in these circumstances, more than ever, that the constitution is seen to possess within itself the power of correcting abuses. For when any one of the three classes becomes puffed up, and manifests an inclination to be contentious and unduly encroaching, the mutual interdependency of all the three, and the possibility of the pretensions of any one being checked and thwarted by others, must plainly check this tendency: and so the proper equilibrium is maintained by the impulsiveness of the one part being checked by its fear of the other.

Caesar Augustus inaugurated the Roman Empire, the political and legal unification of the Mediterranean world. The organization of this "world state" brought a long period of peace to peoples under its rule and created institutions which have entered into the fabric of later civilizations. The goals of many philosophers and statesmen had been attained, and the history of human culture seemed to have reached a glorious plateau. But, as we know, human civilization itself is tremendously active and does not permit man to stand still. New forces and peoples began to stir both within and without the Empire.

The values which existed during this time had had their birth in Greece centuries earlier and had been blended with Roman ideas to form what we call Graeco-Roman culture. As the Empire began to change and disintegrate (as all empires do), a radically new pattern of culture emerged, a transformation of civilization occurred. The energy behind this transformation came from the East in the form of a new religion, Christianity, which in turn drew its strength from Judaism, the religion of the Hebrews. In time, Jerusalem triumphed over both Athens and Rome, and in the wreckage of the Roman Empire, a new civilization was born which was destined to grow in the then-wild forests of Europe, eventually to spread over the world. We must now look upon the climax of ancient civilization.

# UNIT V
# The Climax of Mediterranean Civilization

# 10

# The Ancient World and the Roman Order

The Imperial period of Roman history stretches from the fall of the Roman republic and the reign of Caesar Augustus to the decline of the Empire during the fifth century A.D.—a period of some four hundred years. Many emperors ruled and many events occurred during this period of time, Yet, less space and less detail will be given to the four hundred years of the Roman Empire than was given in Unit IV to the final one hundred years of the republic. The reason for this is the fact that the personalities and events related to the fall of the republic were more significant and important than the isolated events and personalities of the entire Imperial period. The collapse of the republic revolved around the careers of individual men such as Marius, Caesar and Cicero. The greatness and the decline of the Empire, however, forms a slow moving story, one in which ideas, beliefs and gradual changes, rather than individual men, are the dynamic forces of history. Hence, this chapter presents the basic pattern of the Empire, an empire which has haunted the memory of man since its decline.

### The Rule of Augustus

Caesar Augustus moved slowly and carefully in consolidating his power and reconstructing the Roman state. He avoided assuming the title of king and insisted that his tasks were merely to restore the republic and to repair the ravages of the civil wars. He therefore left the senate in existence, along with public offices such as consul and tribune. In so doing, he did not, at least in theory, upset the balanced constitution. He himself bore the title of *Principes,* which means first citizen. In gathering all power into his hands, he did what most Romans knew was necessary, but he did it in a manner which did not cause a violent break with the traditions of the past. Gradually, it became clear that the senate no longer had final power and that the emperor ran the state, no matter what titles he did or did not have. Nonetheless, the forms of the old republic lived on, along with some of its spirit. Gradual change had always been a Roman political virtue.

**The Pax Romana.** The major accomplishment of Caesar Augustus was the establishment of peace and the organization of the many provinces of the Empire into a workable government. It was he who brought about the *Pax Romana*—the Roman Peace—by providing a system of government which produced stability and security throughout the lands ruled by Rome. His success was phenomenal. His claim that he found Rome a city of brick and left it a city of marble was true; Rome, and other major cities of the Empire, were wealthy, secure and impressive. One of the major monuments of this period is a large work of sculpture appropriately called the "Ara Pacis"—the Works of Peace. The period of Augustus' rule (31 B.C.-14 A.D.) is often referred to as the Golden Age of Rome.

Simple war-weariness was perhaps the major cause of this well-being. To most people, peace from any source was preferable

The "Ara Pacis," a detail of which is shown here, was created during the peaceful reign of Caesar Augustus. It has the quality of elegant serenity rather than vigorous strife. The presence of men, women and children shows the importance of the family in Roman society.

*Fototeca Unione*

to the recent destructive battles of the giants. But deeper reasons for the Pax Romana can also be found. The independent power of the kingdoms and cities of the eastern Mediterranean had been broken by Roman rule. Kings and the old ruling classes had been removed, and Roman governors put in their places. Loyalty to Rome was the next logical step, especially since the emperor was seen as a savior, an agent of the gods. National feeling did not exist to any great extent in the ancient world. It was more natural for Syrians, Egyptians or Spaniards to feel loyalty to the emperor than to experience any compelling sense of "Spanishness" or "Egyptianness." The early Romans and Athenian Greeks had been zealous patriots, but by the first century A.D., men were so filled with the universal ideals of Stoicism and so used to traveling throughout the Empire that national differences were insignificant. As Edward Gibbon, one of the great historians of Rome, said, ". . . the nations of the empire insensibly melted away into the Roman name and people."

The breakdown of the polis which had occurred in the Greek world centuries earlier helped to prepare the way for the acceptance of imperial rule. After the conquests of Alexander the Great, educated men had thought of themselves as citizens of the world; in the first century A.D., Rome became "the world." The movement toward unity which had begun centuries earlier reached its completion in the Roman Empire; Augustus was a more effective version of Alexander. Men valued peace, unity and security more than national or city-state independence. The extent of the Roman Peace can be seen in a short phrase from the Bible which reads, "In those days a decree went out from Caesar Augustus that all the world should be enrolled."

**Return to Prosperity.** The end of the civil wars brought about a return of industry and trade, and the acquisition of Egypt brought the richest grain-producing area at that time into the Empire. Personal wealth increased, and the landless men, the proletariat of the cities, could be amply provided with free food and entertainment. Therefore, class friction diminished. Ambitious Romans found outlets for their energies by ruling provinces or conquering new lands. The government was no longer dependent on the old patrician families; in the building of his government, Augustus recruited men on the basis of talent rather than birth. There were even former slaves, called *freedmen*, in high positions in his administration. This kind of policy not only broke the hold of the conservative class but brought about a broad social base for the government, with every class represented.

Some of the provinces were administered by Augustus himself through governors and tax collectors responsible only to him. In this way, he could ensure the fact that imperial rule was fair and just. Other provinces were left to the senate to govern, but over these the emperor kept a close watch to see that exploitation and corruption did not take place. This thorough management of the Empire required a large government, and soon, an efficient civil service grew up, consisting of judges, governors and tax collectors. It was the fundamental fairness of the Roman system which made people willing to accept Roman rule. During the period of the republic, the senate had been unwilling to develop this kind of extensive government but rather had turned whole provinces over to individuals. Augustus recruited a new breed of men who built the kind of government without which an empire is impossible.

**Roman Religion Restored.** To solidify his power and produce confidence in the state, Augustus restored the official religion to an important place in society. The worship of the gods was encouraged, and elaborate temples were constructed. Religion and loyalty to Rome went hand in hand, and Roman religion was, as it always had been, more an act of patriotism than an act of personal devotion. Little spiritual benefit could be gained through this kind of worship, but in the midst of the Pax Romana, the gods of Rome seemed to smile on mankind. In parts of the Empire, the emperor was worshipped as a god, and Rome itself was filled with the presence of divinity. As a final guarantee of success, the emperor himself lived a respectable, proper and long life.

**Weaknesses of the Empire.** The system established by Augustus was not without its flaws, the most important of which was a political weakness—there was no established procedure for the selection of new emperors. As it worked out, sometimes an emperor's son or close relative assumed power, but inheritance never became a guaranteed right to rule. Hereditary monarchy was not developed by the Romans because, in theory, Rome was still a republic. At times, the senate chose the new emperor, but in most cases, the army had the final say. The man who had the support of the army, especially the support of the army stationed in the city of Rome, usually became emperor. This kind of arrangement for succession to the throne could and did lead to difficulty. In the end, it was one of the main political reasons for the decline of Rome.

This sculpture of Caesar Augustus breathes the sense of order and peace which was the hallmark of the Pax Romana. Some of the hardness and realism of earlier Roman faces has been replaced by a Greek idealism and softness. Note the strong hint of the god-like qualities of the emperor.

*Alinari—Art Reference Bureau*

The favorites of the army were not necessarily the best statesmen, and sometimes different groups of soldiers had different favorites. In such cases, civil war broke out, similar to the earlier struggles of men like Caesar, Pompey and Antony. During the year 69 A.D., four emperors held the supreme power in rapid succession.

### The Post-Augustan Empire

During the century after the death of Augustus, the boundaries of Rome expanded, and people ruled by the Romans were absorbed into the Roman way of life. In Gaul in particular, elements of Roman civilization sank deep roots. Through intermarriage, a Gaulo-Roman ruling class grew up which became thoroughly Romanized. In the words of Edward Gibbon:

> The grandsons of the Gauls, who had besieged Julius Caesar, [now] commanded legions, governed provinces, and were admitted into the senate of Rome. Their ambition, instead of disturbing the tranquility of the state, was intimately connected with its safety and greatness.

This pattern of assimilation was to be repeated in other lands as well.

**Expansion.** The island of Britain was brought into the Empire, and lands to the north of Greece up to and beyond the River Danube came under Roman rule. The province of Dacia (DAY shee uh), corresponding roughly to modern Rumania, was added to the Empire in 107 A.D., and this is why the Rumanian language is based on Latin, as is of course, French, Italian and Spanish. But the Empire had its limits. The lands to the east of the Euphrates River, once inhabited by the Persians, never became part of the Empire. In the year 9 A.D., an attempt was made to cross the River Rhine and subdue Germany. The attempt failed, and in a massive battle in the Teutoberg Forest, three entire Roman armies were lost. As a result, Germany was never Romanized. The Rhine remained the boundary between Latin and Germanic cultures, and some historians feel that the future history of Germany can be explained, in part, by this fact.

In the mid-second century A.D., the Empire reached its greatest extent, stretching from northern Britain to the Euphrates River, from the forests of southern Germany to the Sahara Desert. To the area included within these boundaries, the Romans brought the gifts of civilization as they had been developed throughout earlier centuries. In the East, the Romans contributed little more than some governmental and legal practices. The Near East, and Greece, had civilized Rome itself! But to the West and North, the Romans brought industrial skills, a written language, the concept of the state and the artistic and intellectual creations of the Graeco-Roman world. Places such as Gaul, Spain, North Africa and Britain moved beyond the stage of tribal organization and illiterate superstition as a result of Roman rule. The foundations of our own Western civilization were laid in Europe by the Romans.

The Roman Empire and the emperors themselves have captured the imaginations of historians, novelists and moviemakers. Most Hollywood films about Rome are set in the Imperial Period, and a wide selection of historical novels dealing with the Empire have been written. This interest is not without reason; the Empire was one of the wonders of the world.

**Citizenship, Culture and Government.** A common culture (basically Greek) which had been established in the East after the conquests of Alexander was made stronger through the addition of a common Roman citizenship. Roman armies kept the peace, and Roman navies kept the sea clear of pirates. A common legal system and an elaborate network of roads enabled people to trade and travel over large areas in almost total safety. Although local customs still served to separate people from each other, all men were part of one overall unit and under the ultimate protection of a single government. Roman citizenship was gradually extended to peoples living outside of Italy, and by the year 212 A.D., all people living within the Empire became citizens and were granted equal rights. Many of the emperors themselves were not even Italian in origin.

For the most part, the Romans made little attempt to alter the basic patterns of life in the lands they ruled, especially if a congenial kind of culture was there when they arrived. Local customs and laws were unchanged, and taxes were levied with moderation and justice. The worship of the official gods was required, but in a polytheistic world, this routine service to the gods of Rome worked no hardship. All religious groups were, of course, tolerated. In the province of Judea, however, where the Jews refused to worship any god but their own, the Romans made exceptions. Governors in this province were advised to keep the emblems of the divine emperor out of the sacred city of Jerusalem so as not to offend the native population. Jewish religious leaders and the Roman government worked out a practical compromise, a solution which was typical of the Roman method of government.

The Empire, therefore, produced unity in the midst of diversity. In the East, a mixing of Greek and Roman culture took place, with Latin serving as the language of government and Greek as the language of trade and everyday life. Here, in the East, the Romans provided the effective political unity for an already wealthy and sophisticated culture. In the West, barbarian patterns of life tended to disappear as the superior methods of the Romans supplanted them. Because of the Roman Empire, a barbarian chieftain in Britain could learn Greek, and through this knowledge, be capable of conversing with an Athenian scholar or an Alexandrian scientist.

**Roman Law.** Perhaps the greatest element of the Roman Empire was the idea of universal law, an idea which produced a system for settling disputes to which all men, regardless of who they were, could appeal. Through this institution, enforced by Roman courts, men were drawn together by the bonds of common justice. As citizens of Rome, accused men could secure protection from local prejudice and tyranny. Therefore, the rule of law was in many cases substituted for the force of arms.

An example of Roman justice and of the rights held by a Roman citizen can be seen in the following account. A Roman governor, Festus, was asked to decide a case involving a dispute between a citizen of the Jewish faith named Paul and some other members of the same religion. The argument involved a religious question, and Paul felt that the local court was prejudiced against him. The events as recounted below offer a glimpse of the nature of Roman law.

> When he [Festus] had stayed among them now more than eight or ten days, he went down to Caesarea; and the next day he took his seat on the tribunal and ordered Paul to be brought. And when he had come, the Jews who had gone down from Jerusalem stood about him, bringing against him many serious charges which they could not prove. Paul said in his defense, "Neither against the law of the Jews, nor against the law of Caesar have I offended at all." But Festus, wishing to do the Jews a favor, said to Paul, "Do you wish to go up to Jerusalem, and there be tried on these charges before me?" But Paul said, "I am standing before Caesar's tribunal, where I ought to be tried; to the Jews I have done no wrong, as you know very well. If then I am a wrongdoer, and have committed anything for which I deserve to die, I do not seek to escape death; but if there is nothing in their charges against me, no one can give me up to them. I appeal to Caesar." Then Festus, when he had conferred with his council, answered, "You have appealed to Caesar; to Caesar you shall go."
> 
> ACTS 25:6-12

Later, Festus described the encounter:

> There is a man left prisoner by Felix; and when I was at Jerusalem, the chief priests and the elders of the Jews gave information about him, asking for a sentence against him. I answered them that it was not the custom of the Romans to give up any one before the accused met the accuser face to face, and had opportunity to make his defense concerning the charge laid against him. When the accusers stood up, they brought no charge in his case of such evils as I supposed; but they had certain points of dispute with him about their own superstition and about one Jesus, who was dead, but whom Paul asserted to be alive. Being at a loss how to investigate these questions, I asked whether he wished to go to Jerusalem and be tried there regarding them. But when Paul had appealed to be kept in custody for the decision of the emperor, I commanded him to be held until I could send him to Caesar.
> 
> ACTS 25:14-21

Here we see a man who felt that he was being tried in a hostile atmosphere but who was able to be transferred to a different court in Rome itself. Paul's Roman citizenship enabled him to make this appeal, and the Roman governor was interested in the cause of justice, even though he had little interest in the issue which had caused the dispute. In this example, the Roman legal system can be seen as being both tolerant and just. As might be gathered from this short account, Roman law is the basis for some of the legal practices in the United States today.

**Graeco-Roman Culture.** To make generalizations about the nature of any given people is both difficult and dangerous; however, a few observations can be made here. It has usually been said of the Greeks and Romans that whereas the Greeks were artistic, intellectual and politically unstable, the Romans were practical, orderly and rather dull. It is true that the Romans, unlike the Greeks, succeeded in building stable forms of human cooperation. It is true that Roman art and architecture tended to be practical and functional, borrowing most of their artistic elements from the Greeks. It is also true that the Romans produced few penetrating thinkers of the intellectual level of the playwrights and philosophers of Athens. In many ways, the Romans borrowed from the Greeks. Yet, to the Hellenic culture, they added a style of their own, and what they added was of equal merit and of great importance.

The Greek and Latin languages themselves each have a particular structure, style and rhythm which seem to correspond to the peoples who spoke them. Greek is a complicated tongue capable of expressing subtle differences of meaning. It has a penetrating quality, razor sharp and flexible, most suitable for the refined discussion of complex ideas. Latin has a broad, majestic quality, solid and secure. It seems to be a language suited for the presentation of ideas rather than for the creation of them. Indeed, it was Latin which served to implant civilization in the wild lands of Europe and which became the basis for many European languages and literary works. English words dealing with the practice of government are of Latin origin—*law, state, responsibility* and *order*. Words dealing with science and the theory of government are usually of Greek origin—*democracy, atom, biology* and *logic*.

## Roman Literature

**Virgil.** The major Roman writer of the Empire was the poet *Virgil* (VUR jihl), who lived from 70 to 19 B.C. Virgil's great poem, the *Aeneid* (ih NEE ihd), tells of the founding of Rome and is, in many ways, a mirror of Roman virtues. The concept of the long epic poem is as old as, if not older than, the Greeks, but Virgil is distinctly different from Homer. Just as a reading of Homer can serve as an excellent introduction to the Hellenic mind, the *Aeneid* lays bare the Roman style and temperament. Virgil lived during the early years of Caesar Augustus' reign, and his epic poem telling of the history and destiny of the Romans breathes the spirit of the triumphant and humane Empire. The *Aeneid* relates the story of the founding of Rome by Trojan warriors led by *Aeneas,* who left Troy after its destruction by the Greeks. On the way to Italy, Aeneas stopped to visit *Dido* (DIE doe), the Queen of Carthage, whom he angered by leaving and pressing on to the banks of the Tiber, to the Seven Hills of Rome. Dido swore an eternal hatred for Rome, and in such a way, Virgil placed the Punic Wars into his majestic account of Roman history. The *Aeneid* is, therefore, a blend of poetry, mythology and history, and thus is in some ways like the Hebrew Bible. It was to provide the inspiration for writers and thinkers who lived long after the Roman Empire itself had vanished.

The ruins of Timgad in North Africa now stand alone in the desert as a ghost of what was once a flourishing Roman city. It is a striking example of Roman power—and of the impermanence of human empires.

*Fototeca Unione*

**Livy.** The historian *Livy* (59 B.C.-17 A.D.) also told of the history of Rome, and it is from his account that most of the tales of Rome's early history are drawn. Unlike his Greek counterpart Herodotus, Livy did not have the curious and wide-ranging interest which led Herodotus to collect information about various peoples and cultures. Livy's history is a record of the building of a state, told in a patriotic manner. Later generations of political thinkers have gleaned many insights into the nature of human politics from a study of Livy's history.

**Tacitus.** Following Virgil and Livy was *Tacitus* (TAS uh tuhs), who lived from 55 to 118 A.D. Tacitus recorded many interesting events which occurred during his lifetime. His most famous book, called *Germania,* is a study of the Germanic tribes which lived outside of Roman rule. It was he who first described these people and conceived of them as a unit. Therefore he, in a sense, created the concept of a German nation, just as Julius Caesar can be said to have "created" France by giving it a distinct identity through his *Commentaries on the Gallic Wars.* Tacitus' account of the Germans is of additional interest because he used his description of Germanic virtues as a means of criticizing the shortcomings of Roman society as he saw it.

**Plutarch.** One of the most interesting writers of the Roman world was *Plutarch* (46-120 A.D.), who, although he wrote in Greek, lived in the midst of Roman culture. He, therefore, can be seen as a symbol of the joining of Greek and Roman ideas, a living representative of Graeco-Roman culture. Plutarch's major work is the *Parallel Lives,* which is a series of double biographies, each coupling a famous Greek with a famous Roman. In these biographies, Cicero and Demosthenes, Caesar and Alexander, and Pericles and Fabius are compared. By reading any of the *Lives,* we can understand the differences between Greek and Roman culture since we are seeing them through the eyes of a man who lived in both worlds. It was from reading Plutarch's *Lives* that Shakespeare received both the inspiration and information for a number of his plays.

## The Roman Mind

The lack of any effective involvement on the part of individuals in the political life of the Empire might account for the lack of a vibrant creativity among the Romans. In the realm of intellectual and spiritual insight, the creations of the Athenian polis in the fifth century B.C. were, and perhaps remain to this day, unsurpassed. The close interaction of men and ideas which existed in the Golden Age of Athens did not exist in the Rome of the Caesars. There is a great difference between the entire citizen body of Athens attending a play of Sophocles or listening to Socrates, and the Roman populace witnessing a chariot race or a contest between two gladiators. Roman drama was written mainly for the entertainment of the few and contained little of the profound moral and spiritual elements found in Greek plays.

In fact, the basic view of man and the universe as established by Greek thinkers remained the accepted view of educated Romans. None could equal the creative insights of Plato or the scientific knowledge of Aristotle, or improve on the moral and ethical ideals created by the Stoics. Some of the greatest Stoics of the time were Romans, and Roman boys often went to Athens for their education. All that could be known seemed to be already known, and men accepted the world as they found it, performing their tasks and meeting their end with courage and strength. Good emperors strove to make the Empire more efficient and more just; they tried to retain the high idealism expressed by Virgil and put into practice by Augustus. Even the words of Virgil seemed to suggest that the task of Rome was to maintain rather than to create.

> Others may mould in softer lines the breathing bronze, and cause living features to start from the marble; they may plead their law suits better, and trace the motions of the heavens and the rising of the stars; be it thine, O Son of Rome, to rule the nations; these shall by thy arts, to impose the habit of peace, to spare the vanquished, and to crush the haughty by the sword.

Once these tasks had been completed, there seemed little more that had to be done. The triumph of the Empire came during the reign of *Marcus Aurelius* (aw REEL yuhs), who ruled from 180 to 192 A.D.—the height of the Roman Peace. The poet *Aristides* (ar ih STY deez), who lived during this time, sang the praises of Roman rule.

> Neither sea nor intervening continent are bars to citizenship, nor are Asia and Europe divided in their treatment here. In your empire all paths are open to all. No one worthy of rule or trust remains an alien, but a civil community of the World has been established as a Free Republic under one, the best ruler and teacher of order; and all come together as into a common civic center, in order to receive each man his due. . . .

Thus the present regime naturally suits and serves both rich and poor. No other way of life is left. There has developed in your constitution a single harmonious, all-embracing union; and what formerly seemed to be impossible has come to pass in your time; to treat imperial rule as an occasion for great generosity and at the same time to rule none the less with firmness. . . .

Let all the gods and the children of the gods be invoked to grant that this empire and this city flourish forever and never cease until stones float upon the sea and trees cease to put forth shoots in spring. . . .

A static, unchanging perfection had become the Roman ideal.

## Define

Pax Romana
freedman
Virgil

the *Aeneid*
Livy
Tacitus

Plutarch
Marcus Aurelius

## Review and Answer

1. How and why was Caesar Augustus able to bring about peace and stability to a state which had so recently been torn apart by violence and civil war?
2. What methods did the Romans of the Imperial period use to rule a large area composed of people of widely different traditions?
3. What generalization can be made about the essential differences between the Greek and Roman styles of life and thought?
4. Why is it proper to speak of a "Graeco-Roman culture" as *one* concept?

# 11

# The Great Transformation

The magnificent structure that was the Roman Empire did not last forever, and the fact that it declined and fell has troubled and perplexed historians ever since. Why did this "perfect" structure of political unity and equitable laws fall? In earlier times, before as much was known of ancient history as is today, the fall of Rome was seen as a truly frightening spectacle. Edward Gibbon, writing some two hundred years ago, called "the decline and fall of the Roman Empire the greatest, perhaps the most awful scene in the history of mankind." Perhaps Gibbon was so impressed because more than an empire fell. An entire civilization, a total pattern of life, almost disappeared and gave way to a new organization of human life and thought.

However, we should realize that the migration of peoples, the introduction of new ideas and the gradual collapse of empires is a common thing in the long history of mankind. Hammurabi's empire gradually declined when the Hittites moved into the Near East. The Assyrian and Persian empires fell apart when new peoples, possessing new ideas and better forms of organization, came into being. There should be no reason to be surprised that the course of events in and around the Mediterranean area altered the Empire and eventually brought about its decline. The western portion of the Empire was never far from the "reservoir" of barbarian people. Rome had been attacked by less civilized tribes in 390 B.C. and again in 133 B.C. The failure of the Romans to subdue Germany had left a large number of such people right outside the walls of the Empire. A mass movement by them could well overrun civilization and bring about a dark age, just as the early Greeks had once overrun the Mycenaean and Cretan civilizations. The fall of Rome, if it can be called that, should be seen as a normal event.

## Causes of the Decline

**Barbarian Influences.** The continual existence of less civilized peoples close to the Empire was one important circumstance of its decline. Yet, for many centuries, the Romans had managed to incorporate these people into the Roman pattern of life and to make them defenders of Roman values. Gallic chieftains had become senators, and Spanish rulers had become emperors. However, in the second and third centuries A.D., Roman society and culture became less able to absorb new peoples. Groups who were hostile to Roman values moved into or near the Empire, and Romanization did not take place quickly enough. Rather, the Romans themselves were "barbarized." Therefore, the ultimate cause of the decline of Rome is not to be found in outside pressure, which had always been there, but in internal weaknesses. These weaknesses may not have been known to the Romans, and they are clear to us only because we can see the Empire from such a long perspective of time. It would be interesting, but impossible, to know what people living centuries from now will see as the weaknesses of our own civilization.

**Economic Factors.** The existence of a large class of poor, landless people either living in the cities of the Empire or eking out a meager livelihood as farm laborers was a constant reminder of a basic economic weakness. Roman society's massive governmental structure was too large for the productive forces of the time. The economic support of Roman prosperity rested on slaves, precious metals and food taken as the reward of successful wars. Wealth was made in shipping, retailing and some manufacturing, but productive activity tended to center in the eastern portions of the Empire. The West, including the city of Rome, purchased more than it produced.

**Technological Problems.** The spread of the Empire had brought thousands of people out of barbarism and had increased the number of cities, the very centers of civilization. Yet, the Romans did not develop the technological means to produce new sources of wealth needed to sustain an active and enlarged urban life. Roman cities were consumers rather than producers of wealth. What was needed was some kind of technological revolution, a rapid thrust forward in man's control over his material environment. In earlier centuries, the discovery of farming (the Neolithic Revolution) and of iron had been revolutions of this sort, making possible an expansion of human activity. In the eighteenth and nineteenth centuries A.D., the discovery of an effective form of power—what is usually called the Industrial Revolution—produced the economic resources required for our present way of life. However, in the Roman world, no such revolution took place; the techniques of farming and manufacturing remained as they had been for centuries. As a result, there was a limited amount of wealth for a large number of people. How different ancient Rome probably would have been if huge factories had existed to provide employment for the masses!

**Cultural Deficiencies.** In the field of intellectual and artistic creativity, the Romans were highly advanced, being the receivers of the long traditions of the past. Although the technology of the ancients might be laughable, the insights of their thinkers and their works of art are equal, if not superior, to modern creations. But this gap between material progress and intellectual achievement in the Empire made Graeco-Roman culture a possession of only the few. The ideals of this culture revolved around leisure, beauty and refined discussions, but only a small minority of people could practice these ideals. Most Romans did not live a beautiful life, and few had the means to become educated. Therefore, there was a profound spiritual gap between the few and the many; the great majority of Romans had little knowledge or appreciation of the culture on which the Roman Empire rested. There was no mass culture. The values of the civilized man did not sink deep roots into the society, and so, in a sense, Rome was threatened by internal barbarians—masses of people who, like the external barbarians, were increasingly alienated from prevailing cultural values.

Gaps in human society had always existed, but the political unity brought about by Roman rule made people more aware of each other and of the world in which they lived. A common language and easy communication made mass movements possible. The lack of any mass culture produced a kind of spiritual vacuum which was ready to receive new values and ideas. Graeco-Roman culture had reached its limits; as the poet Aristides said, "No other way is left." Without a technological revolution to change the material basis of life, change would have to come from another source. The second and third centuries A.D. were ripe for a *spiritual revolution*—the creation of new patterns of thought and new values by which to live.

*Alinari*

Shown here is the colossal bronze statue of the emperor Marcian, or possibly Valentinian I. By comparing this with the statue of Caesar Augustus (page 164), one can see the increasing brutality and despotic quality of Roman rule in the late Empire.

## The Spiritual Revolution

Ever since the creation of civilization, ideas have been multiplied with dazzling speed. During the later years of the Roman Empire, the mixing of people from different backgrounds brought men and ideas into close interaction. Out of such a mixing of old and current ideas, new patterns of thought and life are born. One old idea was that of the polis, the small integrated social unit in which all members shared in the political and cultural life of the state. It was in the small polis that Greek civilization itself had been born. The memory of this ideal union of men haunted thinkers in the large and impersonal Roman Empire.

Within the Empire, there was one group of people whose values and way of life were radically different from others. These were the Jews, living in a closely knit group and sharing a faith in a dynamic God whom they regarded as the only God. Their religion contained not only a complete system of rules for personal behavior but also a rich body of literature and history. There were groups of Jews living in almost every major city in the Empire, but no matter where they were, the Jews had a sense of a special relationship to each other and to their God, as well as a powerful belief in their own destiny as a "chosen people." The idea of the polis and the ideas of the Hebrews were attractive, but one was a dead institution, and the other belonged to a group of people who resisted rather than welcomed outsiders.

**The Mystery Religions.** In Chapter Six, we were introduced to the mystery religions—organizations which drew people to the worship of gods who were not a part of the regular state religion. The membership consisted of people from different backgrounds, and through the sharing of secret ceremonies, a worshipper gained a passionate sense of identification with divine forces. These religions emphasized the spiritual and emotional elements of man and downplayed formal learning; the ceremonies themselves were often wild and frenzied. Unlike the official Roman religions, they did not foster a respect for the state and the social order, although they did not preach against Rome. They were private groups which provided for some men the spiritual food lacking in the official religion, and they grew in number during the later years of the Empire. The mystery religions cut across class lines and offered a kind of close association and personal involvement such as the Empire could not offer. They were an attempt to fill a spiritual vacuum and perhaps provided for the masses what the Stoic philosophy provided for the educated few.

Although some of these religious groups encouraged a feeling of social concern, most were designed to provide personal salvation and individual satisfaction. The gods and goddesses connected with the religions were usually older, pre-Roman gods, shrouded in mystery and magic. Some of the religions offered the hope of personal immortality, a life after death. Most of them lacked any kind of ethical or moral system and served only as a kind of tranquilizer. Members of the cults were, in a sense, withdrawing from the demands of the world. In this regard, mystery religions were like Stoicism, which also urged the wise man to become involved in nothing which could hurt him.

The growth of the mystery religions in the Empire was an indication of a profound shift in values. With their emphasis on emotions and life after death, and with their willingness to accept all sorts of people, these cults stood in contrast to the prevailing values of the times. The official religions tended to reinforce the established order of society, to maintain the graduated order of social rank and to make of man a good citizen. The mystery cults did not do this, and if every Roman joined them, the social fabric might well disintegrate.

The shift in values indicated by the growing popularity of the mystery religions shows the failure of Graeco-Roman culture to provide a system of ideals and ideas which appealed to the whole of society. As the mystery religions increased in number, the culture of the Mediterranean world began to weaken and crumble; the ruling classes began to lose the spiritual bases of their power. A spiritual revolution was taking place, a revolution which was destined to alter the shape of human culture and to bring ancient civilization to its climax.

**The Birth of Christianity.** It was in the midst of this period of change that a new religion came into being, a religious movement which has had perhaps the most important single effect on our own civilization. Most of the mystery religions centered around a god who, if he existed on earth at all, did so in a remote and mythical past. However, this new movement, called *Christianity*, centered around a man who had lived at a specific time, in a specific place, and about whom fairly clear and detailed biographical records had been kept. The man was *Jesus*, a Jew, who had lived in the province of Judea during the reign of Caesar Augustus.

> Jesus, a younger contemporary of Augustus, was a figure in the Hebrew prophetic tradition whose life and teachings show little if any Greek influence. He is depicted in the Gospels as an intensely warm, attractive, magnetic leader who miraculously healed the sick, raised the dead, and stilled the winds. His miracles were regarded as credentials of divine authority. His ministry was chiefly to the poor and outcast, and in Christianity's early decades it was these classes that accepted the faith most readily. He preached a doctrine of love, compassion, and humility; like the Hebrew prophets he scorned empty formalism in religion and stressed the sober, unprepossessing life of generosity toward both friend and enemy and devotion to God. He does not seem to have objected to ritual as such, but only to ritual infected with pride and complacency and divorced from charity and upright conduct. His uncompromising criticism of the moral shortcomings of the established Jewish priesthoods, combined apparently with claims to speak with divine authority, resulted in his crucifixion as a subversive.

As a Jew, Jesus fell heir to the long Hebrew tradition of monotheism, an emphasis on the ethical life and a sense of purpose in the course of history. Jesus taught his followers in a simple way, free from the elaborate intellectualism of the Greek philosophers. His powerful personality and simple yet profound ideas on the good life appealed to many people. His sense of a single God who had created the world and yet cared for the individuals he had created contrasted greatly with the rather impersonal gods of Greek and Roman mythology. Jesus preached a doctrine of personal salvation, a faith in God which would bring about a radical change in a person's life and a feeling of closeness to divinity. He said that men must be "born again" into a new kind of life, one which would give them a sense of harmony with God.

Some of Jesus' followers saw him as the leader who would expel the hated Romans from Judea, restore the Hebrew monarchy and usher in the time when their God would become the God of all men. In fact, it was the fear of such a revolution which, in part, led the Roman governor, Pontius Pilate, to have Jesus executed. Jesus, however, did not claim earthly power, saying that his kingdom was "not of this world." Most of his followers disbanded after his death, but among some, the belief grew that he had risen from the dead. They believed that Jesus was more than a mere man, that he was a manifestation of God revealing himself to men in the form of a human. Ideas such as this had an appeal beyond the world of Judaism and led to the formation of a religion centering around the life, teachings and death of Jesus.

**Paul of Tarsus.** One of the most important believers in Jesus was *Paul of Tarsus,* a Jew who was familiar with Greek ideas. Paul, who never knew Jesus personally, had a vision of him and immediately became a believer in his resurrection from the dead. Paul presented the teachings of Jesus and explained the purpose of his death in a manner which non-Jews could understand. He called Jesus *Christus,* a Greek word meaning chosen one. Paul taught that Jesus was indeed God revealing himself to man. As he said, "God was in Christ reconciling the world to himself. . . ." He also believed that the spirit of Jesus would remain with men who believed in him until he would come once again to destroy all earthly kingdoms and usher in the Kingdom of God. In this hope, we can see the Hebrew idea of a future kingdom linked to an idea of a divine personality, an idea also found among the mystery religions.

**The Spread of Christianity.** The fact that the teachings of Jesus embodied so much of the moral ideas of the Hebrews gave Christianity more substance than the emotional mystery cults. Here was a union of mystery and moral teaching—a religion which offered personal salvation, a code of behavior and a sense of purpose in the progression of events. Groups of Christians began to form in major cities, first in the Greek-speaking East and then in Rome itself. It is interesting to note that these early groups took the name of *ekklesia,* the name which had been given to the assembly of the Athenian citizens in the polis. The early church was therefore seen as a kind of spiritual polis. Paul's basic ideas and instructions for the early Christians were presented in the form of letters which are now included in the Bible under the name of *Epistles.* They were written in Greek, the common language of most of the Empire, as were the four accounts of the life of Jesus, called *Gospels.* The words of Jesus, a Jew, were therefore presented to the Roman world in Greek, the language of Graeco-Roman culture.

The definite relationship between Judaism and Christianity can be seen in the fact that each religion had a sacred book, a collection of writings which set forth historical and theological truth. The

"The Spoils of Jerusalem" from the Arch of Titus celebrated the Roman conquest of the city of Jerusalem. Among the items taken from the Jewish temple was a menorah, or candleholder. This sculpture contrasts markedly with the "Ara Pacis" (page 161) and shows the military side of Roman rule.

Alinari

Christian book, a collection of Gospels and Epistles, was called the New Testament. "Testament" here means promise or agreement, and to Christians, the revelation of God through Jesus was the New Testament, as opposed to the earlier revelation of God to the Hebrews, which is called the Old Testament. This is why the two parts of the Bible as we know it are so named by Christians today.

The early appeal of Christianity was mainly to the poor, especially to those living in the cities, those who were rootless and without security or hope. We must remember that Jesus had not been a phantom of mythology. He was a common man who spent his earthly life among the poor of Judea and preached the idea of the equality of all men before God. The movement was scorned by wealthy and sophisticated Romans, as well as by educated Greeks, who saw it as a religion of slaves. However, Christianity combined so many elements lacking in Graeco-Roman culture that its appeal began to spread beyond the lower classes. Although the teachings of Jesus were simple and direct, they also contained a depth and subtlety which intrigued the philosophers.

**Philosophical Interest.** Philosophers, especially those who lived after Plato, were interested in the relationship between the world of men and the world of the ideal forms. The two worlds appeared to be distinct, and as Plato argued, only the true philosopher could gain a knowledge of the true but unseen world (Reading III, pages 104-111). Christ, however, was thought to be both man and God; he was the symbol of the union of the two realms, the means for all men to attain that which only the Platonic philosopher had possessed. The opening words of the Gospel of John make this point clear. "In the beginning was the Word, and the Word was with God, and the Word was God. . . . And the Word became flesh and dwelt among us. . . ." As Christian thought developed, the argument grew that in Jesus, both worlds conjoined, the divine touched the mortal, eternity crashed into time. This kind of idea was not totally new to the Greeks, for Zeus had often assumed human form for various purposes. But in the case of Jesus, it was thought that the creator of the entire universe had taken human form for the purpose of teaching men the truth and offering them eternal life.

The appeal of this kind of religion was obvious, and the challenge it presented to thinkers was enticing. What was the true nature of Jesus? Was he man, or God or a mixture of the two? Was he a flesh and blood teacher who walked the dusty roads of an obscure province, or was he one of Plato's pure and perfect forms moving in the world of mere human reality? The same intellectual tools used to debate the meaning of piety could be turned to a question of great importance. Not only was the actual nature of Jesus a significant question, but his teachings were as profound as those of any Greek philosopher. In time, educated Greeks and Romans were drawn into the Christian movement, and they were confronted with the powerful legacy of Hebrew historical and ethical thought. Compared with the Hebraic-Christian concept of God and his dramatic role in human history, the mythology of the Greeks appeared frivolous, and the state religion of Rome seemed unrelated to man's basic spiritual needs.

## The Empire in Turmoil

**The Christian Element.** Christianity was clearly a threat to the Roman order. Like the Jews, Christians refused to worship anyone but the true God. To them, emperor-worship was a sin. However, the worship of the emperor was bound up with the stability of the Roman order; he was the head of state. Also, the Christian prohibition against killing ran against the needs of the army. The Jews could be tolerated, as they were a separate and clearly recognizable nation. Christians, however, were Romans and on the surface were indistinguishable from other Romans. But underneath, a Christian was a Christian first and a Roman second. The following instructions to Christians makes this point clear.

> But you are a chosen race, a royal priesthood, a holy nation, God's own people, that you may declare the wonderful deeds of him who called you out of darkness into his marvelous light. Once you were no people but now you are God's people....
> I Peter 2:9-10

Here we see the Christians depicted as a separate nation, an empire within an empire, no longer loyal to the official Roman state and priesthood. It is interesting that the writer of this passage regarded the Christians of Rome as having been "no people" before they became "God's people." Clearly, the sense of belonging to Rome, of being a Roman citizen, had lost its compelling power, and the Christian Church was becoming for many a new state. Hence, various emperors began to attempt to stamp out Christianity by persecution.

**Political Difficulties.** At the same time, the Empire was experiencing increasing political difficulties. Some of the basic weaknesses began to have a telling effect as barbarian tribes pressed into Roman lands and people under Roman rule began to revolt. A leader of the Britons spoke out against the Pax Romana, saying, "Robbery, butchery, rapine, the liars call Empire; they create a desolation and call it peace." Roman rule was gradually dismantled in Britain and also along the Rhine and the Danube. The eastern half of the Empire fared better, as it had always been wealthier and more civilized; the West had always been the frontier. Therefore, it would be accurate to say that the Empire *shrunk* to the East rather than declined. This process occurred at the same time that the Christian Church was increasing in strength and membership. Therefore, some have said that Christianity destroyed the Roman Empire.

The truth is not so clear. The basic political weakness of the Empire was the lack of any fixed method for choosing new emperors. During the third century A.D., it was the soldiers who did the choosing, and there were many civil wars between rival candidates leading separate armies. Many of these leaders were of lower class origins, and so even the emperors had only a smattering of the basic elements of Roman culture. Prominent Romans who might have worked together for stability and good government tended to remove themselves from public life, retiring to their great estates in the country. The tendency toward this kind of withdrawal can be clearly seen in Christianity as well as in Stoicism.

**Economic and Military Problems.** Economically, the Empire was unable to provide employment or to increase the supply of wealth. Productive forces declined, especially in the West. Trade dropped off, and heavy taxation drove many men out of business. Those who could no longer support themselves became attached to large landowners as perpetual tenants. With the decline of city life, the very basis of not only Rome but of civilization itself was seriously weakened. Some Roman cities took on the appearance of ghost towns, and even Rome itself decreased in population. Many Romans moved to the East where city life was still strong and opportunity for advancement existed. Others moved to the country where agricultural labor provided at least some kind of security. The substitution of rural for city life was the clearest sign of the "barbarization" of Roman society.

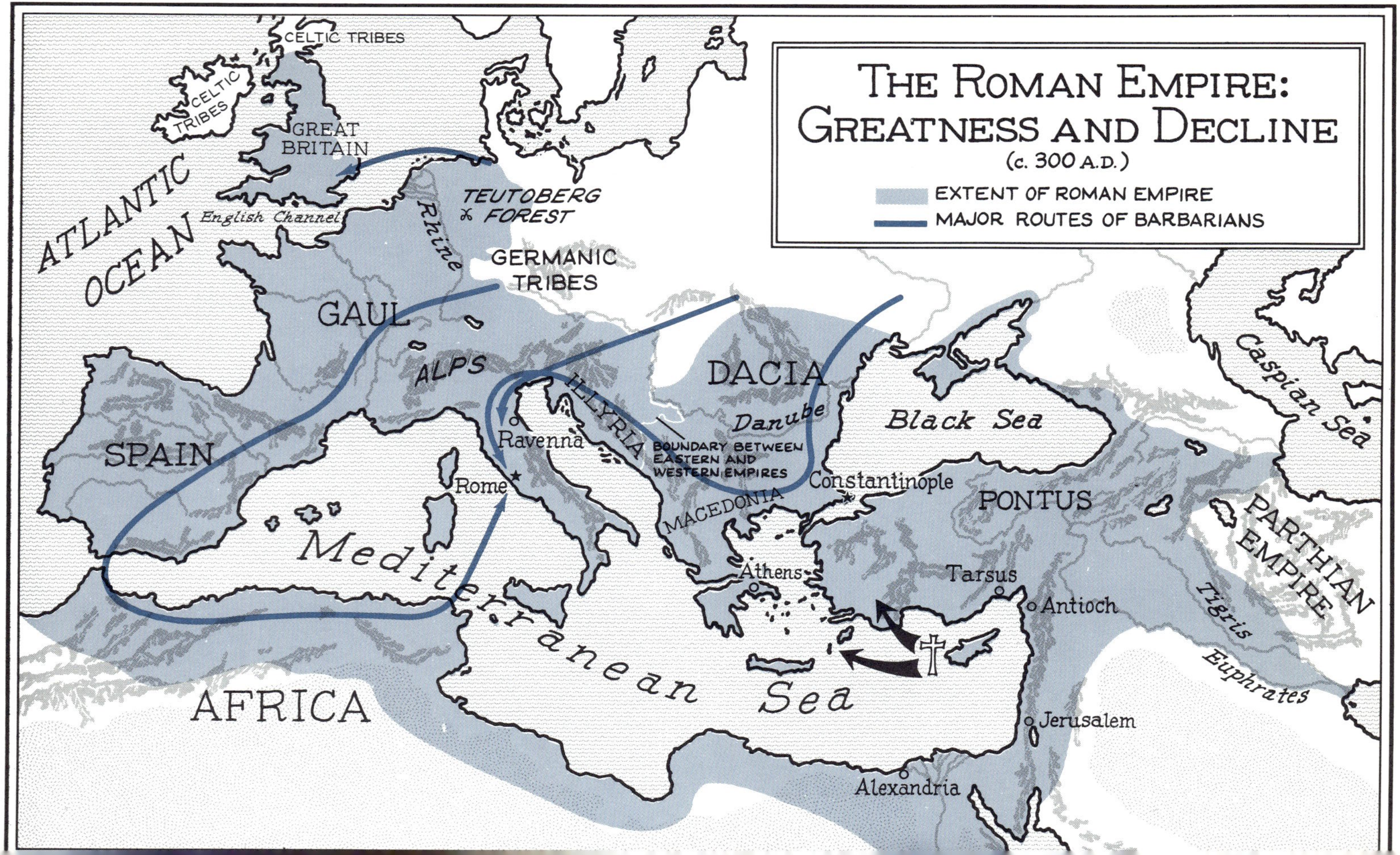
THE ROMAN EMPIRE:
GREATNESS AND DECLINE
(c. 300 A.D.)
EXTENT OF ROMAN EMPIRE
MAJOR ROUTES OF BARBARIANS
CELTIC TRIBES
CELTIC TRIBES
GREAT BRITAIN
ATLANTIC OCEAN
English Channel
TEUTOBERG FOREST
Rhine
GERMANIC TRIBES
GAUL
ALPS
SPAIN
DACIA
Danube
ILLYRIA
BOUNDARY BETWEEN EASTERN AND WESTERN EMPIRES
Ravenna
Rome
MACEDONIA
Constantinople
Black Sea
PONTUS
Caspian Sea
PARTHIAN EMPIRE
Athens
Tarsus
Antioch
Tigris
Euphrates
Mediterranean Sea
Jerusalem
Alexandria
AFRICA

It became increasingly difficult to recruit men for military service. In earlier days, service in the army had been the main route to citizenship. Now that all men were citizens, a major incentive was taken away. Therefore, generals often had to fill the ranks of the army with men whose knowledge of Roman ways was slight and whose loyalty to Rome was doubtful. Thus, the process of Romanization slowed to a halt, and indeed was reversed. A fundamental weakness can be seen in the declining birthrate. With growing uncertainty and political confusion, many Romans saw a bleak future and so were unwilling to have large families; the family itself, that foundation stone of Roman morality and stability, became fragmented and weak. The Empire was sick. It has been said of the Roman Empire of the third century A.D. that it suffered anemia in the provinces and apoplexy at the center.

**Diocletian.** In the face of this kind of situation, the Empire appeared to be about to break up into its component parts, with its people reverting to an uncivilized pattern of life. This process had occurred before; it had been the fate of the Assyrian, Persian and Macedonian empires. The Roman Empire was too large for the economic resources its technology was capable of producing. It was threatened by vigorous tribes of land-hungry barbarians; its ruling ideas and cultural values no longer commanded the loyalty of the majority of its citizens. However, in the year 284 A.D., an emperor assumed power who for awhile checked this process of disintegration. He was *Diocletian* ( die uh KLEE shuhn ), a man of peasant origins. He established a strong central government and divided the Empire into new districts, each called a *diocese*. He no longer called himself merely the first citizen ("Principes") of the state but set himself up as a divine ruler and established an elaborate royal court, much in the manner of a Persian king or an Egyptian pharaoh. As a last desperate attempt, Rome became a divine monarchy.

Diocletian decreed that people were forbidden to leave their chosen trades, even though the occupation might no longer be profitable. He also decreed that sons must take on their father's

---

As the map on page 184 shows, "Empire" to Rome meant Britain, Gaul, Spain, Dacia, Egypt, the Near East and parts of Africa—territories never before under one, united rule. Outside pressures, however, as well as internal weaknesses, would cause a gradual crumbling of Roman imperial power.

trade. In such ways, he hoped to keep basic and essential occupations filled. He regulated prices and wages, and he attempted to increase the supply of money. By strengthening the power of the government and regulating the private lives of citizens, he established what is called a *totalitarian state*—a government which is not only absolute but unlimited in its power.

Diocletian also tried, unsuccessfully, to solve the religious and political problems of the Empire. He launched a severe campaign against the Christian Church, which was growing both in numbers and in organizational strength. He devised a system for appointing a successor, but it had only limited success, and civil war developed during his reign. Realizing that the Empire was too large for one capital, especially a capital in the declining western portion, he established a second seat of government in the East. He himself spent most of his time outside of Rome on his huge estate in Illyria (uh LIHR ee uh), an area corresponding to modern Yugoslavia.

By the time of Diocletian, Rome was no longer recognizable as the Rome of Fabius, Caesar and Cicero. It was no different from the divine monarchies which had once flourished in the ancient Near East. Politically speaking, the history of the ancient world had come a full circle.

## Alliance and Assimilation

With the decline of effective government in the western portion of the Empire, the Christian Church began to take on many political functions. The leaders of individual churches, called *bishops,* were in charge of their people, who looked to them rather than to imperial officials for direction and security. The bishop of Rome, because of his location, became a leader among the bishops. The Church also adopted some of the Roman governmental forms, and subdivisions of the Church came to be called *dioceses.* The political unity which had been established by Rome and the legal system which had sustained it served the Church as it grew— much like a new empire. The Church merely took over institutions which had already been developed and infused them with new meaning. The life of Jesus, and the writings of early Christians such as Paul, provided a body of sacred writings to serve as a basis for the Church. Membership in this new body was of greater significance than citizenship in the crumbling Empire.

This sixth-century Byzantine mosaic, "The Betrayal," portrays the betrayal of Christ just before his execution. The style is radically different from the standard Graeco-Roman style. The figures are two-dimensional and have an intense spiritual and other-worldly quality. The mosaic represents the triumph of Christian values.

Christians claimed that Rome was doomed and was being punished by God for its persecutions of the faithful. Here is how a Christian writer predicts the destruction of Rome.

> ... the great city which has dominion over the kings of the earth ... has become a dwelling place of demons, a haunt of every foul spirit, a haunt of every foul and hateful bird. ... Come out of her, my people, lest you take part in her sins, lest you share in her plagues; for her sins are heaped high as heaven, and God has remembered her iniquities. ... Alas, alas, for the great city that was clothed in fine linen, in purple and scarlet, bedecked with gold, with jewels, and with pearls! In one hour all this wealth has been laid waste. ... Rejoice over her, O heaven, O saints and apostles and prophets, for God has given judgment for you against her!
>
> REVELATION 17:18; 18:2-20

In many ways, this prediction was correct. The Roman government was forced to come to terms with the Christians and ally itself with the Church. Legend says that in a battle, the emperor

Constantine saw a vision of a cross (the symbol of Christianity) bearing the inscription, *In hoc signo vinces,* which means conquer by this sign. Constantine was victorious. Attributing his victory to the Christian God, he issued, in 313 A.D., the *Edict of Milan,* which granted toleration to the Christians. Constantine not only ratified the power of the Church but then became a Christian himself. Soon Christianity became the official and only religion of the Empire; Christians joined with Roman civilization rather than letting it collapse.

**The Eastern Empire.** Constantine realized that "the Empire" meant, in reality, the eastern portion of the Empire. Therefore, he established his capital in the city which bore his name, Constantinople. This city, the "second Rome," was in an excellent location on the site of the old Greek city of Byzantium. It had good defenses and was to remain the capital of the now shrunken Roman Empire for centuries to come. In the West, barbarian tribes roamed at will through Gaul, Italy and Spain. The western capital was shifted from Rome to the more easily defended city of Ravenna; the city of Rome itself was invaded and plundered in 410 A.D., and in 476 A.D., a Germanic king assumed the title of emperor. This date—476 A.D.—is usually given as the official date for the fall of Rome. However, we must realize that the Roman Empire still existed in the East, in Constantinople. This eastern Roman Empire, sometimes called the Byzantine Empire, lasted for a thousand more years, until 1453, not long before the discovery of the new world.

**The Empire in the West.** In the West, the Church took over the defense of Roman civilization. The emperor gave up the title of Pontifex Maximus (high priest) because the Roman gods were no longer worshipped. The bishop of Rome assumed these priestly functions, and this is why the Pope today is sometimes referred to as the Pontiff. When the *Huns,* a fierce and savage tribe led by the brutal *Attila* (AT ih luh), swept into Italy and threatened to take and destroy the city of Rome, it was the leader of the Christian Church, Pope Leo, not the emperor, who met the barbarian. Attila was so impressed with the Pope's spiritual power that he turned back. What Leo said to Attila remains unknown, but what is significant is the fact that it was the Pope and not the emperor who stood at the gates of Rome. The Roman Empire had become the Christian Church.

The Rome of the Caesars and of Graeco-Roman culture had been destroyed by both material and spiritual forces coming from within and from without the Empire. What remained among the wreckage was a mixture of Christian, Roman and Germanic ideas and institutions from which a new civilization would arise—a civilization quite different from that which had existed on the shores of the Mediterranean, a civilization of which the Roman Empire had been the final expression.

## Define

| | | |
|---|---|---|
| ekklesia | Diocletian | Constantine |
| Epistles | diocese | Pope Leo |
| Gospels | totalitarian | |
| New Testament | bishop | |

## Review and Answer

1. What were the major weaknesses of Roman society and culture?
2. How did these weaknesses lead to a disintegration of the Roman Empire?
3. What was the "spiritual revolution" which took place along with the decline of Rome?
4. What were the basic elements of Christianity, and why did it eventually become the major religion of the Roman Empire?
5. How did Diocletian and Constantine attempt to save the Roman state from decay?

## Reading V
# The Transformation of Values
## Selections from the New Testament

The New Testament consists primarily of two parts: (1) four biographies of Jesus, called Gospels, each written by a different author (Matthew, Mark, Luke and John), and (2) a series of letters, called Epistles, written in large part by Paul to groups of Christians in major cities of the Roman world. Once Christianity became an established religion, these writings were gathered together into what eventually became the Christian portion of the Bible. (They were first written down in Greek, the language of everyday life in the eastern portion of the Roman Empire.) Since Christians believe that God revealed himself first to the Hebrews and then to all men in the person of Jesus, the sacred writings of the Hebrews are a part of Christian sacred writings.

Although the ideas of the Greeks and Romans have had a great influence beyond their times, it was the Christian religion which was the predominant element in the formation of European civilization. Hence, the New Testament is, without doubt, the most influential book written in Greek, even though at the time of its composition, it was read by only a small portion of the population. Although today Christianity is only one of several world religions, and although there are many people who follow no religion at all, the impact of Christianity on the formation of modern culture has been tremendous. Therefore, a person who would understand the development of the modern world must become familiar with this influential collection of writings. Selected parts appear here.

### The Teachings of Jesus

Unlike the Greek teachers who placed great emphasis on logical argument and the accurate definition of terms, Jesus expressed his ideas in simple form. He used direct sayings (proverbs), or he told simple stories with profound meanings (parables). In this, he was very much like the Hebrew prophets; he was a part of the Hebraic religious tradition rather than the Hellenic intellectual tradition.

---

*The Holy Bible,* Revised Standard Version (New York: Thomas Nelson & Sons, 1953).

In fact, Jesus often scorned sophisticated learning and elaborate argumentation.

Seeing the crowds, he [Jesus] went up on the mountain, and when he sat down his disciples came to him. And he opened his mouth and taught them, saying:
"Blessed are the poor in spirit, for theirs is the kingdom of heaven.
"Blessed are those who mourn, for they shall be comforted.
"Blessed are the meek, for they shall inherit the earth.
"Blessed are those who hunger and thirst for righteousness, for they shall be satisfied.
"Blessed are the merciful, for they shall obtain mercy.
"Blessed are the pure in heart, for they shall see God.
"Blessed are the peacemakers, for they shall be called sons of God.
"Blessed are those who are persecuted for righteousness' sake, for theirs is the kingdom of heaven.
"Blessed are you when men revile you and persecute you and utter all kinds of evil against you falsely on my account. Rejoice and be glad, for your reward is great in heaven, for so men persecuted the prophets who were before you.
"You are the salt of the earth; but if salt has lost its taste, how shall its saltness be restored? It is no longer good for anything except to be thrown out and trodden under foot by men. You are the light of the world. A city set on a hill cannot be hid. Nor do men light a lamp and put it under a bushel, but on a stand, and it gives light to all in the house. Let your light so shine before men, that they may see your good works and give glory to your Father who is in heaven.
"Think not that I have come to abolish the law and the prophets; I have come not to abolish them but to fulfil them. For truly, I say to you, till heaven and earth pass away, not an iota, not a dot, will pass from the law until all is accomplished. Whoever then relaxes one of the least of these commandments and teaches men so, shall be called least in the kingdom of heaven; but he who does them and teaches them shall be called great in the kingdom of heaven. For I tell you, unless your righteousness exceeds that of the scribes and Pharisees, you will never enter the kingdom of heaven.
"You have heard that it was said to the men of old, 'You shall not kill; and whoever kills shall be liable to judgment.' But I say to you that every one who is angry with his brother shall be liable to judgment; whoever insults his brother shall be liable to the council, and whoever says, 'You fool!' shall be liable to the hell of fire. So if you are offering your gift at the altar, and there remember that your brother has something against you, leave your gift there before the altar and go; first be reconciled to your brother, and then come and offer your gift. Make friends quickly with your accuser, while you are going with him to court, lest your accuser hand you over to the judge, and the judge to the guard, and you be put in prison; truly, I say to you, you will never get out till you have paid the last penny.

"You have heard that it was said, 'You shall not commit adultery.' But I say to you that every one who looks at a woman lustfully has already committed adultery with her in his heart. If your right eye causes you to sin, pluck it out and throw it away; it is better that you lose one of your members than that your whole body be thrown into hell. And if your right hand causes you to sin, cut it off and throw it away; it is better that you lose one of your members than that your whole body go into hell.

. . . . . . . . . . . .

"You have heard that it was said, 'An eye for an eye and a tooth for a tooth.' But I say to you, Do not resist one who is evil. But if any one strikes you on the right cheek, turn to him the other also; and if any one would sue you and take your coat, let him have your cloak as well; and if any one forces you to go one mile, go with him two miles. Give to him who begs from you, and do not refuse him who would borrow from you.

"You have heard that it was said, 'You shall love your neighbor and hate your enemy.' But I say to you, Love your enemies and pray for those who persecute you, so that you may be sons of your Father who is in heaven; for he makes his sun rise on the evil and on the good, and sends rain on the just and on the unjust. For if you love those who love you, what reward have you? Do not even the tax collectors do the same? And if you salute only your brethren, what more are you doing than others? Do not even the Gentiles do the same? You, therefore, must be perfect, as your heavenly Father is perfect.

"Beware of practicing your piety before men in order to be seen by them; for then you will have no reward from your Father who is in heaven. Thus, when you give alms, sound no trumpet before you, as the hypocrites do in the synagogues and in the streets, that they may be praised by men. Truly, I say to you, they have their reward. But when you give alms, do not let your left hand know what your right hand is doing, so that your alms may be in secret; and your Father who sees in secret will reward you.

"And when you pray, you must not be like the hypocrites; for they love to stand and pray in the synagogues and at the street corners, that they may be seen by men. Truly, I say to you, they have their reward. But when you pray, go into your room and shut the door and pray to your Father who is in secret; and your Father who sees in secret will reward you. And in praying do not heap up empty phrases as the Gentiles do; for they think that they will be heard for their many words. Do not be like them, for your Father knows what you need before you ask him.

. . . . . . . . . . . .

"And when you fast, do not look dismal, like the hypocrites, for they disfigure their faces that their fasting may be seen by men. Truly, I say to you, they have their reward. But when you fast, anoint your head and wash your face, that your fasting may not be seen by men but by your Father who is in secret; and your Father who sees in secret will reward you.

"Do not lay up for yourselves treasures on earth, where moth and rust consume and where thieves break in and steal, but lay up for yourselves treasures in heaven, where neither moth nor rust consumes and where thieves do not break in and steal. For where your treasure is, there will your heart be also.

. . . . . . . . . . . . .

"No one can serve two masters; for either he will hate the one and love the other, or he will be devoted to the one and despise the other. You cannot serve God and mammon.

"Therefore I tell you, do not be anxious about your life, what you shall eat or what you shall drink, nor about your body, what you shall put on. Is not life more than food, and the body more than clothing? Look at the birds of the air: they neither sow nor reap nor gather into barns, and yet your heavenly Father feeds them. Are you not of more value than they? And which of you by being anxious can add one cubit to his span of life? And why are you anxious about clothing? Consider the lilies of the field, how they grow; they neither toil nor spin; yet I tell you, even Solomon in all his glory was not arrayed like one of these. But if God so clothes the grass of the field, which today is alive and tomorrow is thrown into the oven, will he not much more clothe you, O men of little faith? Therefore do not be anxious, saying, 'What shall we eat?' or 'What shall we drink?' or 'What shall we wear?' For the Gentiles seek all these things; and your heavenly Father knows that you need them all. But seek first his kingdom and his righteousness, and all these things shall be yours as well.

"Therefore do not be anxious about tomorrow, for tomorrow will be anxious for itself. Let the day's own trouble be sufficient for the day.

"Judge not, that you be not judged. For with judgment you pronounce you will be judged, and the measure you give will be the measure you get. Why do you see the speck that is in your brother's eye, but do not notice the log that is in your own eye? Or how can you say to your brother, 'Let me take the speck out of your eye,' when there is the log in your eye? You hypocrite, first take the log out of your own eye, and then you will see clearly to take the speck out of your brother's eye. Do not give dogs what is holy; and do not throw your pearls before swine, lest they trample them underfoot and turn to attack you.

"Ask, and it will be given you; seek and you will find; knock, and it will be opened to you. For every one who asks receives, and he who seeks finds, and to him who knocks it will be opened. Or what man of you, if his son asks him for a loaf, will give him a stone? Or if he asks for a fish, will give him a serpent? If you then, who are evil, know how to give good gifts to your children, how much more will your Father who is in heaven give good things to those who ask him? So whatever you wish that men would do to you, do so to them; for this is the law and the prophets. Enter by the narrow gate; for the gate is wide and the way is easy, that leads to destruction, and those who enter by it are many. For the gate is narrow and the way is hard, that leads to life, and those who find it are few.

"Beware of false prophets, who come to you in sheep's clothing but inwardly are ravenous wolves. You will know them by their fruits. Are grapes gathered from thorns, or figs from thistles? So, every sound tree bears good fruit, but the bad tree bears evil fruit. A sound tree cannot bear evil fruit, nor can a bad tree bear good fruit. Every tree that does not bear good fruit is cut down and thrown into the fire. Thus you will know them by their fruits.

"Not every one who says to me, 'Lord, Lord,' shall enter the kingdom of heaven, but he who does the will of my Father who is in heaven. On that day many will say to me, 'Lord, Lord, did we not prophesy in your name, and cast out demons in your name, and do many mighty works in your name?' And then will I declare to them, 'I never knew you: depart from me, you evildoers.'

"Every one then who hears these words of mine and does them will be like a wise man who built his house upon the rock; and the rain fell, and the floods came, and the winds blew and beat upon that house, but it did not fall, because it had been founded on the rock. And every one who hears these words of mine and does not do them will be like a foolish man who built his house upon the sand; and the rain fell, and the floods came, and the winds blew and beat against that house, and it fell; and great was the fall of it." And when Jesus finished these sayings, the crowds were astonished at his teaching, for he taught them as one who had authority, not as their scribes.

MATTHEW 5, 6, 7

## *The Kingdom of Heaven*

Like the Hebrew prophets, Jesus expressed a hope for the coming of a kingdom in which God's truth would be fully revealed. In his parables of the kingdom of heaven, he not only gave hope to men for future justice but revealed some of his ethical values.

"Again, the kingdom of heaven is like a net which was thrown into the sea and gathered fish of every kind; when it was full, men drew it ashore and sat down and sorted the good into vessels but threw away the bad. So it will be at the close of the age. The angels will come out and separate the evil from the righteous, and throw them into the furnace of fire; there men will weep and gnash their teeth."

MATTHEW 13:47-50

"For the kingdom of heaven is like a householder who went out early in the morning to hire laborers for his vineyard. After agreeing with the laborers for a denarius a day, he sent them into his vineyard. And going out about the third hour he saw others standing idle in the market place; and to them he said, 'You go into the vineyard too, and whatever is right I will give you.' So they went. Going out again about the sixth hour and the ninth hour, he did the same. And about the eleventh hour he went out and found others standing; and he said to them, 'Why do you stand here idle all day?' They said to him, 'Because no one has hired us.' He said to them, 'You go into the vineyard too.' And when evening came, the owner of the vineyard said to his steward, 'Call the laborers and pay them their wages, beginning with the last, up to the first.' And when those hired about the eleventh hour came, each of them received a denarius. Now when the first came, they thought they would receive more; but each of them also received a denarius. And on receiving it they grumbled at the householder, saying, 'These last worked only one hour, and you have made them equal to us who have borne the burden of the day and the scorching heat.' But he replied to one of them, 'Friend, I am doing you no wrong; did you not agree with me for a denarius? Take what belongs to you, and go; I choose to give to this last as I give to you. Am I not allowed to do what I choose with what belongs to me? Or do you begrudge my generosity?' So the last will be first, and the first last."

MATTHEW 20:1-16

*The Mercy of Forgiveness*

Although Jesus wished people to obey established moral laws, he displayed an uncommon concern for individuals who had strayed from the path of proper behavior. His was a strong morality but one tempered with mercy. Consider the passage which follows in this light.

Now the tax collectors and sinners were all drawing near to hear him. And the Pharisees and the scribes murmured, saying, "This man receives sinners and eats with them." So he told them this parable: "What man of you, having a hundred sheep, if he has lost one of them, does not leave the ninety-nine in the wilderness, and go after the one which is lost, until he finds it? And when he has found it, he lays it on his shoulders, rejoicing. And when he comes home, he calls together his friends and his neighbors, saying to them, 'Rejoice with me, I have found my sheep which was lost.' Even so, I tell you, there will be more joy in heaven over one sinner who repents than over ninety-nine righteous persons who need no repentance."

. . . . . . . . . .

And he said, "There was a man who had two sons; and the younger of them said to his father, 'Father, give me the share of property that falls to me.' And he divided his living between them. Not many days later, the younger son gathered all he had and took his journey into a far country, and there he squandered his property in loose living. And when he had spent everything, a great famine arose in that country, and he began to be in want. So he went and joined himself to one of the citizens of that country, who sent him into his fields to feed swine. And he would gladly have fed on the pods that the swine ate; and no one gave him anything. But when he came to himself he said, 'How many of my father's hired servants have bread enough and to spare, but I perish here with hunger! I will arise and go to my father, and I will say to him, "Father, I save sinned against heaven and before you; I am no longer worthy to be called your son; treat me as one of your hired servants."' And he arose and came to his father. But while he was yet at a distance, his father saw him and had compassion, and ran and embraced him and kissed him. And the son said to him, 'Father, I have sinned against heaven and before you; I am no longer worthy to be called your son.' But the father said to his servants, 'Bring quickly the best robe, and put it on him; and put a ring on his hand, and shoes on his feet; and bring the fatted calf and kill it, and let us eat and make merry; for this my son was dead, and is alive again; he was lost, and is found.' And they began to make merry.

"Now his elder son was in the field; and as he came and drew near to the house, he heard music and dancing. And he called one of the servants and asked what this meant. And he said to him, 'Your brother has come, and your father has killed the fatted calf, because he has received him safe and sound.' But he was angry and refused to go in. His father came out and entreated him, but he answered his father, 'Lo, these many years I have served you, and I never disobeyed your command; yet you never gave me a kid, that I might make merry with my friends. But when this son of yours came, who has devoured your living with harlots, you killed for him the fatted calf!' And he said to him, 'Son, you are always with me, and all that is mine is yours. It was fitting to make merry and be glad, for this your brother was dead, and is alive; he was lost, and is found.'"

LUKE 15

### *"Who Is My Neighbor?"*

Although Jesus was a Jew who never left his native land, his teachings had a universal quality to them, enabling the religion which grew around him to spread throughout the world. His concept of "neighbor" was far more than a person who merely lived near him. Consider the following parable.

And behold, a lawyer stood up to put him to the test, saying. "Teacher, what shall I do to inherit eternal life?" He said to him, "What is written in the law? How do you read?" And he answered, "You shall love the Lord your God with all your heart, and with all your soul, and with all your strength, and with all your mind; and your neighbor as yourself." And he said to him, "You have answered right; do this, and you will live."

But he, desiring to justify himself, said to Jesus, "And who is my neighbor?" Jesus replied, "A man was going down from Jerusalem to Jericho, and fell among robbers, who stripped him and beat him, and departed, leaving him half-dead. Now by chance a priest was going down that road; and when he saw him he passed by on the other side. So likewise a Levite, when he came to the place and saw him, passed by on the other side. But a Samaritan, as he journeyed, came to where he was; and when he saw him, he had compassion, and went to him and bound up his wounds, pouring on oil and wine; then he set him on his own beast and brought him to an inn, and took care of him. And the next day he took out two denarii and gave them to the innkeeper, saying, 'Take care of him; and whatever more you spend, I will repay you when I come back.' Which of these three, do you think, proved neighbor to the man who fell among the robbers?" He said, "The one who showed mercy on him." And Jesus said to him, "Go and do likewise."

LUKE 10:25-37

## Testaments Old and New

The continuity between the Old and New Testaments—between Judaism and Christianity—can be seen in the following poem spoken by Mary after the angel of the Lord had told her that she would be the mother of Jesus. It is strikingly similar to the words spoken by Hannah when she had given birth to Samuel (I SAMUEL 2:1-10).

> And Mary said,
> "My soul magnifies the Lord,
> and my spirit rejoices in God my Savior,
> for he has regarded the low estate of his handmaiden.
> For behold, henceforth all generations will call me blessed;
> for he who is mighty has done great things for me,
> and holy is his name.
> And his mercy is on those who fear him
> from generation to generation.
> He has shown strength with his arm,
> he has scattered the proud in the imagination of their hearts,
> he has put down the mighty from their thrones,
> and exalted those of low degree;
> he has filled the hungry with good things,
> and the rich he has sent empty away.
> He has helped his servant Israel,
> in remembrance of his mercy,

as he spoke to our fathers,
to Abraham and to his posterity for ever."

LUKE 1:46-55

## Jesus as the Christ

Jesus conceived of himself as being more than a prophet. He saw himself, as did others after him, as the son of God—as much a divine person as a human person. The words of John make this belief quite clear.

The true light that enlightens every man was coming into the world. He was in the world, and the world was made through him, yet the world knew him not. He came to his own home, and his own people received him not. But to all who received him, who believed in his name, he gave power to become children of God; who were born, not of blood nor of the will of the flesh nor of the will of man, but of God. And the Word became flesh and dwelt among us, full of grace and truth; we have beheld his glory, glory as of the only Son from the Father.

JOHN 1:9-14

For God so loved the world that he gave his only Son, that whoever believes in him should not perish but have eternal life. For God sent the Son into the world, not to condemn the world, but that the world might be saved through him.

JOHN 3:16-17

In the words of Jesus:

"Let not your hearts be troubled; believe in God, believe also in me. In my Father's house are many rooms; if it were not so, would I have told you that I go to prepare a place for you? And when I go and prepare a place for you, I will come again and will take you to myself, that where I am you may be also. And you know the way where I am going." Thomas said to him, "Lord, we do not know where you are going; how can we know the way?" Jesus said to him, "I am the way, and the truth, and the life; no one comes to the Father, but by me. If you had known me, you would have known my Father also; henceforth you know him and have seen him."

JOHN 14:1-7

Jesus said to them, "I am the bread of life; he who comes to me shall not hunger, and he who believes in me shall never thirst. But I said to you that you have seen me and yet do not believe. All that the Father gives me will come to me; and him who comes to me I will not cast out. For I have come down from heaven, not to do my own will, but the will of him who sent me; and this is the will of him who sent me, that I should lose nothing of all that he has given me, but raise it up at the last day. For this is the will of my Father, that every one who sees the Son and believes in him should have eternal life; and I will raise him up at the last day."

JOHN 6:35-40

When Jesus was handed over to the Roman governor Pontius Pilate to be executed, Pilate questioned him carefully.

Pilate entered the praetorium again and called Jesus, and said to him, "Are you the King of the Jews?" Jesus answered, "Do you say this of your own accord, or did others say it to you about me?" Pilate answered, "Am I a Jew? Your own nation and the chief priests have handed you over to me; what have you done?" Jesus answered, "My kingship is not of this world; if my kingship were of this world, my servants would fight, that I might not be handed over to the Jews; but my kingship is not from the world." Pilate said to him, "So you are a king?" Jesus answered, "You say that I am a king. For this I was born, and for this I have come into the world, to bear witness to the truth. Every one who is of the truth hears my voice." Pilate said to him, "What is truth?"

JOHN 18:33-38

## Christianity and Hellenic Thought

Jesus never responded to the question "What is truth?" a question which would have launched a Greek philosopher into a lengthy dialogue on the nature of truth. Jesus was more concerned with an emotional faith in simple truth than with an intellectual argument about the complexity of true reality. In this, Christianity was true to its Hebrew roots, and Christians needed only faith in the fact that Jesus had died for them and would come again to reward the faithful.

Such a simple faith would have little appeal to sophisticated Greeks or Romans. However, it was the teachings of Paul of Tarsus which fused the simple faith of the Hebrews with the logical reasoning of the Greeks and Romans. Paul used the logical tools developed by the Greek philosophers to argue the truth of Christianity as he saw it. By so clothing the teachings of Jesus in Hellenic dress, he helped to spread Christianity far beyond the confines of Judea. Here is an example of this kind of logical style.

Now if Christ is preached as raised from the dead, how can some of you say that there is no resurrection of the dead? But if there is no resurrection of the dead, then Christ has not been raised; if Christ has not been raised, then our preaching is in vain and your faith is in vain. We are even found to be misrepresenting God, because we testified of God that he raised Christ, whom he did not raise if it is true that the dead are not raised. For if the dead are not raised, then Christ has not been raised. If Christ has not been raised, your faith is futile and you are still in your sins. Then those also who have fallen asleep in Christ have perished. If in this life we who are in Christ have only hope, we are of all men most to be pitied. But in fact Christ has been raised from the dead, the first fruits of those who have fallen asleep. For as by a man came death, by a man has come also the resurrection of the dead. For as in Adam all die, so also in Christ shall all be made alive. But each in his own order: Christ the first fruits, then at his coming those who belong to Christ."

I CORINTHIANS 15:12-23

But some one will ask, "How are the dead raised? With what kind of body do they come?" You foolish man! What you sow does not come to life unless it dies. And what you sow is not the body which is to be, but a bare kernel, perhaps of wheat or of some other grain. But God gives it a body as he has chosen, and to each kind of seed its own body. For not all flesh is alike, but there is one kind for men, another for animals, another for birds, and another for fish. There are celestial bodies and there are terrestrial bodies; but the glory of the celestial is one, and the glory of the terrestrial is another. There is one glory of the sun, and another glory of the moon, and another glory of the stars; for star differs from star in glory.

So is it with the resurrection of the dead. What is sown is perishable, what is raised is imperishable. It is sown in dishonor, it is raised in glory. It is sown in weakness, it is raised in power. It is sown a physical body, it is raised a spiritual body. If there is a physical body, there is also a spiritual body. Thus it is written, "The first man Adam became a living being"; the last Adam became a lifegiving spirit. But it is not the spiritual which is first but the physical, and then the spiritual. The first man was from the earth, a man of dust; the second man is from heaven. As was the man of dust, so are those who are of the dust; and as is the man of heaven, so are those who are of heaven. Just as we have borne the image of the man of dust, we shall also bear the image of the man of heaven. I tell you this, brethren: flesh and blood cannot inherit the kingdom of God, nor does the perishable inherit the imperishable.

Lo! I tell you a mystery. We shall not all sleep, but we shall all be changed, in a moment, in the twinkling of an eye, at the last trumpet. For the trumpet will sound, and the dead will be raised imperishable, and we shall be changed. For this perishable nature must put on the imperishable, and this mortal nature must put on immortality. When the perishable puts on the imperishable, and the mortal puts on immortality, then shall come to pass the saying that is written:

> "O death, where is thy victory?
> O death, where is thy sting?"

The sting of death is sin, and the power of sin is the law. But thanks be to God, who gives us the victory through our Lord Jesus Christ. Therefore, my beloved brethren, be steadfast, immovable, always abounding in the work of the Lord, knowing that in the Lord your labor is not in vain.

I CORINTHIANS 15:35-58

We know that in everything God works for good with those who love him, who are called according to his purpose. For those whom he foreknew he also predestined to be conformed to the image of his Son, in order that he might be the firstborn among many brethren. And those whom he predestined he also called; and those whom he called he also justified; and those whom he justified he also glorified. What then shall we say to this? If God is for us, who is against us? He who did not spare his own Son but gave him up for us all, will he not also give us all things with him? Who shall bring any charge against God elect? It is God who justifies; who is to condemn? Is it Christ Jesus, who died, yes, who was raised from the dead, who is at the right hand of God, who indeed intercedes for us? Who shall separate us from the love of Christ? Shall tribulation, or distress, or persecution, or famine, or nakedness, or peril, or sword? As it is written,

"For thy sake we are being killed all the day long;
we are regarded as sheep to be slaughtered."

No, in all these things we are more than conquerors through him who loved us. For I am sure that neither death, nor life, nor angels, nor principalities, nor things present, nor things to come, nor powers, nor height, nor depth, nor anything else in all creation, will be able to separate us from the love of God in Christ Jesus our Lord.

ROMANS 8:28-39

It was this image of God, expressing a concern for the faithful and a promise for the future, which filled the spiritual vacuum of the Graeco-Roman world. In the writings of Paul and in the developed Christian religion, faith and reason combined to provide the foundation on which civilization would be built after the collapse of the Roman order. The principles of European culture can be seen in an early Christian statement of belief (the Nicene Creed), which is itself a fusion of both faith and logic.

I believe in one God the Father Almighty, Maker of heaven and earth, And of all things visible and invisible:
And in one Lord Jesus Christ, the only-begotten Son of God; Begotten of his Father before all worlds, God of God, Light of Light, Very God of Very God; Begotten, not made; Being of one substance with the Father; By whom all things were made: Who for us men and for our salvation came down from heaven, And was incarnate by the Holy Ghost of the Virgin Mary, And was made man: And was crucified also for us under

Pontius Pilate; He suffered and was buried: And the third day he rose again according to the Scriptures: And ascended into heaven, And sitteth on the right hand of the Father: And he shall come again, with glory, to judge both the quick and the dead; Whose kingdom shall have no end.

And I believe in the Holy Ghost, The Lord, and Giver of Life, Who proceedith from the Father and the Son; Who with the Father and the Son together is worshipped and glorified; Who spake by the Prophets: And I believe one Catholic and Apostolic Church: I acknowledge one Baptism for the remission of sins: And I look for the Resurrection of the dead: And the Life of the world to come. Amen.

# Epilogue: The Legacy of Greece and Rome

The collapse of the Roman order, the disintegration of civilization itself in the West and the conversion of the eastern portion of the Empire to Christianity all seemed to indicate a total end of Graeco-Roman culture. In Italy, Spain, Gaul and Britain, the thread of human civilization which stretched back through thousands of years to Egypt and Mesopotamia seemed to be broken. Cities, the very life source of civilization, fell into ruin; public life declined and people had to fight for mere survival; illiteracy and ignorance grew. It seemed as if the Neolithic age of "precivilized" man had returned.

In the East, Constantinople remained a large flourishing urban center, but it was no longer the city of Constantine, the Roman emperor. Scholars no longer studied Plato and Herodotus; poets no longer sang the epics of Homer and Virgil. Men of learning and art turned their attention to the transcendent God of the Christians and to Jesus Christ. Scholars studied the Bible rather than Socrates, and artists portrayed saints and holy men rather than athletes and warriors. The books of the Greeks and pagan Romans were regarded as evil, and eventually, many of the centers of Graeco-Roman learning were destroyed. Both the Pope in Rome and the emperor in Constantinople were religious rulers who directed their subjects to a vision of life after death.

The culture which eventually developed in Europe out of the turmoil following the decline of Rome was substantially different from the culture of the ancient Mediterranean. A fundamental shift in the style of civilization had taken place. European civilization had for its very base the Christian religion which had played such a major role in the decline of Graeco-Roman culture. The basic political structure of European culture rested upon forms of organization used by the barbarians who overran the Empire. Even the overall physical environment of European culture was different from that of Greece and Rome. Deep forests, rich soil and the cycle of four distinct seasons contrasted markedly with the sparse rugged landscape and warm clear skies of Mediterranean lands. The medieval\* Gothic cathedral and the Greek temple can be seen as clear architectural symbols of this difference.

Yet, the massive accomplishments of Greece and Rome were not swept into oblivion even though Christ had replaced Caesar and dark pine forests had replaced olive groves. All ages are influenced by what has gone before them; the continuity of civilization has never yet been completely broken. The legacy of Greece and Rome is not a dead artifact, a museum piece. Its influence can be seen on two levels, both of which are a part of our own culture.

## Graeco-Roman Influences in Europe

First of all, much which was Graeco-Roman remained interwoven in the fabric of European culture. Ironically, the Christian Church, the single most important institution in European history, was patterned on the Roman imperial government. Roman law was adopted by the Church and provided an important legal framework for the emerging culture. As the only institution existing in all parts of Europe, the Church brought elements of Roman culture into the entire continent, although in different forms and for different purposes. The Church was a shadow, or ghost, of the Roman Empire, providing a common government for the many separated tribes and nations. For good reason, it is sometimes called the Roman Catholic (meaning universal) Church. The very idea of a single European government, an idea very much alive today, stems from the world unity once attained by the Romans.

In addition to political institutions, the obvious presence of the Latin language in European culture is a clear example of the legacy. For centuries after the fall of Rome, the language which had once united the Mediterranean world united the educated classes of the European world. Literacy meant the ability to read Latin! Even those who spoke the local European languages felt

---

\* *Medieval* means of or relating to the Middle Ages, a period in history which extended from about 500 to 1500 A.D.

the influence of the Romans. Many modern languages have Latin as a major ingredient. The English words *duke, prince, senate* and *consul* are of obvious Latin derivation; others, such as *victory, navigate, personality* and *chant*, are variations of words which were originally Latin. Therefore, the Roman legacy and European culture were, and are, intertwined. Even the city of Rome itself was a major city in both Roman and European civilization. Rome, the center of the Mediterranean world, became the spiritual center of European culture.

Although the immediate threads from Rome to Europe are clearer than those from Greece, Greek as well as Roman elements became an integral part of European culture. The view of the physical world and of the universe as seen by Greek scientists (and expressed in particular by Aristotle) became the accepted view for centuries to come. The system of logic developed by thinkers such as Socrates and Plato was used by Christians to present and defend their religious beliefs. The basic ideas of Christianity itself, although of non-Greek origin, were chiseled out with the fine instrument of the Greek language. These ideas became housed in the Roman Empire and were implanted in Europe by churchmen using the Latin tongue. The future is always built upon the past.

Yet, the past is always transformed and sometimes distorted when it is moved beyond its original historical setting. The Christian Church was not the Roman Empire, and a medieval assembly of knights or the United States Congress was not the Roman Senate, even though the same name might be used. The legacy of Greece and Rome was present in European culture, but it was submerged and altered; men were not always conscious of its presence.

## The Rebirth of Graeco-Roman Culture

There was, however, a second and perhaps more significant level on which the Graeco-Roman experience influenced Western culture. During the fourteenth and fifteenth centuries A.D., about one thousand years after the decline of Rome, substantial changes took place in Europe. There was a shift in values and cultural forms as the attention of learned men was directed back to the ancient world.

Discontented with their present age, artists and thinkers (at first, just in Italy) sought knowledge of a civilization which was radically different from their own. Through research and discovery, men were able to reconstruct a fairly accurate picture of pre-Christian, Graeco-Roman culture. The study of the Greek language was introduced so that the literary and philosophical works of the Greeks could be read. The Latin style of Cicero and other Roman writers was used to replace the form of Latin used by the Church. Principles of Greek and Roman architecture were studied and used to construct buildings in the Greek style. With these insights and tools, men used Greek and Roman ideas and accomplishments to criticize their own society and to serve as models for educated men to follow. The ancient world was reborn and exalted during the fourteenth and fifteenth centuries, an era we rightly call the *Renaissance* ("rebirth").

Ciceronian prose became a standard by which to judge writing, just as Greek temples and statues were used as guides for artists. Even statesmen and political thinkers began to use ancient writers and governmental forms as models to follow. Writers such as Livy, Polybius and Solon were studied, and the Roman republic was seen as the ideal form of government. Many of the ideas which went into the formation of the United States republic had their origin in this revival of Greece and Rome. The fact that legislative bodies are often called senates, that public buildings are often imitations of Greek temples and that a number of American cities have been given the names of ancient cities is some indication of the effect of this renaissance of the ancient world.

During the time of the Renaissance, Latin and Greek in their ancient form became the basic ingredients of a formal education. A man was considered educated only after he had read the major Greek and Roman writers in the original language. It was believed that these ancient thinkers had somehow grasped the ideal forms of human culture. Therefore, a knowledge of the ancients provided a person with a set of standards by which to order his life. To many, this admiration of the Greeks and Romans became a kind of religion, and as such, its influence was widespread. Western culture since the Renaissance has had a layer of Graeco-Roman culture spread through its educated classes.

It should be clear by now that the Greek and Roman experience is very much alive in modern culture—first, as a formative and civilizing influence in the early years of European history, and second, as a later and deliberate addition which has shaped art, education and patterns of thought, providing models for men to follow. In one sense, the ideas and artistic forms of the ancient Greeks and Romans have exerted a kind of tyranny over Western European culture. The accomplishments of the ancients were regarded as *classical* works, that is, accomplishments which were both perfect and applicable to any age. This is why ancient history is sometimes called *classical history.*

On this deepest level, the value of the legacy of Greece and Rome can be seen regardless of whether Latin words are used in the English language or Greek names are used for American cities. This kind of classical legacy points to the ability of the ancients to probe to the depths of the human condition and, in truth, to speak to men of all times. Consider, by way of quick review, some of the things touched on in this book—man's sense of joy in the use of his mind as shown by Herodotus when pondering the Nile flood or Plato when reaching for absolute truth; Thucydides' brutal exposure of those forces which drive nations to war and men to civil strife; the deep wisdom of the Stoics who understood the limitations of the individual man in an impersonal world, and the profound simplicity of Jesus who sought to tap the sources of human love and morality in that same world; the patriotism, sense of duty and respect for law of the early Romans and the burning concern for social justice shown by the Gracchi; the spectacle of the gradual and almost inevitable disintegration of the Roman Empire and the birth of a new culture from its ruins. All of these things form a legacy of permanent value to the human race. The experience of the ancients must not go unnoticed, for our present condition, although different in outward form, is the same as theirs. The men who lived during this past epoch spanned the full spectrum of human thought and action. This small book has but glimpsed at this panorama. Much lies beyond for those who wish to understand their past, and in so doing, to understand themselves.

# INDEX

# INDEX

Achilles, 11
Acropolis, 16
Acts of the Apostles, 167
Aeneas, 169
*Aeneid*, the, 169
Aeschylus, 46-47
Agamemnon, 46
Agora, 16, 43
Alcibiades, as cosmopolite, 75; importance of, 54-56; as individualist, 76; and polis, 74; and Socrates, 62, 64; as Socrates' pupil, 57
Alexander the Great, assumption of the throne, 80; as conqueror, 83-85; deeds of, 81-86; and Diogenes, 94; impact of, 162; *map* of empire, 84; in retrospect, 85-86; and the Romans, 142; successors, 86
Alexandria, founding of, 85; in Hellenistic period, 90; as important city, 88; and philosophers, 91
Alphabet, 4
Amon, 83, 99
Anaximander, 13-14
*Antigone*, 48
Antigonus, 86
Antioch, 88, 90, 91
Antiochus IV, 102
Antony, Marc, 149-51
*Antony and Cleopatra*, 151
Apennines, 114
Aphrodite, 5, 7
Apollo, 5, 7
"Ara Pacis," 161
Archimedes, 90, 115
Architecture, 50, 206
*Arete*, definition, 11; Hesiod on, 19; and Rome, 142; and society, 24; and sophists, 58; in Sparta, 22
Aristides, 171-72, 175
Aristocracy, definition, 16; and Greek democracy, 40; after Peisistratus, 26; and Plato, 94; role of, 17-18; Roman, 123-24; of Roman officeholders, 133; and Roman republic, 120; warrior, 18
Aristophanes, 49
Aristotle, and European culture, 205; as individualist, 76; and Judaism, 101; in Macedonia, 79; and natural law, 92; and polis, 91; and political organization, 77; and Romans, 171; as tutor, 75; view of non-Greeks, 94; world view of, 99
Army, Julius Caesar's, 146; and Christians, 182; Greek, 20; in Hellenistic period, 89; Roman, 143
Art, Greek, 89; individualism in, 76; Roman, 175; and Roman conquest, 134
Asia Minor, after Alexander's death, 86;

Greeks in, 6; and Pompey, 143; and Roman expansion, 135; in Selucid kingdom, 88
Assyria, 29, 80-81, 173
Athena, 7, 9, 40
Athenian, 38, 43-44
Athens, breakdown of unity, 52, 53-54; buildings of, 40; Julius Caesar in, 144; civilization of, 28; and commerce, 75; constitution of, 23; culture of, 49-50; defeat of, 56; and Delian League, 38-41; democracy of, 26-27, 43; education in, 57; empire of, 41-45; fifth century B.C., 91; funerals in, 66; government, 27; Herodotus in, 14; importance of, 5; under Macedonia, 80; military leaders of, 27; organization of, 22-26; and Peloponnesian War, 74; and Persian Wars, 28-29, 74; population—fifth century B.C., 40; revolution of 510 B.C., 26; and Socrates, 62; under Sparta, 56-57; treatment of smaller states, 51; war with Sparta, 51-57
Attica, 5
Attila, 188
Augustus, Caesar, 151, 160-64, 178. *See also* Octavian
Autarky, 93

Babylon, 29
Babylonia, and Alexander, 83; and Assyria, 80; creation story of, 12; and Hebrews, 98; religion, 9
Barbarians, under Constantine, 188; and European politics, 204; in Gaul, 136; internal, 175; pressure from, 183; and Roman decline, 174; threat of, 185
Barcas, 129
Bible, Christian part, 190; epistles in, 180; and ethics, 99; and Old Testament, 98; parts of, 181; and scholars, 203. *See also* New Testament; Old Testament
Bishops, 186
Black Sea, 3
Bribery, 144
Britain, 165, 183, 203
Brutus, Lucius Junius, 120, 149
Brutus, Marcus, 149, 150
Byzantine Empire, 188
Byzantium, 188

Caesar Augustus. *See* Augustus, Caesar
Caesar, Julius, and Cicero, 148; death of, 148-49; and France, 170; versus Pompey, 145-46; rise of, 144-45; and Roman republic, 150; struggle for reform, 148-49; in Triumvirate, 145

210

## INDEX

Calendar, 148
Cannae, 131
Carthage, background of, 127; and barbarians, 136; defeat of, 133; during Hellenistic period, 89; as important city, 88; revenge of, 129; Roman attack on, 132; and Roman expansion, 134; and Rome, 127; as sea power, 128; and Third Punic War, 135; trade with Etruscans, 115
Catiline, 147
*Catiline Orations*, 148
Chaeronea, 80
Chariot races, 142
Christ, 181, 198-99. See also Jesus
Christian Church, 186, 188, 204
Christianity, appeal of, 181; birth of, 178-79; conversion of eastern Roman Empire to, 203; and faith, 199; and Greek, 205; and Hellenistic thought, 199-202; and Judaism, 180-81, 197; and modern culture, 190; persecution of, 182; spread of, 180-81; as threat to Rome, 182, 183
Christians, and Diocletian, 186; and Roman religion, 182; on Rome's doom, 187; and scholars, 203; toleration of, 188
Christus, 179. See also Christ; Jesus
Cicero, on Julius Caesar, 148; on Julius Caesar's assassination, 149; death of, 150; importance of, 146-48; study of, 206
Cincinnatus, 117, 137
Cisalpine Gaul, 136, 142, 148
Cities, alliance with Rome, 125; decline of, 183; Etruscan, 115; after fall of Rome, 203; Greek, in Italy, 125; in Hellenistic period, 89; revolt against Romans, 142; and Romans, 174
Citizenship, Athenian, 40; and Julius Caesar, 148; concept of, 25; and the Gracchi, 140; granting, 142; of Hellenistic period, 90-91; for non-Romans, 124; Roman, 165-66, 168
City-states, 89. See also Polis
Civilization, and Christian Church, 188; of Crete, 2; European, 190; and Greece, 2, 3; Greek, 14, 76, 104; Greek, and Homer, 7; Greek, and humanism, 9; Hellenic, 5-6, 28; Ionian, 6-12; Mycenaean, 2-3; Roman, 102-03; and Rome, 151; spread of, 4; weakening of, 183; Western, 165, 203
Classes, 122
Cleon, 54
Cleopatra, 150, 151
Clients, 123
Clytemnestra, 46
Coinage, 4, 17

Colonies, 20, 25
*Commentaries on the Gallic Wars*, 144, 170
Constantine, 188
Constantinople, 188, 203
Constitution, 23, 24, 153-57
Consul, under Augustus, 160; elected, 123; and plebians, 121, 122; Pompey as, 145; in provinces, 129; in republic, 120
Corinth, and challenge to Athens, 41; and commerce, 75; location of, 5; and Peloponnesian War, 53; Roman destruction of, 134
Corinthians, 199-201
Cosmopolitan, 89
Cosmopolite, 94
Council of Five Hundred, 26, 27, 42
Courts, 17
Covenant, 99, 100
Crassus, 143-44, 145
Crete, civilization of, 2; destruction of civilization of, 4; and Greeks, 173; influence of Mycenaeans, 2-3
Culture, and Alexander, 83; Athenian, 49-50; Egyptian, 61; European, 201, 203, 205; Graeco-Roman, 168, 170, 175, 178, 181, 203; Graeco-Roman, rebirth, 205-07; Greek, 61, 76, 77, 85, 102; Greek, and Alexander, 81, 83, 86; Greek, as dominant, 85; Greek, and Romans, 134; Hellenic, 7, 75, 125, 142; in Hellenistic period, 88; mass, 175; modern, 190; and polis, 66; Roman, 130, 175; and Romans, 165-66; spread of Greek, 21; Western, 111
Cumae, 116
Cyrus, 76

Dacia, 165
Danube River, 165, 183
Darius, 28, 29, 81-83
Delian League, 38-41, 74
Delos, 38
Democracy, Athenian, 26-27, 52, 56, 57; and Athenian empire, 40; direct, 26, 40, 58; Greek, 40; Herodotus on, 33; and Peisistratus, 26; and Peloponnesian War, 54; and Pericles, 42-43; and Pericles' *Funeral Oration*, 66-69; and Persian Wars, 30; and polis, 42, 77; representative, 26; and Rome, 124; and Socrates, 62, 94; and Stoics, 94
Demosthenes, 79-80, 148
Dialogue, 59, 106-10
Dictator, 120
Dido, 169
Diocese, 185, 186

## 212　INDEX

Diocletian, 185-86
Diogenes, 94
Dionysius, 75, 110
Dionysus, 46
Divination, 115
Drama, definition, 45; Greek, 43, 45-49, 76, 171; Roman, 171

Earth, 90
Edict of Milan, 188
Education, 57
Egypt, and Alexander, 83; and Antony, 150; attacks on, 4; drama, 46; fall of, 83; fertility, 2; geography, 6; and Herodotus, 31; and Pompey, 143; population of, 20; and Ptolemy, 86; in Roman Empire, 151, 162; and Thales, 12; and Xerxes, 29
Ekklesia, 26, 180
Electra, 46
Emperor, German as, 188; selection of, 163, 183; worship, 163, 182
Employment, 183
English Channel, 151
Enlil, 5
Epictetus, 93, 95-96
Epistles, 180, 190
Equality, 94, 95
Ethics, 93, 99
Etruscans, 115, 119
Euclid, 90
Euphrates River, 82, 151, 165
Euripides, 48-49, 76, 79
Europe, 204
Euthyphro, 106

Fabius, 131
Family, 117, 118
Farmer-soldier, 117, 137
Farming, 174
Farms, 138
Festus, 167
Florence, 115
France, 170
Freedmen, 162
Furies, 46

Gaul, barbarians in, 188; Julius Caesar in, 144, 148; civilization in, 203; Roman influence in, 164, 174; and Romans, 136, 165
Gaul, Cisalpine, 136, 142, 148
Gaul, Transalpine, 136
Generals, 138, 141, 142
Genius, 117
Geometry, 90
*Germania*, 170
Germany, 165, 173
Gibbon, Edward, 162, 164, 173

Gladiatorial contests, 115, 142
God, and Christians, 190; Hebrew, 9; image of, 201; and Jesus, 179; Jewish, 98, 101, 176; and Rome, 187; and scholars, 203
Gods, under Augustus, 163; Babylonian, 9; Greek, 5, 10, 11, 104, 109, 179; in Greek plays, 48; and Hesiod, 18; in Homer, 7-8, 9; and Jews, 99; of mystery religions, 97, 177; and natural law, 14; and Pericles, 42; and provinces, 166; Roman, 118, 179; Roman household, 117; and Stoics, 92
Gospels, 180, 181, 190
Government, Athenian, 22-27; under Augustus, 162; under Julius Caesar, 148; Cicero's philosophy of, 147; early Greek, 16; Greek, 17, 21-26; Greek, criticism of, 49; in Hellenistic period, 88; and Herodotus, 15, 34; of Pax Romana, 161; republic as, 120; Roman, 121, 137, 145, 153; and Romans, 165-66; Spartan, 21-22
Gracchus, Gaius, 140
Gracchus, Tiberius, 139-40
*Graecus*, 116
Granicus River, 82
Greece, under Antigonus, 86; and Athens' leadership, 74; civilization in, 2, 3, 14, 28; climate, 6, 26, 44; culture of, 61; culture, world-wide, 86; early, 16; early invasion of, 4; economy of, 75; fertility of, 2; geography of, 6; government, 21-26; in Hellenistic period, 89; historians, 99; in Iron Age, 4; legacy of, 204, 207; Macedonian control of, 80; Mycenaeans, 114; and Peloponnesian War, 52, 74; after Pericles, 80; Persian invasion of, 38; after Philip's death, 81; political organization of, 16-18; Polybius on, 153-57; and population, 20; religion of, 5-6; Roman contact with, 125; under Rome, 134; social problems of, 18-21; unity of, 74, 77-81. *See also* Hellas
Greek, in European culture, 205; language, 168; as language of New Testament, 190; study of, 206
Greeks, books of, 203; as Christians, 182; civilization and Homer, 7; colonies, 20; compared with Hebrews, 60; and ethics, 99; and Homeric poems, 11; and Ionia, 6; in Italy, 115-16; and Mycenae, 173; origin of, 2; political organization of, 5; view of world, 99
Gymnasium, 43

Hammurabi, 173
Hannibal, 129-32, 136

## INDEX

Hanukkah, 102
Heaven, 194-95
Hebrews, and civilization, 4; compared with Greeks, 60; and creation, 12; and faith, 199; and God, 190; and humanism, 9; and idea of future kingdom, 179; influence of, 177; and Jesus' teachings, 180; and Jews, 98; legacy of, 182; and Old Testament, 11; prophets, 49, 190, 194; as slaves, 98
Helen of Troy, 3
Hellas, birth of civilization in, 7; *map*, fifth century B.C., 48; origin of name, 5; spread of culture of, 21, 75. *See also* Greece
Hellen, 5
Hellenes, 5
Hellenic civilization, 5-6
Hellenic culture, 7
Hellenistic period, attitude toward Jews, 101-02; culture in, 88-91; definition, 88; and Syracuse, 115
Hellespont, and Alexander, 81; and Persian invasion, 29; and Sparta, 55-56; and Troy, 3
Helots, 21, 41
Hermes, 7
Herodotus, and Athens' government, 27; importance of, 14-15; on law, 23-24; and Livy, 170; Readings from, 31-35; on Thermopylae, 29
Hesiod, 18-19, 19-20
Hippocrates, 59-60
Historians, 90
History, 99
History, classical, 207
Hittites, 2, 114, 173
Homer, and aristocracy, 16; and divinity, 10; emphasis in, 11; and gods, 92; and the *Iliad*, 3; image of man, 11-12; importance of, 7; influence of, 25; and Judaism, 101; and *Orestia*, 46; and Romans, 134; and Socrates, 60
Hoplites, 20
Humanism, Greek, 44; and Greek civilization, 9; and Peloponnesian War, 57-58; and Plato, 110; and Socrates, 58-59
Huns, 188

Idealism, 106
*Iliad*, the, and Alexander, 82; educational value of, 11; importance of, 7; and man, 9; and Romans, 142; tale of, 3
Ilium, 3. *See also* Troy
Illyria, 186
Immortality, 177
India, 83
Individualism, 76-77, 89
Indo-Europeans, 114

Indus River, 83
Industrial Revolution, 175
Ionia, 6, 38
Ionians, 6-15
Iran, 83
Iron, 3, 4, 174
Iron Age, 4
Isaiah, 9, 10
Isis, 97
Isocrates, 78, 79
Israel, 98, 100
Issus, 82
Italians, 114-17
Italy, barbarians in, 188; civilization in, 203; fertility of, 124; geography of, 114; Greeks in, 125; in Hellenistic period, 89; people in, 114

Jerusalem, and Hellenization, 102; and Jews, 98; Pompey in, 143; and worship of Roman gods, 166
Jesus, biography of, 178; as Christ, 198-99; and Christian Church, 186; and faith, 199; and forgiveness, 195-96; and heaven, 194-95; and Hebrew tradition, 179; and mythology, 181; nature of, 181-82; in New Testament, 190; and Pilate, 199; preachings of, 179; and scholars, 203; teachings of, 180, 190-94; universality of teaching, 196-97. *See also* Christ
Jews, definition, 98; in Hellenistic period, 101-02; Jesus as, 178, 179; and Roman religion, 182; values of, 176-77; and worship of Roman gods, 166
John, 181, 190; quoted, 198-99
Judah, 29
Judaism, nature of, 98-101; in perspective, 100-101; relation to Christianity, 180-81, 197
Judas Maccabaeus, 102
Judea, 166, 178
Jugurtha, 140
*Julius Caesar*, 151

Lacedaemonia, 5, 21
Lake Trasimene, 129
Languages, 205
Latin, 168, 204, 206
Latin tribes, 114, 116-17
Laws, in Athens, 27; Christian Church, 204; Greek, 17; and plebians, 122; and polis, 47; Roman, 166-68; Solon's, 23-25
Legal system, 165
Literature, Etruscan, 115; Greek, 49; Roman, 119, 168-70
Livy, on Rome's founding, 103; study of, 206; work of, 170; writing of, 153
Luke, 190; quoted, 195-98

Macedonia, under Antigonus, 86; Aristotle in, 75; Euripides in, 76; and Greece, 81; and Greek culture, 85; military success of, 82; rise of, 79-81; Roman defeat of, 134; as Rome's rival, 133, 134
Macedonian Wars, 133
Man, 9, 44-45, 110
Marathon, Battle of, 28-29, 38
*March Up Country, The,* 76
Marcus Aurelius, 95, 171
Marduk, 12
Marius, Gaius, 140-41
Mark, 190
Mars, 117
Matthew, 190
Medieval, 240 (footnote)
Mediterranean, and Alexander, 86; control, 127; fertility of area, 2; and Greek culture, 85; *map* of area, c. 1000 B.C., 8; and mystery religions, 98; *map* of Roman Empire in, c. first century B.C., 149; and Romans, 103
Melos, 39
Mesopotamia, and Assyria, 80; fertility of, 2; in Selucid kingdom, 86, 88
Messina, 127
Miletus, 6, 12, 14
Military, 79, 131-32, 185
Millennium, 6 (footnote)
Mithra, 96
Mithridates, 135
Mithridatic Wars, 135
Monarchy, 33, 88, 185
Monotheism, 179
Monotheist, 5-6
Mount Olympus, 7
Mycenae, 2
Mycenaeans, buildings of, 3; civilization, 2-3; destruction of civilization of, 4; and Greeks, 173; language, 3; location of, 5; migration of, 114
Mythology, definition, 6 (footnote); Greek, 6, 182; Greek and Roman, 179; and Greek drama, 46; and Homer, 7-11; and Jesus, 181

Naples, 116
Nation-state, 77
Natural law, 14, 31, 92
Navies, 89
Neolithic Revolution, 174
Neopolis, 116
New Testament, 181; Readings from, 190-202. *See also* individual books
Nicene Creed, 201-02
Nicias, 54
Nile, Alexander at, 83; Alexandria, 85; and Isis, 97; under Rome, 151

Nobility, 26
North Africa, 165

Octavian, 150-51. *See also* Augustus, Caesar
Odysseus, 7, 9
*Odyssey,* the, educational value of, 11; importance of, 7; and man, 9; and *Orestia,* 46; quoted, 9-10
Oedipus, 47-48
Old Testament, on creation, 12; and Hebrews, 98; as history, 99; nature of, 11, 181; translation into Greek, 101
Oligarchy, 18, 33
Orestes, 46
*Orestia,* the, 46, 47
Osiris, 11, 46
Ostracism, 27
Ostrakon, 27

Palestine, 4
Panhellenic, 78
Parables, 190
*Parallel Lives,* 170
Parthenon, 40, 50
Parthians, 145
Patricians, 120, 121
Patriotism, 118
Patrons, 123
Paul of Tarsus, deeds of, 179; epistles of, 180, 190; impact of, 199-202; writings of, 186
Pax Romana, 161-62, 183
Peisistratus, 25-26, 28
Peloponnesian War, and humanism, 57; impact of, 74; nature of, 51-57; polis during, 69; and thinkers, 64
Peloponnesus, 5, 41
Pericles, and Athens, 42-43; death of, 52; *Funeral Oration* of, 66-69; humanism of, 44; and Peloponnesian War, 53; and polis, 91
Pericles, Age of, 50, 57
Persia, aid to Sparta, 56; and Alexander, 81-83, 85; fall of, 173; and Greek civilization, 14; and Hebrews, 98; influence over Greece, 75; invasion of Greece, 38; and Isocrates, 78; migration of, 2; and Philip, 79; in Selucid kingdom, 88; and Sparta, 76; threat to Greece, 28-30
Persian Wars, 28-29, 74
Peter, 182
Phalanx, 82, 134
Philip, 79-80, 81
*Philippics,* 80, 148
Philistines, 4
Philo, 101
Philosophers, 12, 181, 199

INDEX 215

Philosophy, 91-97, 104-11
Phoenicia, and Alexander, 83; and alphabet, 4; and Carthage, 127; and Xerxes, 29
*Pietas*, 119
Pilate, Pontius, 179, 199
Pindar, 81
Piraeus, 40, 56
Planets, 90
Playwrights, 46, 90. See also individual playwrights
Plato, and Christians, 205; and humanism, 110; ideal government of, 94; and idealism, 106; as individualist, 76; influence of, 111; and Judaism, 101; philosophy of, 93; and polis, 91; and political organization, 77; on politics, 75; Readings from, 104-11; on real and ideal, 181; and reason, 105; and Romans, 171; and Socrates' Dialogues, 59, 106-10; as Socrates' pupil, 104; and true knowledge, 110-11; world view of, 99
Plebians, 120-22, 133
Plutarch, 51, 170
*Poenicus*, 128
Poets, 46, 90. See also individual poets
Polis, Aeschylus' depiction of, 47; breakdown of, 162; and culture, 66; decline of, 76; definition, 16; democratic, 30; failure of unity of, 74; and Greek culture, 86; and Greek greatness, 77; ideal, 91; importance of, 41; independence of, 78; influence of, 176, 177; and Jews, 101; loss of independence of, 80; and Peloponnesian War, 64, 69; and religion, 96; Rome as, 116. See also City-state
Politics, Greek, 77; and Herodotus, 33; invention of, 34; Thucydides on, 69
Polybius, 206; Readings from, 153-57
Polytheist, 5
Pompeius, Gnaeus. See Pompey
Pompey, versus Julius Caesar, 145-46; and Crassus, 144; rise of, 143; in Triumvirate, 145
Pontifex Maximus, 119, 188
Pontus, 135
Pope Leo, 188
Population, 20, 22, 124
Po River, 136
Poseidon, 5
Priesthood, 115, 118
Principes, 160
Pro-consuls, 129
Proles, 139
Proletariat, 139, 142, 143
Protagoras, 44, 60
Proverbs, 190

Provinces, administration of, 139; consuls of, 129; Greece as, 134; origin of, 128; and wealth, 134
Psychology, 111
Ptolemaic kingdom, 143
Ptolemy, 86, 88, 90
*Punicus*, 128
Punic Wars, First, 128; nature of, 127-33; Second, 129; Third, 135; in Virgil, 169
Pylos, 2
Pyrrhus, 125

Ravenna, 188
Reason, 105
*Religio*, 119
Religion, under Caesar Augustus, 163; and drama, 45; Etruscan, 115; Greek, 5-6, 104, 109; Homeric, 12; and humanism, 9; Judaism, 98-101, 176-77; monotheistic, 98-101; mystery, 96-98, 101, 177-78, 179; official Greek, 96; official Roman, 177, 178; Roman, 115, 118-19, 182
Renaissance, 205-07
Republic, 120
Resurrection, 179
Revelation, 187
Rhetoric, 58
Rhine River, 165, 183
Roads, 165
Roman Empire, after Caesar Augustus, 164-68; eastern, 188; economic and military problems of, 183-85; fall of, 173; internal, 142-48; internal crises, 139-42; map, c. first century B.C., 149; map, c. 300 A.D., 184; under Marcus Aurelius, 171; origins of, 133-36; period of, 160; political and social problems of, 142-43; political difficulties of, 183; and proletariat, 139; spiritual revolution of, 176-82; in turmoil, 182-86; and universal law, 166; weakness of, 163-64; western, 188-89
Roman republic, 206; fall of, 148-51, 160; nature of, 119-24; political structure of, 120-21
Romans, and absorption of new people, 174; army, 143; and assimilation of foreign culture, 80-81; and authority, 117-18; birthrate of, 185; books of, 203; and Carthage, 127; and Christianity, 182, 183; concept of state, 122; contact with Greece, 125; and culture, 175; early society of, 117-19; in the East, 165, 166; and expansion, 133-34; in First Punic War, 128; and Germany, 173; versus Hannibal, 129-30; in Hellenistic period, 102-03; influence of Etruscans on, 115; as Italian tribe, 114;

## 216  INDEX

and Latin tribe, 116; leaders during Empire, 143-44; literature of, 168-70; middle class, 128; military leaders, 131-32; mind of, 170-72; and provinces, 166; view of man, 171; and urban areas, 174; in West and North, 165
Romans, quoted, 201
Rome, and the *Aeneid*, 169; alliances of, 124; attack by barbarians, 173; balance of trade, 174; bishop of, 186; causes of decline, 174-75; Christians in, 180; Christians on, 187; as city, 205; and civilization, 151; and Cumae, 116; date of fall, 188; destruction of, 189; as divine monarchy, 185; during Age of Pericles, 114; effects of expansion on, 137-39; and Etruscans, 119; first century B.C., 142-43; founding of, 116; government of, 124; and Hannibal, 131, 132; in Hellenistic period, 89; and holdings of Carthage, 133; as important city, 33; influence in Gaul, 144; invasion of, 188; and landless men, 138; legacy of, 204, 207; Livy's history of, 170; loyalty to, 162; and Messina, 127; no longer capital, 188; and plebian reform, 122; Polybius on, 153-57; rise of, 125; Virgil on role of, 171; war with Macedonia, 133; weakening of, 183; and wealth, 128; as world power, 136. See also Roman Empire; Roman republic
Rubicon River, 146
Russia, 20

Sabines, 114
Salamis, 29-30, 38
Samnites, 114
Sardinia, 128
Schools, 58
Science, 90
Scipio, 141
Sculpture, 50, 89, 134
Seleucus, 86
Selucid kingdom, Israel in, 98; nature of, 88; and Pompey, 143; and Rome, 143
Senate, under Caesar Augustus, 160; after Julius Caesar, 149; and civil war, 142; decline of prestige of, 141; during Empire, 142; after Hannibal, 132-33; during Hannibal's invasion, 130; after plebian revolt, 123; plebians in, 122; and republic, 120; during Roman expansion, 139; in Roman government, 137
Seneca, 93
Shakespeare, 151
Sicily, Carthaginian colonies in, 127; and First Punic War, 128; in Hellenistic period, 89; Syracuse on, 20

Slavery, 18, 94, 95
Slaves, Athenian, 44; and farms, 138; and Pompey, 143; and Roman expansion, 134; and Rome, 174; Spartan, 21; and steam power, 90
Society, 90, 117-19, 137-39
Socrates, as Athenian patriot, 94; and Athens, 75; and Christians, 205; and class war, 74; concept of evil, 61; concerns of, 92; death of, 62-64; and democracy, 94; Dialogues of, 59, 106-10; importance of, 57-64; and Peloponnesian War, 52; and Plato, 104; and Romans, 134; and sophists, 59
Socratic Method, 59-60
Soldier, Athenian, 28; farmer-, 117, 137; Greek, hired by Persia, 76; long-term, 138; Roman, 125, 137-39
Solon, 22-25, 28, 206
Sophists, 58-59
Sophocles, 45, 47-48
Soul, 111
Spain, barbarians in, 188; and Caesar, 144; Carthaginian colonies, 127; civilization in, 203; and Greek colonies, 20; Romanization of, 174; as Roman province, 136; and Romans, 165
Sparta, and Alcibiades, 55; area of, 5; Athens' truce with, 54; and Greek unity, 74; Homer on king of, 10; organization of, 21-22; and Peloponnesian War, 74; and Persians, 29, 38; power of, 41; victory of, 56; war with Athens, 51-57; and Xenophon, 75
Steam power, 90
Stoicism, and Cicero, 146; influence of, 94-96; and Judaism, 101; and nationality, 162; nature of, 91-97, 101
Stoics, 171, 177
Sulla, Cornelius, 142
Sumer, 80
Sun, 90
Syracuse, Athenian attack on, 54-55; and Dionysius, 110; as Greek colony, 20; importance of, 75, 115; Plato in, 75
Syria, Alexander in, 82, 83; and Pompey, 143; in Selucid kingdom, 86, 88; and Xerxes, 29

Tacitus, 170
Tarquin, 120, 149
Tax, 139
Technology, 174-75
Telemachus, 9, 10
Temple of the Muses, 90
Teutoberg Forest, 165
Thales, 12-13, 14
Thasos, 39
Thebes, and Alexander, 81; in Pelopon-

nesian War, 53; versus Philip, 80; rise of, 75
Themistocles, 29
Thermopylae, battle at, 29
Thirty Tyrants, 57
Thucydides, on Alcibiades' speech, 55; on Athens, 43; on Cleon's speech, 54; on Greek experience, 64; on Melos, 39-40; and Peloponnesian War, 52, 53; Readings from, 66-71; and sense of history, 99
Tiber River, 116
Totalitarian state, 186
Toynbee, Arnold, 44
Trade, 134
Tragedy, 46
Transalpine Gaul, 136
Tribes, 26
Tribune, 122, 160
Triumvirate, 145
Trojan War, 3, 7, 17
Troy, 3
Twelve Tables, 122
Tyrant, 25
Tyre, 83

United States, 206
Universalism, 94
Universe, 12-13, 92

Varro, 131-32
Verres, 147
Veto, 122
Virgil, 168-69, 171

War, civil, Roman, 140, 142, 146, 164, 183, 184; class, Roman, 140; and early Romans, 117; Greek, class, 74; Thucydides on, 69-71
*Works and Days*, 18

Xenophanes, 44-45
Xenophon, 75-77
Xerxes, 29, 38

Zeno, 91, 94
Zeus, and Amon, 99; Hesiod on, 20; in Homer, 7; nature of, 5, 12, 181; Stoic view of, 92